To

MW00891547

Norill Dorothy, NP

March 3, 2006

Feeling Terrific

Feeling Terrific

Four Strategies for Overcoming Depression Using Mood Regulation Therapy

Namir F. Damluji, M.D.
Renee Robinson Sievert, R.N., M.F.T.
Michele LaPorte Downey, R.N., M.F.T.

iUniverse, Inc.
New York Lincoln Shanghai

Feeling Terrific
Four Strategies for Overcoming Depression Using Mood Regulation Therapy

Copyright © 2005 by Namir Damluji, Renee Sievert, Michele Downey

All rights reserved. No part of this book may be used or reproduced by any means, graphic, electronic, or mechanical, including photocopying, recording, taping or by any information storage retrieval system without the written permission of the publisher except in the case of brief quotations embodied in critical articles and reviews.

iUniverse books may be ordered through booksellers or by contacting:

iUniverse
2021 Pine Lake Road, Suite 100
Lincoln, NE 68512
www.iuniverse.com
1-800-Authors (1-800-288-4677)

ISBN-13: 978-0-595-35508-2 (pbk)
ISBN-13: 978-0-595-79996-1 (ebk)
ISBN-10: 0-595-35508-0 (pbk)
ISBN-10: 0-595-79996-5 (ebk)

Printed in the United States of America

To Our Families

To my wife, Gina, and my children, Mona, Omar, and Nadim, with admiration and gratitude for their continuing love, encouragement, and support throughout the nine years of writing this book.

Namir F. Damluji, M.D.

To my family and my loving husband. Thanks for your support, belief in me and the work I love.

Renee Robinson Sievert, R.N., M.F.T.

... the song in my heart since

Michele LaPorte Downey, R.N., M.F.T.

You ought to know yourself as you really are, so that you may understand of what nature you are and whence you have come to this world and for what purpose you were created and in what your happiness and misery consist.

Al-Ghazali

TABLE OF CONTENTS

>What is mood regulation? ~ Understanding depression from a mood regulation perspective ~ Feeling terrific

>The history of emotions ~ Defining the terms ~ What is the value of detecting an emotion? ~ Why is being aware of our mood important? ~ The foundations of mood regulation ~ Defining mood regulation ~ Homeostasis and mood regulation ~ Understanding the role of the emotion center ~ Characteristics of moods ~ When do mood regulation skills begin? ~ When do we regulate our moods? ~ Mechanisms of mood regulation ~ How are moods regulated? ~ Understanding the four mood regulation processes ~ Identifying mood dysregulation

>The nature of depression ~ How common is depression? ~ Types of depression ~ One feeling, many presentations ~ Can depression be normal? ~ The manifestations of depression ~ Masked depression ~ Proper evaluation of the person with depression ~ Theories of causation of depression ~ Current approaches to treating depression ~ A mood dysregulation perspective for understanding depression ~ Depression as a mood regulation disorder: A paradigm shift ~ Feeling terrific with MRT

>Defining Mood Regulation Therapy ~ The approach to change with MRT ~ The four goals of MRT ~ Feeling terrific ~ The phases of MRT ~ Moving from depression to feeling terrific ~ Tools for feeling terrific ~

PREFACE

The individual pursuit and attainment of happiness and finding ways to give our life meaning are topics that were always close to my heart as a psychiatrist and a person. In that effort, I have spent the last twenty-five years studying, researching, and working with individuals who became depressed and lost their ability to enjoy any of the small nuances of their life. In my role as a psychiatrist, I have been privileged in confidence to listen to many life stories, mostly of pain, suffering, and helplessness. Even though no two stories were the same, the misery and hopelessness were. In an effort to help my depressed patients feel better, I tried working with all the traditional modalities of treatment available, but found that they all fell short and their results were unsatisfactory over time. My main focus was always on achieving an outcome of wellness and well-being that is lasting and enduring.

My teacher at Johns Hopkins Hospital, Dr. Paul McHugh, taught that psychiatry could not be understood from one perspective only. If we wanted to truly help our patients, we had to rise above the small details and allow ourselves to think and treat from multiple perspectives. How precious his teachings were. Following Dr. McHugh's enlightened teaching allowed me to get "out of the box" as I started to study and approach the treatment of depression from multiple perspectives. No longer were the symptoms of depression the only focus of treatment; the person who is depressed and his whole life were. I began to ask new questions: Who is this individual? What's going on in his or her life? What has been lost? What outcome does he or she want from therapy? This line of inquiry and study led to research into various disciplines: biology, psychology, psychiatry, anthropology, sociology, philosophy, spirituality, religion, cognitive science, and genetics, among others, all of which played a role in defining who the person was, had an impact on what he felt and experienced, and made him the person he was. From these perspectives emerged the theory and practice of mood regulation therapy, the subject of this book.

This book is the outgrowth of more than twenty years of clinical practice, research, and teaching conferences, primarily in San Diego. The conferences and clinical work were conducted at our outpatient clinics and at several hospital

xiv • *Feeling Terrific*

programs that I established and/or directed, including the Depression Treatment Program at Alvarado Parkway Institute (API), the Woman's Program at Vista Hill Hospital, the Adolescent Outpatient Program and Crisis Center at Rancho Park Hospital, the Eating Disorders program at API, and the Mood Disorders Clinic at Psychiatric Centers at San Diego. Lectures and teachings were also conducted with medical students and psychiatry residents at the University of California-San Diego and the American University of Beirut. Clinicians and participants in these conferences and programs offered many thoughtful and knowledgeable observations and suggestions that helped in our theory development. We are grateful to them all.

This book is based on the contributions of several researchers, clinicians, clergy, academicians, philosophers, sociologists, and most importantly, our patients. The ground-breaking research of Dr. James Gross on emotion regulation has been invaluable, and we are most appreciative of his pioneering work and publications. Dr. Paul Wong has also been pivotal in our progress, and we are most grateful to him for allowing us to quote him and reference his work. We are also indebted to all of the researchers and scientists whose work we have quoted, including Drs. Aaron Beck, David Burns, Reid Creech, and Maxie C. Maultsby, Jr. with regard to cognitive therapy, and Drs. Gerald Klerman and Myrna Weissman with regard to interpersonal therapy. We thank Dr. Anthony Damasio for his lucid writing on emotions and the brain, and we thank Drs. Gordon Bower, P. Ekman, Ralph Erber, J.P. Forgas, N.H. Frijda, L. Joseph LeDoux, Vicky Rippere, and T. Strauman, and all of the pioneering researchers in the field of emotion that are too numerous to name. We also want to thank Dr. Elizabeth MacKinlay for her original work on spirituality and depression. Special thanks go to Dr. David Wexler and Dr. Frank Faltus, who reviewed the manuscript and offered invaluable comments and suggestions.

This book is the outgrowth of theory and our practice. Our starting point in treating anyone with depression is defining the expected outcome, which we call *feeling terrific*. Our book describes the theoretical and clinical bases of mood regulation therapy (MRT) of depression and offers a guide to achieve that outcome.

The book is divided into four parts. The first part is Chapter 1, which discusses the theory of mood regulation in detail. The second part is Chapter 2, which provides an overview of depression types and causes and offers our view of depression as a mood regulation disorder. The third part is about mood regulation therapy. Chapter 3 introduces the concept of mood regulation therapy (MRT), and in Chapters 4 through 7 the significance and application of each mood-regulating strategy are discussed in detail.

The book concludes with the fourth part, including case histories in Chapter 8, where we present examples of individuals treated with mood regulation therapy and their outcome of treatment. In Chapter 9 we summarize our theory and findings in an integrative approach.

The first three chapters are best read in sequence, as they are all connected; understanding one chapter depends on having read the chapter before it. Chapter 4 to 7 can be read in any sequence. The case histories and integration, best read after completing earlier chapters, may be helpful in clarifying the theory and practice of mood regulation therapy.

We have written this book in such a way that we believe it will be beneficial to the public. It includes medical and psychiatric terminology because we believe that the educated public should be as equally informed as professionals regarding new theories and approaches to treatment as they are published. We strongly believe in the public's ability to understand and comprehend the medical and psychiatric concepts presented and to discuss with their treating physician or therapist the information they have gained. When the depressed person or family member is better informed, he or she is better able to make informed choices about treatment and discuss expected outcomes.

Our purpose of writing this book is twofold: to share with you what we have learned through our research and clinical work in the treatment of depression with mood regulation therapy, and to let you know that you can overcome depression and feel terrific to enjoy life more fully than ever before.

Namir F. Damluji, M.D.
March 2005
San Diego, California

ACKNOWLEDGEMENTS

We are indebted to our superb editor, Susan Ferguson. Her continuous inquiry, searching questions, and ability to organize and edit made many improvements to the text. Her editorial guidance, patience, and support made this project possible.

We owe special gratitude to our patients who have expressed their confidence in us and worked with us over the years. All case histories have been substantially changed to obscure the identity of any one person. Any similarity between the stories and any individual living or dead is purely coincidental.

ABOUT THE AUTHORS

Namir F. Damluji is a clinical professor of psychiatry at the University of California-San Diego. He completed his residency training at Johns Hopkins Hospital and has since been in private practice in San Diego, California. He is the medical director of the Damluji Research Clinic. Dr. Damluji pioneered the study and treatment of Mood Regulation Therapy (MRT) in depression. Dr. Damluji is a Distinguished Fellow of the American Psychiatric Association.

Renee Robinson Sievert is a clinical education consultant and national trainer. She has more than twenty-five years' experience and has advanced certification in psychiatric and mental health nursing, alcoholism/addiction treatment, and HIV/AIDS. She is a licensed marriage and family therapist and lives in San Diego, California.

Michele LaPorte Downey is a registered nurse, master addictions therapist, and a marriage/family/child therapist. Since 1987 she has had a private practice in Carlsbad, California, specializing in families affected by addictions.

INTRODUCTION

Feeling terrific is the yearning of every soul. Often sought and seldom realized, feeling terrific is a state of good health in body, mind, and spirit. It is characterized by well-being, contentment, serenity, self-acceptance, meaning, purpose, and self-transcendence. Feeling terrific creates in us an enhanced sense of self and a positive state of mind that allows us to fully experience and enjoy life.

Our life experiences are bittersweet, typically resulting in a mixture of positive and negative feeling states. If feeling terrific represents the positive feeling state, then depression represents the negative state. The two states have a complex and dynamic relationship, like the inseparable duality of light and shadow or day and night, where one is a continuation of the other. When we look at the relationship between feeling terrific and feeling depressed, we see that they are counterparts, each occupying a pole on the emotion continuum. The depressed state is the counterpart of the feeling-terrific state. If we understand the nature of one state, our knowledge may lead to realization of the other.

Several authors have written about depression as an opportunity for finding more satisfaction and meaning in life. In *The Secret Strength of Depression,* author Frederic Flach M.D. observed, "To experience acute depression is an opportunity for a person not just to learn more about himself but to become more whole than he was." We find that depression, if treated properly, may be an opportunity for transformation by examining old negative patterns of thoughts and behaviors and relinquishing them to open new possibilities in life. Effective treatment also allows you to achieve a better mood state than you had prior to the depression, permitting you to reach new levels of awareness and creativity. Accordingly, depression is our point of departure in this book, and from it we journey to the state of feeling terrific.

What does "being depressed" really mean? The word *depression* has been used to represent a feeling, a mood state, an illness, a character deficit, an attitude in life, the state of bereavement after the loss of someone close or something meaningful, or the state of having a "sick soul." We use the word depression throughout this book to designate a specific mood state characterized by feeling down, blue, or dejected, accompanied by a loss of pleasure or indifference, negative thoughts, and other physical or behavioral changes.

During the last three decades, great strides have been made in the conceptualization of the causes and treatment of depression. Many theoretical models have been advanced and are in wide use for the treatment of depression. The best-known theories are the cognitive, biological, and behavioral approaches. Each of these modalities postulates that depression is caused by a malfunction in the area it represents. Therefore, cognitive theory assumes that depression is caused by cognitive distortions or faulty thinking, biological theory assumes that depression is caused by a chemical imbalance, and behavioral theory assumes that depression is caused by maladaptive behaviors and learned helplessness. These theories are unitary in their explanation of the causation of depression, and proponents of each theory adhere to their causation almost exclusively. This bird's-eye view of depression's causation has limited treatment options and has led to dismal treatment outcomes.

For instance, studies in the treatment of depression with medications have shown that only 20 percent of patients recover completely, while 45 percent of patients get partial improvement in their symptoms. The rest get no help. That is why many drop out of treatment prematurely and why two out of three people who are prescribed medication stop taking it too soon. Additionally, a high proportion of those who have been diagnosed with clinical depression and treated with cognitive therapy or medication continue to experience significant residual symptoms and suffer a high rate of relapse. The suicide rate in depression has been unchanged over the last thirty years in spite of all the advanced pharmacological and cognitive therapies. Why?

An important variable that determines how well people recover from depression is the interface between the belief that the depressed person brings into treatment and the reasoning that the treating therapist offers to explain the cause of depression and the rationale of the treatment method being proposed (McLean and Hakstian 1979). People with depression who are seeking treatment usually have their own views on causation of their depressed mood. In our experience, depressed individuals usually offer multiple reasons as precipitants of their depression, such as when the patient says, "I'm under stress at work, and I just started on new blood pressure medication, and I ended my two-year relationship with my girlfriend." Therapists and psychiatrists who strictly adhere to one theory of causation are doomed to fail if they suggest that the single theory is the only cause of a person's depression without reconciling it with the depressed person's own theory of causation. People suffering from depression often go from therapist to therapist, searching for a modality they can understand and accept in the hope of attaining full recovery.

In the last twenty years, research in the field of psychology has been more advanced than the clinical practices of psychology and psychiatry with regard to depression. Studies by Dr. James Gross and others in the area of emotion regulation have shown that the ability to regulate one's emotions is a very important function for healthy development, necessary for emotional stability and well-being. The construct of mood regulation emerged from the theory of self regulation, which is related to the concept of homeostasis. Research into mood regulation (which in the literature is referred to as *emotion regulation*) was first done with children, where it was noted how mood regulation evolved developmentally during childhood and adolescence. From there, research moved to adults in health and disease. Dr. Gross has written about the importance of the emotional regulation process in mental health and healthy functioning (Gross and Munoz 1995).

The majority of clinical psychiatric disorders have been found to have an element of mood dysregulation (Gross and Levenson 1997). Physical conditions such as hypertension and coronary heart disease have been associated with dysregulated moods, specifically long-term hostility and the inhibition of anger (Julkunen et al. 1994). Inhibition of emotions has also been found to exacerbate cancer growth (Gross 1989).

We view depression as arising from a central breakdown in mood regulation; the resultant dysregulated mood state is called depression. This dysregulation in mood is a joint outcome of the interactions of a person's biological dispositions, cognitive deficits, social difficulties, and spiritual emptiness.

The Mood Regulation Therapy (MRT) approach is an educational and skill training process based on twenty-five years of clinical experience. MRT teaches men and women how to use emotional information in a problem-solving manner and how to regulate mood toward the goal of feeling terrific. The ultimate goal in MRT treatment is a person who has full command of his or her moods at all times by having the appropriate skills to self-regulate them. The aims of this book are:

- To introduce you to the concept of mood regulation and the four dimensions that influence it
- To teach you how to identify and rate your mood
- To assist you in understanding depression from a mood regulation perspective
- To discuss the strategies that lead to feeling terrific
- To define the "feeling-terrific" state and set it as a goal of recovery from depression.

What is mood regulation?

Mood regulation refers to the processes in which our moods are consciously and unconsciously adjusted. The mechanisms by which moods are regulated include biological, cognitive, social, and spiritual influences. Mood regulation is related to W.B. Cannon's theory of homeostasis (Cannon 1932). Cannon defined homeostasis as the coordinated actions and reactions in the body and mind needed to maintain a stable steady state. To maintain our body homeostasis in a well-regulated state twenty-four hours a day, all of our systems must function in synchronicity with each other. Examples of operant regulatory systems are body temperature, oxygen concentration, and the sleep-wake cycle. Homeostasis aims at keeping the individual balanced at all times, able to respond to and accommodate changes in his or her environment. With respect to mood regulation, there is a constant interface between the biological, cognitive, social, and spiritual factors to bring about this homeostatic regulatory state.

We will use two tools to help you identify and rate your mood. The Depression Questionnaire will help you find out if you are depressed, and if so, how severely. The Daily Mood Scale will teach you how to rate your mood on a daily basis, then graph it in order to detect certain patterns and cycles.

Understanding depression
from a mood regulation perspective

Depression is a state that occurs when there is dysregulation in mood. Dysregulation leads to changes within the body and the mind, affecting a person's thinking, feeling, behavior, and his or her physiological functions. The disorders that can arise from these changes are called the depressions, each caused by a combination of biological, cognitive, social, and spiritual influences of varying intensities. They range on a continuum of severity from clinical depression to depressive personality to grief and are not fragmented or unrelated.

A particular type of depression (for example, clinical depression) may arise more from the biological than the other influences, but no type of depression is all biological, all social, or all spiritual. Change may start in one domain (as biological, for example) but then lead to changes in the other domains.

People who are depressed have inadequate or maladaptive mood-regulating skills. We will discuss the skills that can be acquired in the biological, cognitive, social, and spiritual domains to recover from depression and feel terrific. The therapist using the MRT approach first makes a thorough evaluation of the cause of the mood dysregulation. Once the cause is identified, the depressed person starts using mood regulation strategies to work on skill building in all or most of the four domains. Only by attending to all of the areas can a person recover fully from depression and feel terrific. Anything less leads to partial improvement.

Feeling terrific

We believe the depressed person should not settle for partial improvement from depression; you have the right to feel the best that you can and should. MRT teaches you how to feel terrific by working through your depression and emerging from that negative mood state to a feeling state that is better than the one you had before. A feeling-terrific state that is born out of the adversity of depression is enduring because you will be aware of and knowledgeable about ways to keep your mood stable and prevent future depressions.

There is joy in life. Our goal is to help you understand your feelings and have the mastery to guide them so you may experience this joy and feel terrific all the time.

The information in this book has been gathered from treatment and therapy sessions with our patients over the last twenty-five years. It should be a reference for self-understanding and growth and is meant to help you feel terrific. It is not meant as a substitute for therapy. There is no substitute for the caring of a therapist to accompany you through the journey towards feeling terrific.

CHAPTER 1
Mood Regulation

The history of emotions

Since antiquity, philosophers and scientists have had difficulty understanding and explaining human emotions and how our emotional life relates to other aspects of our being, such as thoughts and behavior. Early philosophers had complex and confusing notions of what emotions were, and multiple theories were advanced to explain the origin of emotions and their role in life. In essence most philosophers positioned reason and emotion as opposites: Reason was the higher moral ground that defined our humanity, and emotions were disruptive influences on thinking and behavior.

Plato (427–347 B.C.) was one of the first to connect emotions to one's mental life, stating that a person had three basic mental faculties: reasoning, desiring, and emotions. Plato placed the source of some emotions, such as the love of beauty, in the brain, which he described as the immortal soul, while other "regular" emotions were distributed all over the body, or mortal soul.

For Aristotle (384–322 B.C.) emotions were of three types. The first type was a product of our natural predisposition, like the emotions that allow us to experience the passions of life. The second type of emotions developed from social pressures and repeated experiencing of the passions; these were learned emotions. The third type of emotions accompanied pain and pleasure experiences. To Aristotle the expression of emotions was essential for the experience of emotions.

In the seventeenth century, Rationalist philosophers René Descartes (1596–1650) and Baruch Spinoza (1632–1677) believed emotions represented different forms of desire or will. Descartes was known for the Cartesian mind-body theory, where he proposed a separation of the thinking mind from the body as two independent entities. To Descartes, emotions were secondary to the general character of the individual. This became the basis of education, which attempted to develop a child's character in order to produce certain emotions.

1

Descartes identified six "simple" passions—wonder, love, hatred, desire, joy, and sadness. He stated that all other emotions were made up of some or part of these six passions (Descartes 1967). Spinoza claimed that persistence, attainment, and necessity were central to one's emotional life. The emotional dimensions of desire, pleasure, and pain were derived from these concepts.

In the eighteenth century, David Hume (1711–1776) presented the viewpoint that put emotion in a central role when he stated, "Reason is, and ought to be, the slave of the passions" (Solomon 2000).

Moses Mendelssohn (1729–1786) was among the first to plainly divide mental life into three faculties: feeling, understanding, and the will. Immanuel Kant (1724–1804) later expanded on this tripartite division, which he classified as cognition, conation, and affect (Forgas 2000). This separation between body and mind remains with us to this day and influences many aspects of our daily lives. This division is most obviously seen in the practice of medicine, where physical diseases are treated as completely separate and independent entities from psychological disorders.

In the last century, psychologists adopted this tripartite theory of mind and went further into separating the three mental faculties from each other, declaring that each functioned in isolation from the other. The major paradigms in the field of psychology that emerged in the twentieth century were psychoanalysis, behaviorism, and cognitivism. Psychoanalysis was concerned with unconscious motives, wishes, and drives. All mental events were seen as occurring secondarily to changes in these unconscious processes. Behaviorism defined emotions in terms of reinforced behavioral patterns and focused on motivation, action, and will as determining mental life. Cognitivism focused on information processing; emotions were seen as by-products of thoughts and beliefs. Some cognitive researchers (Laird 1989) didn't even consider emotions an entity, noting that "the experience of emotion is a cognition."

All of these paradigms ignored emotions and considered them an impediment to normal mental life. Emotions were seen as dangerous influences on thinking and behavior; as J. Elster noted in 1985, whenever emotions are "directly involved in action, they tend to overwhelm or subvert rational mental processes" (Forgas 2000). Accordingly, emotions were found unworthy of scientific study and were ignored for a long time.

In the last twenty years there has been a radical change in the study and research of emotions. With recent advances in understanding of brain function in health and disease, and extensive research in the field of psychology, there has been a new appreciation for the central role of emotions in our mental life. Dr. Antonio Damasio and other researchers have demonstrated that emotions are necessary for rational thinking and reasoning and that there is close interdependence between emotions and thinking; they are not separate entities, as was proposed earlier (Damasio 1994, 1999). Emotion theory has become well developed, and as Dr. Forgas (2000) points out, "The available research clearly points to a bidirectional rather than a unidirectional link between affect (emotions) and cognition (thoughts). There is much evidence for affect influencing attention, memory, thinking, associations, and judgments."

Mental functions are no longer seen as three separate entities operating in isolation but as interdependent and complementary functions integral to a normal mental life. The most prominent theory of emotion focuses on emotion regulation, which has been defined (Kokkonen and Pulkkinen 1996) as "those adaptive processes which direct, inhibit, and shape emotions and limit inappropriate behavior."

The study of emotion regulation began in the 1980s in an effort to understand the healthy development of children (Barrett and Lamb 1983). Shortly after that, the field of research in emotion regulation expanded into the study of how adults regulate their emotions in order to explain how emotions are expressed and experienced (Gross 1998). The emotion regulation process is rooted in the biological functions of the body and brain and is influenced by internal events in the body and brain and by external environmental factors.

With the new theories and understanding of the important role of emotions in our life, new terms and concepts have emerged, specifically the terms *emotional intelligence* and *emotional well-being*. Emotional well-being is defined as a person having a positive mood state and high self-esteem (Schutte et al. 2002). Another definition offered by researcher Sarah Stewart-Brown (2000) is "a holistic, subjective state which is present when a range of feelings—among them energy, confidence, openness, enjoyment, happiness, calm, and caring—are combined and balanced."

Emotional intelligence is the ability to understand and regulate mood successfully, combined with the ability to perceive, understand, and harness emotions in one's self. Higher emotional intelligence is associated with emotional well-being, less depression (Martinez-Pons 1997), and greater life satisfaction (Ciarrochi et al. 2001). Our work in this book is based on the premise of understanding emotions from a regulatory perspective and on learning how to achieve emotional well-being through the proper and deliberate regulation of our emotions and moods.

Defining the terms

Terms we will use in this book include *stimulus, emotions, mood, feeling, affect,* and *emotion center.* Different people use these terms to mean different things. The definitions we will use are the ones commonly used by therapists and researchers in the field. We have also used Dr. Damasio's classification of emotions and feelings, as we find it consistent with our understanding and approach of mood regulation therapy (Damasio 1999).

Stimulus: A stimulus is a trigger capable of producing an emotion. This stimulus is picked up by the sensory part of the brain as a signal and is then identified and processed in the emotion center to produce an emotion; this process is illustrated in FIGURE 1.

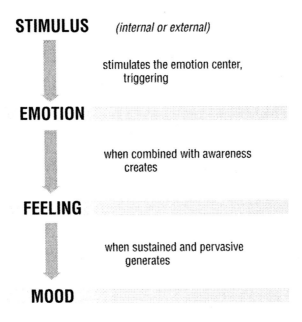

STIMULUS   *(internal or external)*

stimulates the emotion center, triggering

EMOTION

when combined with awareness creates

FEELING

when sustained and pervasive generates

MOOD

FIGURE 1. THE AFFECT/EMOTION/FEELING/MOOD CONTINUUM. A MOOD STATE DEVELOPS IN STAGES, STARTING FROM A TRIGGERING STIMULUS, FOLLOWED BY EMOTION AND FEELING, AND CULMINATING IN A MOOD STATE.

The emotion center is a network of areas in the brain that process the emotions that result from the stimulus. Stimuli are of two types: external and internal. External stimuli occur in the environment that surrounds us and are identified as visual, auditory, tactile, olfactory, or through the sense of taste. Internal stimuli occur within and are comprised of thoughts, memories, or recalled images. Any change in the environment around us, such as a change in temperature, noise level, light level, and so on, can generate a stimulus. We do not need to be conscious of a stimulus for it to produce an emotion, and often we are not.

Emotions: Emotions are a collection of chemical and neural responses produced by the activation of the emotion center in the brain by an external or internal stimulus. Emotions are biologically determined processes depending on innately set brain systems. They arise from the chemical, hormonal, and electrical circuitry in the nervous system. An emotion is triggered by a stimulus that is perceived as a signal in the brain. The signal then activates the emotion center.

Emotions are generated in the emotion center in the brain and get expressed throughout the body (as in the heart, lung, skin, gut, endocrine glands, and musculoskeletal systems) in a manner that is characteristic of that emotion; for instance, if one is shy, one's skin flushes. Emotions also lead to changes in behavior and the generating of thoughts that are consistent with that emotion. The triggering of an emotion also causes changes in the immune system.

Effects on the body systems are carried out by chemicals called peptides that are released from the brain to the blood and then to the whole body, neural signals that are carried through the autonomic nervous system to the end organs, neural signals to the muscles (affecting facial expression and body posture), and neurotransmitters that are released in the brain.

With certain types of emotions, such as primary emotions, we are "wired" to respond with a specific emotion for certain stimuli in our environment. For example, in an earthquake the sudden movement of the ground underneath our feet startles us and leads us to fear. A stimulus is detected and processed in the emotion center. Emotional states can cause various changes in the body and brain, including:

- Changes in the body organs (heart, lungs, gut, skin, adrenal gland, pituitary gland)
- Changes in the muscle contraction of the face, throat, trunk and limbs
- Changes in body posture
- Changes in thoughts and cognitive processing
- Autonomic changes such as flushing or pallor.

In the case of the earthquake, the startle-and-fear response will lead to our jumping from our seat and running toward a safe location in the house. Our facial expression may show pallor and wide-open eyes, our heart may beat faster, we feel tense, and all of our thoughts will be directed to the earthquake, our safety, or what's happening right then and there.

There are three types of emotions, according to Dr. Damasio (1994, 1999). The first type is called *primary* or *universal emotion.* The second type is the *secondary* or *social emotion,* like embarrassment, jealousy, guilt, and pride. The third type is *background emotion.*

Primary Emotions: The six primary emotions are happiness, sadness, fear, anger, surprise, and disgust. These are universal across cultures. Primary emotions are defined as pre-wired emotional states that occur in response to a stimulus from within our body or from the environment. Primary emotions are innate and have been hard-wired into our brain over the course of evolution, according to Dr. Damasio. This wiring causes us to respond in a predetermined fashion to certain stimuli. Joseph LeDoux (1998) describes these emotions as adaptive responses that are crucial to survival by helping a person deal with specific situations or threats. The emotional response allows the body to make the required adjustment, thus helping deal with key changes posed by the environment or body.

For example, an infant will cry when hungry so the mother can take notice and feed him. At six weeks, an infant will smile in response to hearing the mother's voice or if he is being carried by her, his or her smile inviting further nurturing or contact. Another example: If, while you are walking, a snake slithers in front of you, most likely you will respond by jumping away to avoid the risk of getting bitten. The primary emotion of fear is what allows you to react instantly to the snake, a stimulus you perceive as dangerous, and allows you to move away from it to a place of safety. As these examples show, primary emotions are usually triggered by specific events or stimuli, and the stimulus is usually detected before it reaches consciousness. Through experience and learning, primary emotions move into the realm of becoming secondary emotions.

Secondary Emotions: These are acquired or learned emotions. According to Dr. Damasio, secondary emotions arise when we make connections between certain thought processes and situations on one hand and primary emotions on the other. Secondary emotions are different from primary emotions in that they begin with a thought or cognition and then follow a pathway that has been established by learning, rather than evoking a response more evolutionary and preset. Through experience, the brain retains mental images (which are thought processes) associated with emotions; when new events trigger these images, the past associated emotions are triggered, as well. With secondary emotions, the stimulus begins in the frontal lobe, which is the thinking center of the brain, and travels to the limbic system, which is the emotion center of the brain; from there, it completes the emotional circuit exactly like the primary emotions. Secondary or social emotions include embarrassment, jealousy, guilt, pride, stress, shyness, optimism, love, humiliation, and hope.

Here is an example of a secondary emotion: You are standing in line in the grocery store. You see someone that reminds you of a good friend you had several years ago. You know that this person is not your friend, but there are similarities in the posture and in the face of the stranger that remind you of the good friend that you had. The images that result from seeing this stranger evoke specific positive thoughts which in turn trigger the emotion center. You start having pleasant feelings as you are reminded of your friend. Emotions that are triggered through secondary emotions usually follow a previous or learned experience. In this case, when you saw the stranger, it reminded you of someone that was a good friend in the past that you had not seen for a long time but for whom you had a lot of feelings. Intuition is thought to be a subtle form of secondary emotion.

Background Emotions: Background emotions originate in the "background" resting state of the body and are always present, monitoring the body's mental state. Background emotions work like a small power generator, flowing continuously as they monitor the condition of the body and brain in the background to create emotional responses that we are not readily aware of. While primary and secondary emotions are triggered by environmental or internal changes or thoughts that get our attention and make us aware of our inner state, background emotions are more subtly detected and enduring. Their responses target both the body and brain. Background emotions include well-being, malaise, calm, tension, feeling down, cheerfulness, and enthusiasm.

When a person says he or she is tense, edgy, discouraged, enthusiastic, down, or cheerful, that person is experiencing a background emotion. These ongoing emotional states do not dominate a person's thoughts and actions and can be detected by subtle changes in body posture or movement and in muscle contraction.

According to Dr. Damasio, the triggers of background emotions are usually internal triggers and include the body organs and the musculoskeletal system, among others. In comparison to primary and secondary emotions, background emotion's target is more internal than external. Background emotions reflect the internal milieu, which is the inner state of the body.

An example of background emotion is when somebody feels relaxed or comfortable after doing yoga for an hour. The body has been stretched and relaxed, and the person carries a body posture of relaxation. In contrast, when somebody is worried about an examination and is tense, the person will experience physical tension, which may be demonstrated by pacing or grimacing and a sense of feeling preoccupied; the background emotion in this situation is tension or edginess. As you can see, background emotions can occur by different means, including thoughts, physical efforts, or any change within the internal state, whether it is physiological or occurs through an interaction with the environment.

What is the value of detecting an emotion?

Every emotion serves a distinct function, which is to bring our conscious attention to the triggering event. For instance, if a man speaks in an angry tone to his wife, he will notice that her face is flushed, she is flinching, and her eyes are wide open—responses that should bring to his attention that she is angry. Most likely, the triggering event for her anger is what he said.

Emotions are adaptive, active, and ongoing processes and are thought to be the brain's interpretation of reactions to changes in the environment. One of the important functions of emotions is that they lead to action. Again using the snake as an example, if a person working in the garden sees a snake, he or she may be startled, feel scared that the snake may bite, and run away from the snake. What prompts the behavior of running away is emotion, which is the combination of feeling startled upon seeing the snake plus the memory that snakes are dangerous and can bite.

The behaviors that follow an emotion are usually very specific and relevant to the stimulus that prompted the emotion and to the recall of a unique memory or experience concerning that stimulus or emotion. Because each person's experiences and memories are unique, two people can be exposed to the same stimulus and have two very different responses. In the snake example, a person who likes snakes and collects them as pets may be drawn to the snake, while a person who has previously been bitten by a snake may run away as fast as he can.

Emotions are at the heart of the human experience. They play a big role in our survival and continuity in life. The emotion of fear, for example, protects us from dangerous situations. Aggression drives us to find food and shelter. The emotions of love and emotional bonding lead to attachment behavior, intimacy, mating, and parenting. Emotions help us make decisions, conduct reasoning, and make judgments. Other important functions that emotions serve include

- Shaping our thoughts in accordance with the demands of the situation at hand (Clore 1994)
- Promoting the process of decision making (Oatley and Johnson-Laird 1987)
- Preparing the individual for action and physical response (Frijda 1986)
- Promoting the process of learning (Cahill and Prins 1994)
- Giving the person a sense of whether what he or she is experiencing is good or bad (Gross 1999)
- Helping the individual to effectively manage complex social situations (Walden 1991).

Emotion Center: The emotion center is an integrated anatomical system in the brain responsible for the identification of emotionally relevant information, the generation of emotional behaviors and experiences, and the regulation of mood. The emotion center is connected through a neural circuitry system and is anatomically located within the cortical and subcortical regions of the brain. (This will be presented in detail in FIGURE 2 later in this chapter.) The connections between these two areas are bidirectional. The emotion center is connected to the rest of the brain through the neural circuitry of the brain and to the rest of the body through hormones and other messengers that travel through the bloodstream.

Dr. Donald Nathanson (1996) states that if we are aware of something in our environment, we are aware of it in relation to an emotion. The emotion center therefore acts as a filter through which we process and interpret our experiences in the world (Nathanson 1988). We will use the terms *emotion center* and *mood center* interchangeably in this book.

Affect: The word *affect* is used in two ways. It can be used in a general way to denote the whole subject matter of emotions, mood, and feelings. For instance, when we talk of "affective disorders," we are referring to all of the emotional disorders that have an effect on feelings and mood, such as manic-depressive illness, depression, and the like. More specifically, affect is used to designate an emotional tone that a person displays or emotes. Affect is thus the expression of a person's emotion that can be externally observed, as on the face, in body posture, or from the tone of the voice. For instance, if an acquaintance named John were emoting restlessness, muscle tension, and a loud voice indicative of irritability, an observer would say, "John's affect is irritable." A person's affect can be described as flat, labile, appropriate, inappropriate, excited, irritable, blunted, or constricted.

Feeling: A feeling is the conscious awareness of an emotion. It is what we become conscious of and pay attention to after an emotion has been triggered. With feelings we can become aware of the trigger and pay attention to the ensuing emotional state and the thoughts associated with it. Feelings are continuously generated during wakefulness and sleep. During sleep, we experience them in dreams or nightmares. We are always experiencing feelings in reaction to events in our lives, thoughts, dreams, and so on. A feeling is our individual and personal mental interpretation of an emotional response evoked in us. It is conscious, subjective, and internally experienced. Feelings and emotions are part of a functional continuance. Emotions are about being, while feelings are about experiencing.

Feeling is an individual's conscious mental experience of an emotion. A feeling is inwardly directed and private, as when we say, "I feel...." Feeling occurs when we pair our emotional response to past experiences of people, objects, and situations. Feelings are important because they reflect our experience of reality and determine our reaction to that reality. For example, a nightmare may feel very real and we may be scared or panicky, which leads to our screaming or jumping out of bed. Once we wake up, the nightmare will no longer be real and our feelings will change.

Identifying, labeling, and expressing feelings are typically skills learned in childhood. Many people, however, have great difficulty identifying feelings and labeling them appropriately. They end up ignoring them or suppressing them and thus are not aware of them.

Dr. Damasio coined the term *background feelings*, which are feelings stemming from our background emotions. At times we are aware of these feelings; other times we don't pay attention to them. According to Dr. Damasio, background feelings play a role in defining our mental state and are an index of a momentary condition of our inner state. We consider background feelings to depend on many levels of representation, including the cognitive, social, and spiritual influences. Examples of background feelings are excitement, wellness, harmony, discord, tension, and relaxation.

Mood: Mood is defined as an emotion that lasts for a long period of time with the consequent feeling (Davidson 1984). It is the conscious, prevailing, sustained emotional tone that a person is experiencing or displaying at any given moment. Mood and emotion generally convey the same meaning; the difference is in the longer duration and pervasiveness of mood states. If a person considers mood to be a melody played on a piano, then emotion could be considered a single specific note in that melody.

Moods define our conscious state and color our life. Mood is subjectively experienced when someone says "I'm in a good mood today." Moods are usually scattered and diffuse and have no set target. For example, when a person says "I'm in a bad mood today," there is usually no special target or purpose for that mood state. When a person expresses an emotion, such as "I am angry," the anger is targeted at a specific person or subject and is provoked by a specific internal or external stimulus (Erber 1996).

A unique way to look at mood (Weissman and Kasl 1976) is to conceptualize it as the "pervasive and sustained emotional climate," as opposed to emotions, which are the "fluctuating changes in emotional weather." Moods are more diffuse and prolonged than emotions. Every mood state is expressed through a coordinated set of responses, which are behavioral, cognitive, emotional, expressive, and physiological. Mood usually leads to physiological responses that characterize emotions, which include the endocrine, autonomic, immune, and nervous systems, and musculoskeletal changes.

For instance, we all experience a happy mood state as a positive and enjoyable experience associated with positive thoughts and good feelings; we may smile or laugh and look relaxed, assuming a comfortable body posture. Words used to describe mood states include irritable, depressed, euphoric (ecstatic), grief, dysphoric (sad), mood swings, happy, terrific, or euthymic (normal).

Researchers (Forgas 1992) have found that the operational differences between mood and emotion are difficult to ascertain, which has prompted some to use the two terms interchangeably, as is seen often in the literature (Kokkonen and Pulkkinen 2001). The key term we use in this book to describe a person's emotional state is *mood,* as it carries with it a broader and longer-lasting emotional experience (Ekman 1994; Kagan 1994). The mood regulation processes we will be discussing have been shown to directly modulate emotion and mood. Because mood is the predominant and prevailing emotional experience, we refer to our approach as *mood regulation.*

> *Mood reflects our evaluation of the enduring features of our life—ourselves, and the overall structure of our life circumstances.*—Paul Wender, M.D., and Donald Klein, M.D.

Why is being aware of our mood important?

Professor Gordon Bower of Stanford University reviewed research by himself and many others (1994) showing that people usually determine their daily activities in accordance with their mood state. He specifically stated that "depending on their mood, people tend to become interested in or attracted to activities, people, stories, movies, and music that are 'in tune' with their mood." Dr. Bower went on to describe how mood states influence affect, thinking, memory, judgment, self-perception, and perception of others. Dr. Bower's studies also identified these other areas that are directly impacted by a specific mood state:

Mood memory: When people try to recall events from the past, they will recall events that agree with their current mood state and will use information from the past that agrees with their current mood state. When people are happy, they will remember happy events from their childhood; when people are depressed, they will recall their childhood as an unhappy and deprived one. After their depression lifts, they recall a far happier childhood than they did when depressed. Therefore, mood determines the memory recalled.

Mood perseverance: Individuals prefer to be in situations with or in the company of people complimentary and confirming of their current mood. For instance, sad people often prefer the company of others who are down and sad like them, and happy people like to be around people who are happy.

Researchers have found that sad people, when given a choice to listen to any type of music, choose to listen to sad or nostalgic music and watch depressing and somber films—thus the saying, "misery loves company."

Thought associations: Every mood state has the potential of triggering a stream of thoughts consistent with that mood. When a mood state is aroused, it brings with it concepts, words, themes, and inferences that the person associates and links with that mood state. For instance, if a person is in a depressed mood, then the thoughts and associations that person makes will be negative and depressive in nature.

Life satisfaction: An individual's mood state influences his or her momentary opinions about personal matters and how he or she reports satisfaction in life. Accordingly, when a person is in a good mood, he or she is likely to report satisfaction with life; when in a bad mood, that person will likely report dissatisfaction with his life.

Health evaluation: Researchers have found that mood states determine how people report their physical health status, their perception of their current health, and their medical history. When people are sad, they report more physical complaints, recall more times that they were sick, and complain of more pain and discomfort than those who are in a good or neutral mood.

Future health appraisal: Mood influences how a person rates his or her vulnerability to future illnesses and whether any preventive health measures could help in avoiding these illnesses. Sad individuals were found to predict many health problems in the future and report pessimism about their ability to do anything to prevent them or to effectively treat them once they occur.

Forecasting the future: People's mood affects their judgments and reasoning regarding the likelihood of future events in their lives. People in a happy mood state were found to have high hopes of successful events in their future, with less likelihood of disasters happening to them. Sad individuals, on the other hand, speak of a high probability of future disaster, with a low probability of successful future events.

Judging others: An individual's mood influences judgment about other people's actions or words. Our current mood influences how we interpret other people's behaviors and actions. Research has shown that, when people are in a good mood, they are loving and charitable and forgiving in their relationships with others. When they are depressed, they are critical of others, overly sensitive, and quick to misinterpret remarks said as negative.

Explaining successes and failures: A person's mood state influences how he or she explains personal successes and failures in life. When people are in a good mood, they will take credit for their successes and minimize their failures, while depressed people take full responsibility and blame themselves for their failures, and minimize their successes. For example, people who are in a happy mood state will attribute their success in passing an exam to their studying efforts when they pass, and attribute their failure to bad luck when they fail. On the other hand, when people who are in a sad mood take the test and pass, they attribute their success to an easy exam, and those who fail attribute it to their poor skills and abilities.

Self-evaluation and self-perception: Moods affect our evaluation of ourselves and the world around us. Moods influence our perception of our own behavior. Studies have shown that individuals who are in a good mood judge themselves as friendly and competent and in a positive manner, compared to people in a depressed mood who view themselves as incompetent and unworthy.

Self-confidence: Studies have shown that mood state affects a person's sense of confidence and competence and how confident he or she feels in accomplishing certain tasks. People in a good mood were found to have a high sense of self-confidence, competence, and self-efficacy. On the other hand, individuals who were sad in the studies had a low sense of self-efficacy and self-confidence.

Mood and learning: Research has shown that our mood will sensitize us to learn information that only agrees with that mood state. People who are in a good mood will choose books to read and gravitate towards material that matches their positive mood state.

Dr. Bower concluded his review of research findings with this statement: "The overwhelming results question the age-old belief that people are supremely rational creatures, that we are well-functioning calculators who can set aside our passions, look at the facts objectively, and arrive at our evaluations and judgments rationally and without bias. All of our subjects believed this myth. They believed that they were being totally objective, that their emotions were not influencing their judgments and perception of themselves and their world, but we find that people cannot override their emotions; their emotions appear to leak out in nearly everything they do. Their thinking is suffused with emotion."

The foundations of mood regulation

The field of emotion regulation has been researched and studied extensively over the last thirty years, but progress in the practical application of its principles has been recent, mostly in the last five years. Dr. James Gross of Stanford University has been at the forefront in his work that has outlined the important determinants of mood regulation, which he has called emotion regulation. Emotion regulation, according to Dr. Gross (1998), refers to the methods and processes by which individuals influence which emotions they have, when they have them, and how they experience and express these emotions.

Over the years, we have developed clinical applications based on research in the field of emotion regulation. We have added new strategies, used them with patients presenting with a variety of disorders, and have found great success in assisting patients to improve their moods. We refer to our work as mood regulation rather than emotion regulation and believe that individuals have the ability to change moods from one state to another at will.

Mood regulation refers to processes used for monitoring, measuring, evaluating, and modifying our emotional reactions. Regulating our moods is accomplished by influencing the type of emotions we want to have and their intensity and duration. Mood regulation refers to the way we determine which emotions we experience, when we experience them, how long they last and how strong they are, and how we recognize, identify, and express them.

Defining mood regulation

Regulation is defined as restoring order in a system that has been out of control or dysregulated. It is derived from the verb *regulate*, which means establishing balance, synchronicity, and rhythmicity in a system. Furthermore, the word *regulation* is related to its cousin word, the adjective *regular*. The term regular brings to mind a sense of normalcy, steadiness, and orderliness. Regular conveys uninterrupted "clockwork" functioning day in and day out. These definitions help explain the concept of regulation in mood regulation therapy. All of these adjectives and explanations will help us understand why we emphasize the concept of regulation in our therapy. Successful therapeutic regulations are those that lead to a sense of balance, rhythm, uniformity, and consistency in a person's mood and sense of well-being; regulation is the goal, or the endpoint, of therapy.

Homeostasis and mood regulation

Every person lives with an entity that defines him or her in a unique way and differentiates him or her from others, giving rise to the *I*. This entity is comprised of physical, mental, and spiritual dimensions that collectively give each of us a distinct individual identity and personality. This entity, which we call the *me*, exists within an internal boundary called the human body, which is immersed and interacts continuously within an outer physical and social environment but is separated from it.

Claude Bernard in 1865 stated that living systems maintain their own internal environments within set limits and are independent of the external environment. He called this internal environment the *internal milieu*, which had to be stable at all times for the survival of the person. He defined the internal milieu to include all of the biological and chemical processes that occur within the human body. Nearly seventy years later, Walter B. Cannon introduced the term *homeostasis* to describe those ongoing coordinated processes that serve to regulate and stabilize the body's internal milieu. The term comes from two Greek words meaning "to remain the same." Cannon (1932) defined homeostasis as "the coordinated physiological reactions which maintain most of the steady states of the body…and which are so peculiar to the living organisms."

Homeostasis refers to the coordinated processes needed to provide internal stability in a living organism (Damasio 1999). These processes are essential for maintaining life. As one of the fundamental characteristics of the human body and brain, homeostasis aims to maintain the internal environment within possible and normal limits. Homeostatic regulation also allows the individual to function more effectively by continuously adjusting regulatory function. Homeostasis is a built-in physiological mechanism that allows the body to undergo constant adjustment and readjustment and includes, among other things, temperature regulation; modification of salinity and acidity levels; and regulation of concentrations of glucose, insulin, various ions, oxygen, carbon dioxide, various hormones, and urea. Such readjusting of body systems is what makes it possible for the body to undergo metabolism, sweat to cool the body, shiver to warm the body, and perform other necessary functions. This regulation allows the human body to stay alive and in constant motion.

Homeostasis creates a state of functional balance where the body functions at its best. This state of balance occurs within a range of upper and lower limits and is not a static entity. This state is maintained by ongoing, multiple, re-programmed, consecutive, bio-regularity functions in the body and brain. Corrective regulation occurs when alterations in the state of homeostasis cause a departure from the upper or lower boundaries of normal functioning. This departure beyond the upper and lower limits of normal function can lead to a state of imbalance or dysregulation.

Like all other functions, emotions are an essential part of the body's homeostatic regulatory process and undergo constant adjustment. Moods have a normal range with upper and lower limits. Mania and depression occur above and below these two limits.

At any time there are several processes going on within the body and brain, and between the body and brain on one hand and the environment on another. Each process affects other processes so that there is continuous adjustment within the body and brain. Through a continuous feedback loop, the amount of fluctuation in the internal milieu is kept to a minimum and stability is maintained despite all of the environmental demands and changes. This way the body does more than survive; it adapts itself to and evolves according to modifications in the environment.

Understanding the
role of the emotion center

Mood regulation is part of the body's homeostatic regularity function. The emotion center and associated areas in the brain interconnected to it play a constant regulatory function in maintaining the biological regulation of emotion through feedback received externally from the environment and internally from hormones, electrical impulses, and other chemical messengers and neurotransmitters. Mood is adjusted constantly through these regulatory functions and is kept in a stable state by the steady flow of feedback. The changes seen in depression are caused by a disruption in this homeostatic function.

Dr. Mary Phillips (2003a) has conducted several neuroimaging studies of the brain and has described the anatomical brain regions that comprise the emotion center. Dr. Phillips and her colleagues' overall findings from their research into the neurobiology of emotions reveal that the neurobiological processes of emotions are dependent on the functioning of two neural systems: a ventral and a dorsal system (See FIGURE 2). The ventral system includes the amygdala, insula, ventral striatum, and ventral regions of the anterior cingulate gyrus and ventromedial and ventrolateral prefrontal cortices. This system is responsible for the identification of stimuli and the generation of emotions, feelings, and moods (affective states). The system is also important for the unconscious automatic regulation of the body's responses to the emotions generated.

The dorsal system includes the hippocampus and the dorsal regions of the anterior cingulate gyrus and prefrontal cortex. Through this system, thoughts and cognitions are integrated with the emotional information identified and generated in the ventral system. The dorsal system is also responsible for the regulation of emotions mainly by inhibition so that responses are contextually appropriate.

These two systems have a close interdependent connection and functional relationship. These two systems are what we refer to as the emotion center. Any abnormality or malfunctioning in either or both of these neural systems may result in emotional symptoms and mood disorders as depression.

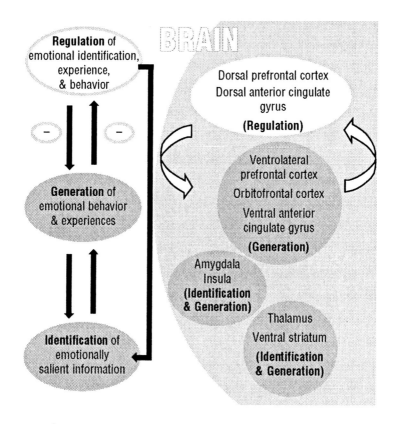

FIGURE 2. EMOTION CENTER ANATOMY. ON THE RIGHT SIDE OF THE DIAGRAM ARE THE ANATOMICAL REGIONS OF THE BRAIN THAT MAKE UP THE EMOTION CENTER. ON THE LEFT SIDE ARE DESCRIPTIONS OF THE ROLES THESE BRAIN REGIONS PLAY IN EMOTIONAL PROCESSING (PHILLIPS 2003B).

So, while the emotion center and the processes related to this regulation are a biological activity of the brain, this function is fully interactive and responsive to all of the body systems and organs, our physical and social environments, and is affected by our spirituality and cognitions. The emotion center is not an isolated biological domain but is affected by the linkages of several disciplines (other biological functions in the body, cognitions, relationships, and spirituality). The emotion center contains neurocircuitry that is modifiable and changeable by experiences of the individual and changes in the environment. Even though the circuitry functions biologically and is preset, it can still undergo adjustments stimulated by new experiences. Paquette and colleagues (2003) conclude in a study of cognitive therapy and its effect on neural circuitry that "changes made at the mind level, within a psychotherapeutic context, are able to functionally 'rewire' the brain…In other words, change the mind and you change the brain." Moods, therefore, are not simply reduced to a brain biological function—because the brain is able to learn and can be modified by new experiences.

Mood regulation processes maintain our mood state within a defined set of variability to enhance our functioning and stability. From moment to moment, our mood continuously varies but only within the range of limits of preset variation, which we define as normal limits. When we go above or below the set limits, our mood may become dysregulated.

Mood regulation is the process in which the brain's emotion center responds to triggers, modifies them, expresses them, and determines which feelings are chosen and how they are expressed or inhibited. This biological activity is impacted by our thought processes (cognitions), by the relationships in our life, and by our spirituality. Mood regulation results from the connected interactions of these four influences. Mood regulation depends on a dedicated multi-dimensional system that is inseparable from biological regulation.

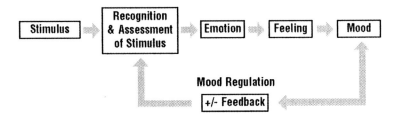

FIGURE 3. THE MOOD REGULATION PROCESS IN THE EMOTION CENTER OF THE BRAIN. THIS STEP-BY-STEP DIAGRAM ILLUSTRATES HOW MOOD REGULATION OCCURS IN THE BRAIN.

The human body is able to maintain functioning with the same consistency and predictability day in and day out through a set of regulatory processes affecting all its vital functions, including sleep, temperature control, appetite, sexual drive, menstrual cycle, and energy level. The hypothalamus in the brain plays a major role in this regulation. While the regulation processes for each function differ from each other, the result is the same—the function is maintained in a range that we all accept as or call the "normal" range. For instance, body temperature is maintained within a normal range between 98 to 100 degrees Fahrenheit. Any change above or below those limits constitutes dysregulation and is an indication of a disease state. In another example, if someone says, "My sleep is off," we understand that it is off the normal rhythm and not regulated and that the person is either sleeping too little, too much, or erratically. In the same way, when a woman says, "My period is irregular," we understand that the menstrual cycle is dysregulated and is occurring at a cycle of either more days or fewer days than the regular 28-day cycle.

In the same manner, our mood is regulated within what we commonly call "normal mood" range. Sometimes we refer to it as an "okay" mood. The body has several mechanisms that maintain our mood within that set range of normalcy; these mechanisms will be discussed in more detail in this chapter and in Chapter 3.

Characteristics of moods

Moods are multi-componential processes that involve the following:

- How we subjectively experience a mood state, including the specific emotions experienced and thoughts evoked
- How we express that mood in our behavior (for example, by screaming or having a temper tantrum when angry)
- Physiological responses (for example, how the face gets red and our pulse increases when we are angry)
- Executive functions of the brain (including how our decisions are influenced and how attention, concentration, and memory function).

Mood regulation involves attempts to influence and change one or more of these components through these means:

- The individual's capacity to modulate, maintain, increase, or decrease both negative and positive emotions
- Occurrence under the individual's conscious control and awareness, although it may also occur unconsciously and automatically at times
- Functioning as an adaptive physiological means that is neither good nor bad.

Mood regulation is dependent on four dimensions—the biological, cognitive, social, and spiritual. The interaction of these dimensions can alter the regulatory circuit in the emotion center and cause changes in mood. These are the four dimensions:

- Biological, which is mediated through chemicals, hormones, and neural connections
- Cognitive, which is mediated through the frontal cortex
- Social, which refers to a person's physical and social environments and relationships
- Spiritual, which is related to a person's faith in God, and his or her sense of purpose and meaning in life.

Functioning collectively, these influences affect the emotion center in a number of ways. They determine what stimulus to respond to and shape it in accordance with a given emotion. They shape some aspects of how the emotion is expressed, and they shape the behavior that follows the deployment of an emotion. Mood regulation, therefore, is the outcome of the interaction of environmental influences, cognitive messaging, and spiritual influences within a biological matrix. Body and brain are the basic biological mechanisms responsible for mood but are influenced by the environment or social experience, by cognitions, and by spiritual experiences; the connection is inseparable.

When do mood regulation skills begin?

Mood regulation skills are developed gradually. Children are born emotionally unregulated in the same way that they are unregulated with their bowel functions, temperament, sleep, and other functions. Through healthy development, children are taught how to regulate their emotions, how to identify proper cues for expressing or holding back emotions, and how to adjust emotional reactions at will. Healthy development depends on healthy role modeling and on skill building, which is normally provided by parents, teachers, and peers.

If a child or adolescent fails to learn these mood-regulating skills, the result at adulthood will be an individual unable to master his mood state who has great difficulty emotionally when confronted with conflict or stress. The person in this situation becomes a servant to his negative mood, whether it is depression, anxiety, rage, or anger. Such a person may eventually seek external dysfunctional regulators such as drugs, alcohol, or food in an attempt to cope and restore his emotions to a state of equilibrium. Not being able to do so, the person continues in a vicious self-destructive cycle, attempting to regulate emotions that have spun out of control.

On the other hand, if a child develops a healthy pattern of mood regulation in childhood, he or she will move into adolescence able to use and test these skills in dealing with the world. Adolescence is a period where mood-regulating skills are clarified and fine-tuned. This leads eventually to adulthood and a state of emotional maturity. A person is considered to have good mood regulation skills when he or she has mastery over his or her moods and emotions in all weathers and terrain. At that point we consider the person to have developed a high *emotional quotient* or what is called E.Q.

These are the healthy skills that are taught to children and adolescents to help them learn to regulate mood:

- Identify, describe, and differentiate emotions and moods
- Accept emotional experiences without fear

- Learn that emotions are an important source of information for decision making and be able to decode that information
- Eliminate the use of worry, denial, suppression, and other ineffective or avoidant emotional strategies
- Develop an increased understanding of how moods affect relationships, and vice-versa.

Mood regulation, therefore, is a dynamic developmental process with its roots in early childhood. It gives each of us our own distinct and unique individual differences in how we are, what choices we make, how we express ourselves, and so on. It eventually is responsible for our sense of wellness and well-being.

When do we regulate our moods?

We can regulate our moods at three key times:
- *Before* emotions are fully experienced and expressed. For example, if you know that taking an exam causes anxiety, then you may decide to do some anxiety-lowering strategies such as meditating or taking an anti-anxiety medication before the test to prevent the anxiety from erupting.
- *During* the time the emotions are being experienced. For example, if riding in an elevator makes you anxious, you may as you enter an elevator start sensing anxiety, develop a feeling of pressure in your chest, and feel fearful. You want to control that fear so you can ride the elevator without an anxiety attack.
- *After* the emotions have been experienced and expressed. For example, you are upset by someone and get angry and start yelling. At this point, you still have an option to regulate and de-escalate by walking away, counting to ten, or taking a time-out.

This ability to regulate mood gives us a wide range of opportunity to access and change our emotions, if we know how. Knowing how to regulate our emotions with consideration to timing allows us to self-monitor and self-correct an emotion if we don't like it at any time before, during, or after its occurrence. Knowing how to regulate our emotions also allows us to prevent a negative emotion from being expressed before it occurs—if we anticipate its occurrence.

Mechanisms of mood regulation

Researchers have described three mood regulation mechanisms. The first two—*mood repair* and *mood dampening*—are called intervening strategies because they seek to change a mood state from a negative to a positive one. The third, *mood maintenance*, is a strategy that is used to preserve the current mood state (Mayer and Stevens 1994; Salovey et al. 1995).

Mood repair applies when a person attempts to change a dysregulated negative mood state to a well-regulated positive one. An example is when a person feels down or depressed and chooses to engage in a pleasurable activity or hobby to change his or her mood. Growing up, we develop various strategies to change our mood, and we use these strategies without being consciously aware of it.

Mood dampening applies when a person tries to dampen, "down-regulate," or inhibit an excited negative mood state to a more stable or neutral one. An example is when a person feels angry and furious at another person and walks away to calm down and de-escalate.

Mood maintenance refers to strategies that a person uses to maintain a current positive mood state. For example, a person who feels good because he is doing an enjoyable activity will continue doing so to maintain his mood state. L.G. Aspinwall (1998) maintains that when an individual feels good, the person will automatically use strategies to maintain that positive mood, whereas when a person is in a negative mood state, he attempts to repair it.

How are moods regulated?

Mood regulation processes refer to the things that we do to influence, adjust, or affect whether a given mood state occurs. In our own research and clinical experience, we have found that four dimensions regulate mood. These dimensions are biological, cognitive, social, and spiritual. Each of these dimensions gives rise to processes, which are the activities occurring within that dimension. For instance, thinking is a process that occurs in the cognitive dimension. These processes play a role in regulating our mood from day to day and moment to moment. These processes are the foundation of mood regulation therapy (MRT).

Mood regulation begins with the physiological functions of the body. The other three regulating processes—cognitive, social, and spiritual—play a significant role in mood regulation by interacting with and influencing the biological regulatory system. For example, sleep regulation is affected by our thoughts or noise in our environment, while a menstrual cycle can be delayed by stress and anxiety. Mood is therefore determined and influenced not only by the physiological mechanism in the brain and nervous system but by our thoughts, beliefs, relationships, and the environment we live in.

Through the emotion center, mood regulation is the tie that binds all four dimensions together. For instance, any change in the environment is detected as a stimulus and processed by the emotion center as a signal. Thoughts, images, and cognitions start in the frontal lobe and are then processed in the emotion center, resulting in secondary emotions. Likewise, spiritual experiences are expressed in the brain through the activity of several regions interconnected with the emotion center. Any physical changes in the body or brain are mediated to the emotion center directly through the neural circuit or indirectly through hormones and other chemicals traveling through the bloodstream. The four dimensions thus all converge and affect the emotion center, each through its own pathways and mechanisms. As regulatory processes, they keep adjusting our emotions upwards or downwards.

Understanding the four mood regulation processes

Mood regulation processes are the activities that occur within the four dimensions (biological, cognitive, social, and spiritual). Mood regulation is an integrative process that allows one or many of the mood-regulating processes to be at work attempting to regulate a person's mood at any time. When we are educated and aware of these processes, we can intentionally use them as strategies to change our mood. Only through knowledge and attention to all these sides of our nature can we develop a sense of balance and well-being and feel terrific. FIGURE 4 illustrates the influences that can affect mood regulation.

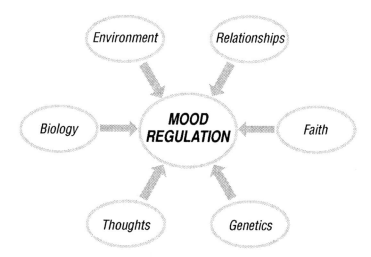

FIGURE 4. MOOD REGULATION PROCESSES. THESE MAJOR INFLUENCES AFFECT MOOD REGULATION.

Biological Influences on Mood: The physiological activities of the body include the endocrine system, nervous system, and cardiovascular system, among other body systems. The emotion center (mood center) is the part of the brain that is responsible for mood regulation. The mood center is connected to and constantly communicates with the other regions of the brain and the rest of the body. The mood center and its regulating processes are affected by and affect the other regions of the brain and the rest of the body. The mood center is made up of a vast network of nerve cells and tracts that are interconnected. The nerve cells communicate with each other through special chemicals called neurotransmitters that generate electrical impulses that flow from one cell to the other, carrying information throughout the neural network. The mood center's key function is to maintain a well-balanced mood state. A well-balanced mood state is what a person experiences when he feels terrific. A normally functioning mood center ensures that the person's mood on a given day does not go too high or too low. A very high mood state is called mania. A very low mood state is called depression.

Cognitive Influences on Mood: Cognitive processes refer to thoughts, opinions, interpretations, reasoning, skills, and attitudes. Our cognitive processes and skills are learned from our parents and influenced by the significant people that we grow up with. Our cognitive skills are further shaped by the experiences we encounter in life. An example of cognitive influence on mood is the person who is a pessimist, always has negative thoughts, predicts gloom and doom, and his mood becomes depressed.

Social Influences on Mood: How we interact with the environment around us and the way relationships affect us and we affect them can also influence our mood. People influence our moods in various ways and intensities. The manner in which people enter our lives and how and when they exit has a profound effect on our mood. People come and go in our lives with or without our permission. This process of entry and exit is *attachment, separation,* and *loss.* It has been extensively studied by psychologists in the last fifty years and has been found to have a profound effect on our emotions. Healthy attachments and close nurturing bonds contribute to stability in our mood and lead to feeling terrific. Abandonment and loss of significant relationships have been well known to cause grief and depression. For example, examine how important your relationship with your parents is in determining your mood state. Can they spoil your mood? Are you affected by their mood? The answer is probably "yes." People are powerful determinants of our moods.

Dr. John Bowlby (1998) developed the attachment theory, which describes our socio-emotional development in childhood and the attachment bonds that we form through attachment behavior that begins early in life and continues throughout our life cycle. He defined attachment bonds as our disposition to seek proximity to an individual for protection, comfort, and assistance. Attachment behaviors are the actions that we do to engage and be close to others, such as hugging or holding hands.

During normal developmental stages, attachment behavior leads to the formation and maintenance of close and secure emotional bonds between child and mother. As the child grows, he or she starts developing attachments with others. These attachments continue to be formed and maintained throughout life.

Attachments shape and form our relationships and are the dynamic of any relationship. Healthy attachments lead to healthy relationships and are an important ingredient for feeling terrific (Schore 2001). Research work by Schore (2002) and others has shown that attachment behavior is biologically mediated through the limbic system and other areas of the brain that are part of the mood center. The mood center is affected and changed by attachment bonds. Schore (2001) states that "attachments can thus be defined as the dyadic regulation of emotion."

This is understandable as the goal of attachment behavior is the formation, maintenance, and renewal of emotional bonds. Attachment behaviors are linked to the emotional center of the brain where they can influence and change our mood and are influenced and changed by our mood. Disruption of attachment bonds leads to disturbance in limbic system activity and inability to regulate the intensity and duration of emotions (Schore 2001) and then to depression.

Dr. Bowlby (1980) states, "In most forms of depressive disorder, including that of chronic mourning, the principle issue about which a person feels helpless is his ability to make and maintain affectional relationships."

Spiritual Influences on Mood: How we define our purpose in life, how we find meaning, and the way we face the questions of life and death are related to our spiritual outlook and beliefs. Individuals with strong faith who have the subjective experience of receiving spiritual support from God have a stable mood and less depression than those who don't have that support. Faith has a direct, consistent, enduring effect on a person's mood. Faith gives people the strength to endure adversity and face life's crises. It offers hope when there is none. In a discussion of perspectives of Tolstoy's *A Confession,* William James (1890) identified faith as a driving force in mankind's existence: "Since mankind has existed, wherever life has been, there also has been the faith that gave the possibility of living. Faith is the sense of life, that sense by virtue of which man does not destroy himself, but continues to live on. It is the force whereby we live."

Faith provides balance and helps restore our mood when it is off. We may not understand how faith heals, but we know of its enduring effect on a person's sense of well-being and feeling terrific.

The lack of faith and spiritual support leads to what James called "religious melancholy," which he described as "a well-marked case of anhedonia, of passive loss of appetite for all life's values." James stated that depression develops in the absence of meaning in a person's life, when there is self-doubt and fear of the universe, when a person has no one to turn to, or when a person struggles with an inner sense of sin and corruption and finds no outlet. He noted that when this melancholia sets in, man's original optimism and self-satisfaction get "leveled with the dust." Some pastoral counselors attribute depression to lack of faith and spiritual emptiness and call it *spiritual melancholy.* The term conveys the same meaning as religious melancholy.

Through faith and participation in a spiritual relationship, a person can overcome the anguish of depression. This faith is to be found in the inner reaches of the self, within the person's spirit, and through a spiritual quest. This quest to faith leads to what Professor James Leuba (1896) called a "faith state."

Many carefully conducted research studies have suggested a direct connection between our spiritual and biological dimensions. Studies by Bouchard and colleagues found that identical twins were twice as likely as fraternal twins to have similar spiritual beliefs. This is an indication that spiritual beliefs may be determined genetically and transmitted biologically (Bouchard et al. 1990, 1999; Bouchard and McGue 2003).

More recently, Newberg's brain imaging research with Buddhist monks has demonstrated that meditative states show a consistent pattern of changes in brain activity (increased activation in the frontal lobe and decreased activation in the parietal lobe) and the neurotransmitter systems (as serotonin and GABA), in conjunction with hormonal and autonomic (heart rate and respiration) changes. He states that the changes in the brain are mediated through the limbic system, which is the central part of the emotion center (Newberg and Iversen 2003).

Michael Persinger's research (1983, 2001) has linked mystical experiences with several interconnecting areas of the brain, central to which is the amygdala, a part of the limbic system and an essential part of the emotion center. Furthermore, in a study by Jacqueline Borg and colleagues (Borg et al. 2003), it was determined that there was a role for the serotonin system in mediating spiritual experiences; she states in the conclusion of her study that "the serotonin system may serve as a biological basis for spiritual experiences." Serotonin neurons originate in the brain stem and innervate several brain regions, including the limbic system. Serotonergic receptors have a major role in mood states, specifically in depression.

We don't know where or how spiritual or religious experiences start within us, or what exactly constitutes the religious experience. But these and other similar studies have clearly demonstrated that spiritual and religious experiences are mediated through several interconnected regions of the brain at a biological level as or after they are experienced. This may be how the brain decodes our spiritual experiences—from a complex level to a simpler biological "signal" level so we may integrate that spiritual experience with the other experiences of our consciousness as emotions and thoughts.

These studies don't suggest that spiritual experiences are caused by biological processes, but that spiritual experiences (as faith, self-transcendence, or religious practices) are biologically expressed in the brain and affect brain performance. Once expressed in the brain, the effects of these spiritual experiences are integrated with the other functions of the body and may modify them and be modified by them.

Identifying mood dysregulation

So far, we have discussed how healthy mood regulation occurs. Like all regulatory systems, things don't always work well. When a person's mood is not well regulated for any reason, it becomes dysregulated.

Mood dysregulation can occur in many forms. For example, some women in the premenstrual period have a dysregulated mood marked by irritability, tearfulness, and depression. People with bipolar disorder have a dysregulation in their mood called *mania*. People who use drugs and alcohol have dysregulated moods characterized by depression, anger, or anxiety states. People with rage have a dysregulated angry mood state. Individuals with panic disorder have a dysregulated mood state marked by anxiety. The list is long. The most common forms of dysregulated mood include anxiety and depression.

Our clinical work over the last twenty-five years has focused on working with people who have mild to severe degrees of mood dysregulation, primarily anxiety and depression. Conceptualizing depression as a mood dysregulation condition allowed us to develop the method we call Mood Regulation Therapy (MRT), which we have found effective and enduring in changing people's moods from feeling depressed to feeling terrific. In the next chapter, we will be discussing depression as a mood dysregulation condition and then we will discuss the specifics of mood regulation therapy.

CHAPTER 2
Depression

For there are...sufferings which have no tongue...—Percy Bysshe Shelley

The nature of depression

Depression is a universal feeling known in all cultures, across all ages, and across all times. It is a feeling that is inherent to our experience as human beings and intrinsic to our daily life and dealings. It is a feeling that we all have experienced at one time or another in response to loss, separation, or unresolved personal conflict.

People use the word *depression* in several different ways to describe different states—as a feeling state, a disease state, or a personality type. Commonly the word depression is used to express and describe a feeling, as when someone says, "I feel depressed." It can also be used as an objective description of someone, as when we say, "His face looks depressed." A doctor will use the term to mean a diagnosable disorder, as when he tells a patient, "You have depression." We also use the term to refer to a person's character, as when we say, "You are a depressive person."

The feelings of depression that occur in response to life circumstances such as loss are normal human experiences and come about as a built-in emotional reaction to the event. When depression occurs as a disorder, we attribute it to an imbalance in brain or body chemistry. When depression occurs as a character trait, it is assumed that the person developed depressive attitudes due to social or psychological problems in his or her formative years.

In spite of this wide variation in how the word is used, depression first and foremost refers to a mood state. People with depression undergo negative mood changes and experience a range of negative feelings such as unhappiness, sadness, indifference, despair, dejection, helplessness, hopelessness, pessimism, and loneliness. This negative mood experience is the core of all that we call depression.

Dr. Gerald Klerman and colleagues (1984) and other researchers (Harlow and Harlow 1971) have proposed that the inherent capacity that we have to feel depressed after an injury, loss, or the disruption of a close relationship is a normal developmental experience. When an infant is separated from its mother, the infant starts crying, becomes tearful, and has a sad, distressed look on his or her face. Dr. Klerman calls this change in the infant's mood a "depressive response," which is an expression of the infant's fear, sadness, and loss of dependence on the mother. Feelings of abandonment, insecurity, and helplessness prevail because the infant depends on his mother for protection, feeding, gratification, love, security, and survival. This depressive response, then, is a normal response that reflects the importance of both attachment and social bonds. It is seen in humans, primates, and many other mammalian species and serves for the survival of the species; anything that threatens to disrupt the attachment bond between infant and parent will lead to this depressive response (Kaufman 1967).

As a child grows into adulthood and is able to care for himself, he retains the ability to respond to certain events and at certain times with the depressive response. Triggering events can be real or anticipated losses, such as the death of a loved one, personal failures, disappointments, not getting one's wishes, and criticism or rejection by others. All of these events can threaten a person's sense of security by threatening the loss of an important social bond or a person on whom he or she is dependent which, in turn, evokes the depressive response. Accordingly, the depressive response becomes a built-in defensive reaction that is wired into the person and under certain environmental changes or threats can be evoked.

As we have discussed, our feelings follow a cyclical pattern from moment to moment and hour to hour, varying from slightly up to slightly down, on a continuum of twenty-four-hour cycles called circadian rhythms. Mood is the sum total of our feelings at any given period of time. Depression is a mood state that occurs when we feel down, and the feeling of depression can range in intensity from mild to very severe.

Dr. Aubrey Lewis in 1938 proposed that the various forms of depression are manifestations of a single underlying condition where the symptoms, severity, and duration of depression occur over a wide continuum. Recent research findings by Dr. Kenneth Kendler (1998) support the continuum theory of depression; Dr. Kendler found that there is a continuum between the various types of depression. Other respected researchers in the field have further demonstrated that all the types of depression occur on a spectrum of severity, not as distinct disorders or entities. Furthermore, research shows that there is considerable mobility as people can move from one end of the depressive spectrum to the other (Angst and Merikangas 1997). For instance, a person may have a grief reaction that turns into a clinical depression, or the two may co-occur.

Our view of depression reflects these findings in that we view depression as a mood regulation disorder that occurs along a continuum of intensity, severity, and scope. What matters when assessing a person along the depression continuum is the severity of the symptoms and how the symptoms are affecting the individual and impacting his daily functioning.

Depression forms a continuum of states and conditions that range from a case of the blues to severe life-threatening or psychotic states. Even the milder forms of depression, which are called minor depression or *dysthymia*, will impair social, personal, and vocational functioning and cause higher mortality from heart disease and other health consequences (Judd et al. 1996; Paykel and Weissman 1978; Hury and Bebington 1987).

Most of us will suffer from an episode of depression in our life. Few of us will seek treatment. Fewer still will have learned anything from it.—Namir Damluji M.D.

How common is depression?

Depression is far more common than most people realize. Father John Powell (1989) wrote, "one third of all Americans wake up depressed every day. Professionals estimate that only 10 to 15 percent of Americans think of themselves as truly happy."

Most studies show that around one in three people has a detectable level of depression of one kind or another at any given time. In a study among people over 60 years old in the general population, Dr. R. Heun and colleagues (2000) found the rate of depression—major, minor and recurrent brief—to be 36.7 percent. In a community study of young adults, Dr. J. Angst, a prominent researcher in the field of depression, found a 29.5 percent prevalence rate for depression (major, minor, and recurrent brief), which broke down to 36.5 percent among women and 22.2 percent among men (Angst and Merikangas 1997). According to the World Health Organization, one million people worldwide commit suicide every year (WHO 2003). The WHO also estimates that by the year 2020 major depression will become the second greatest cause of disability and suffering in the world (WHO 2001). These studies and research reports point to the high rate of depression and its serious complications (disability or death), not to mention the suffering that depression invokes on the depressed person, his family, and friends.

Depression reaches from the poorest inner-city homes to the loftiest palaces. Sylvia Plath, Dick Cavett, Georgia O'Keeffe, Mark Twain, Virginia Woolf, Abraham Lincoln, and Winston Churchill are but a few who have struggled with depression. The tragedy is that, although so many people struggle silently with depression, too few get help. Depression is often dismissed as some sort of moral failure or personal weakness. Because of that, many persons fail to get help and live sad and miserable lives.

Types of depression

Depression occurs in many forms and encompasses varying degrees of severity and intensity across a spectrum, as we have already noted. Researchers in the field have long supported this spectrum concept of depression. In the words of Goodwin and Jamison (1990), "In our view, there is more evidence consistent with the spectrum concept than there is with the idea that depressive disorders constitute discrete clusters marked by relatively discontinuous boundaries."

The concept of the depressive spectrum is not new. Kraeplin recognized the concept in his 1921 article on manic depressive illness: "There is usually an uninterrupted series of transitions to 'periodic melancholia,' at the one end of which those cases stand in which the course is quite indefinite with irregular fluctuations and remissions, while at the other end of the spectrum there are the forms with a sharply defined, completely developed, morbid picture and definite remissions of long duration." TABLE 1 illustrates the concept of the depressive spectrum.

	Normal Depressive Response			Abnormal Depressive Response	
Severity	*Sadness* Grief *Mild*		Moderate	*Severe* Psychotic	
Duration	*Hours to Days to Weeks*			*Months to Years*	
Functionality	*Normal*		Impaired	*Incapacitated*	
Symptoms	*Mood & Thought*			*Moods Thoughts Physical symptoms Behavior*	
Cause	*Mood Dysregulation*				

TABLE 1. THE DEPRESSIVE SPECTRUM. THE VARIOUS TYPES OF DEPRESSION RANGE IN SEVERITY FROM SADNESS TO PSYCHOSIS.

In the last two decades depression has been viewed from a purely categorical approach, classifying depression into separate disease entities as exemplified in the diagnostic categories of the American Psychiatric Association's edition of the *Diagnostic and Statistical Manual* (DSM IV) and the *International Classification of Diseases* (ICD) manual developed by the World Health Organization. The DSM's and ICD's categorical concepts of depression are based on lumping symptom clusters as the major distinguishing variables and not causative reasons or course of the disorder (McHugh and Slavney 1986).

Our own clinical experience and work with patients support the view that depression should be viewed along a dimensional spectrum, while certain types could also be understood as distinct categories along that spectrum. Our work in this book and our discussion of mood regulation therapy will follow that premise. The dimension spectrum approach that we use is based on the fundamental concept that all of the depressive diagnostic categories share the same causation of depression—a central mood dysregulation. Dr. McHugh confirms this when he states, in discussing the validating feature of manic-depressive syndrome, "The pathognomonic feature of the manic-depressive syndrome is the deregulation of the affective domain of mental life, resulting in an unrestrained dominance of mental activity by affect" (McHugh and Slavney 1986).

One feeling, many presentations

There have been many classifications used for depression, and these have varied extensively over the last century—from the neurotic-psychotic division to the current classification used in the DSM IV. Current research findings point to depression occurring along a continuum, where one end is represented by mild symptoms of feeling blue and the other end is represented by severe depressive disorder with psychosis. One of the classifications used in research (Lavretsky and Kumar 2002) is the one that classifies depression into three types based on severity:

- Major depression
- Minor depression
- Sub-threshold depression.

This classification may be helpful in research, but we have not found it helpful in our work with patients. The classification that we find practical and valuable is the one that classifies depression according to the way the word depression is used and descriptively qualified, which are the following types:

- Depression as a reaction, as in bereavement
- Depression as an illness, as in major depressive disorder
- Depression as an attitude, as in the depressive personality.

In all of these types of depression, the symptoms vary in intensity, severity, scope, and configuration. The shared characteristic among all of these types is the dysregulation in mood, which results in a low mood state called depression. This low mood may be temporary and appropriate, as in grief, or it may be persistent and serious, leading to severe disability or suicide, as in major depressive disorder.

For each type of depression described above, there are sub-types that share specific identifying characteristics. TABLES 2-1 AND 2-2 outline the various sub-types of depression and their descriptions.

■ DEPRESSION AS A REACTION: SYMPTOM OR EXPERIENCE

Reactive Depression	Arises following an unhappy or stressful event
Bereavement	Normal grief

■ DEPRESSION AS AN ATTITUDE: TEMPERAMENT

Dysthymic Disorder	Depressed mood for most of the day, more days than not, lasting at least two years
Depressive Personality	A pervasive pattern of depressive thinking and behaviors beginning by early adulthood

■ DEPRESSION AS AN ILLNESS: A SYNDROME

Major Depression (Clinical Depression)	Depressive symptoms that represent a significant change from previous level of functioning lasting two consecutive weeks and including depressed mood or loss of interest or pleasure. Major depression can be a single episode, recurrent, chronic and may have characteristic features, such as melancholia.
Seasonal Affective Disorder or SAD	Recurrent episodes of depression in certain months of the year, alternating with periods of normal mood the rest of the year
Postpartum Depression	Depression that follows the birth of a child

TABLE 2-1. TYPES OF DEPRESSION. THESE ARE THE TYPES AND SUB-TYPES OF DEPRESSION AND THEIR DEFINING CHARACTERISTICS. (CONTINUED ON NEXT PAGE)

■ **DEPRESSION AS AN ILLNESS: A SYNDROME** (continued)

Atypical Depression	Depression that does not fit into the above categories
Bipolar Disorder, Depressed	Depression occurring in the context of bipolar disorder; symptoms are the same as those in major depression
Depression due to a general medical condition	Depression occurring secondary to a medical condition, as hypothyroidism
Psychotic Depression	Depression accompanied by thoughts and beliefs that do not conform to reality; thinking is disorganized; delusions and/or hallucinations usually present
Substance-induced Depression	Symptoms of depression that develop during or within a month of substance intoxication or withdrawal
Cyclothymic Disorder	For at least two years, evidence of numerous periods of hyperactivity (hypomania) followed by numerous periods with depressive symptoms
Pre-Menstrual Dysphoric Disorder or PMDD	Depressed symptoms prior to the menstrual period

TABLE 2-2. TYPES OF DEPRESSION. (CONTINUED FROM PREVIOUS PAGE)

Can depression be normal?

It has been estimated that in a year four out of every ten persons in the United States complain of feeling depressed or unhappy (Bradburn 1977). The feeling of depression is a normal human experience and it is part of our everyday life; most of us have said at one time or another, "I feel down today" or "I'm in a funk" or the like. When we lose someone close or something valuable, we feel depressed.

When we are rejected or devalued by people we care about, we also may feel depressed. These are normal experiences that we go through in our normal life.

Even though the feeling of depression may be a normal experience, there are clear boundaries where depression is considered abnormal and where intervention and treatment are warranted. When we talk about depression, we have to be clear what we mean because, as we have seen, it can be a reaction, an attitude, or an illness. Depression can start as a normal response to stress in one's environment and escalate into an abnormal state of a depressive illness.

Dr. Vicky Rippere did several studies in an effort to understand how people normally respond on their own when they get depressed. Her research showed that people respond to getting depressed with what she calls the "anti-depressive response." This response is their coping mechanism, which they employ in an effort to get out of the depressed state or adjust to it. The most common anti-depressive response behaviors that Dr. Rippere found among depressed and non-depressed groups were watching television, keeping busy, talking to someone about how they feel, reading a newspaper or magazine, and doing something they enjoy (Rippere 1976). The manner and level of success in which individuals manage and respond to these anti-depressive behaviors with regard to their depression determines the outcome. Dr. Melanie Klein (1948) noted that learning to manage depression occurs during the early developmental stages, where children learn through example to control their feelings of fear and raise their self-esteem with the correct feedback. She called that the "depressive position."

All the terms that researchers have used to describe our normal response defenses to depression (anti-depressive behaviors, depressive position, depressive response) point to how depression is part and parcel of our lives and how under normal developmental circumstances we should be well-equipped to cope with most types of depression. (See FIGURE 5.) We think that the experiences we get from responding to depression in a normal corrective way (through developing our own functional anti-depressive responses) contribute to our emotional maturity and to the development of healthy defenses and coping skills. Dr. Klerman points out that it also contributes to the development of healthy social bonds and social learning and assists in the survival and growth of the human spirit (Klerman et al. 1984).

Depression becomes abnormal when there is an exaggeration and amplification of the intensity and duration of the depressive feeling and when the depressed person experiences the following:

- Considerable disturbance in the person's physical or psychological functioning
- An almost complete loss of pleasure in activities that were pleasurable
- No control over changing how he feels
- Interference with personal, social, and vocational functioning.

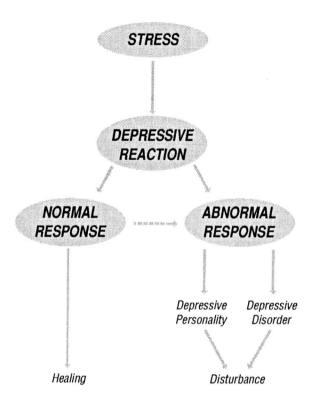

FIGURE 5. RESPONSES TO DEPRESSION. WHEN A DEPRESSIVE REACTION IS TRIGGERED BY STRESS, A PERSON MAY RESPOND IN A NORMAL OR ABNORMAL MANNER (ADAPTED FROM MITCHELL 1981).

We don't understand our sadness, and when we try we become confused.—Dorothy Rowe

The manifestations of depression

Depression is a pervasive emotion, one that affects multiple systems. When a person feels depressed, he may experience a variety of symptoms associated with the depressive feeling. The change in mood that is experienced in depression is accompanied by changes in a person's behavior, physical state, thinking, emotions, and social functioning. TABLE 3 lists some of the more common symptoms of depression.

Emotional	Cognitive	Behavioral	Physical	Social & Vocational
Feeling down	Negative thinking	Tearfulness	Change in appetite	Avoids family
Anxiety	Low self-esteem	No motivation	Sleep disturbance	Withdrawn from friends
Guilt	Obsessive	Increased alcohol use	Loss of sexual drive	Stops working
Anger	Suicidal thoughts	Illegal drug use	Lack of energy	Stops going to school
Irritability	Poor concentration	Talk and move slowly	Bodily complaints	
Hopelessness	Slowed thinking	Hostile	Aches and pains	
Worthlessness	Indecision	Neglect personal care	Increased or decreased weight	
Feeling empty	Poor judgment	Looks sad		

TABLE 3. COMMON SYMPTOMS OF DEPRESSION. DEPRESSION IMPACTS AND CHANGES A PERSON'S EMOTIONS, COGNITIONS, BEHAVIOR, PHYSICAL, AND SOCIAL FUNCTIONS.

Many men transmute their depression into other pathologies. Some seek relief in alcohol or drugs—solutions that only compound the problem—while others express their unhappiness through reckless or violent behavior. Researchers sometimes call these pathologies 'depressive equivalents'…—Michael C. Miller, M.D.

Masked depression

Individuals at times do not complain of feeling depressed but describe other disturbances of mood, such as nervousness, anger, or anxiety; physical complaints, such as pain, muscle weakness, or loss of appetite and energy; or certain compulsive behaviors, such as overeating or drug use, probably because these are more acceptable or more comfortable to talk about. In these instances the depression is said to be "masked" by other symptoms called depressive equivalents. These depressive equivalent symptoms (See FIGURE 6) mask an underlying depression, and the underlying depression has to be inferred from other symptoms or behaviors.

Depressive equivalents may be the presenting emotion or behavior when a person is feeling depressed. For instance, a person may present with the chief complaint of having bouts of anger and rage, underneath which may exist a depressive disorder. It may be easier for him to be angry and critical and say, "I'm pissed off" than to say, "I feel depressed." An adolescent may display his depressed feelings through impulsivity or acting out through shoplifting or self-injurious behaviors to bring attention to himself, when he is actually depressed. Depression presents in various ways, with varying intensities, and in varying ways of expressing the depressed feeling. A person may express depression directly and say, "I feel depressed," or mask and express it through a depressive equivalent.

- Drug and alcohol abuse
- Self-injurious behaviors
- Pessimistic attitude
- Worrying a lot and obsessing
- Aggression, anger, or rage
- Impulsivity or acting out
- Socially withdrawn or isolated
- Lack of motivation accompanied by inertia
- Compulsivity (overeating, compulsive shopping, gambling)
- Hypochondriacal complaints
- Physical symptoms that have no detectable underlying cause
- Atypical pain

FIGURE 6. DEPRESSIVE EQUIVALENTS. PEOPLE WITH DEPRESSION MAY PRESENT PRIMARILY OR EXCLUSIVELY WITH THESE "DEPRESSIVE EQUIVALENT" SYMPTOMS INSTEAD OF THE USUAL SYMPTOMS OF DEPRESSION.

Proper evaluation of the person with depression

When a person is feeling depressed and the depression is affecting the ability to function, he or she should seek help with a doctor or therapist to obtain a comprehensive evaluation and recommendations for treatment. It is important to see a doctor or therapist you can trust and with whom you feel open and comfortable. The doctor should be knowledgeable about various different types of depression, their treatments, and be open minded to new treatment approaches. Here are some of the basic tenets of a thorough evaluation as recommended by the Depression and Related Affective Disorder Association (Lipsey 2005):

- The doctor or therapist has to know the different types of depression. Some people have symptoms of depression as a reactive depression; others, as a manifestation of a major depressive disorder. One cannot tell from the degree of a person's depression alone which type of depression it is. If the therapist doesn't know the difference between the different types of depression and treats everyone with depression with medications, or treats all depression as a response to life problems with psychotherapy alone, the outcome will be disastrous.
- An evaluation includes taking a detailed history of the person's symptoms, how and when the depression began, the current stressors, coping skills, and how the depression affects functioning.
- The evaluation also involves taking a detailed family history of psychiatric disorders and any past history of being treated for any substance abuse or psychiatric problems.
- The next step in the evaluation involves taking a thorough medical history to rule out potential medical causes of depression. For example, neurological disorders such as multiple sclerosis, endocrine disorders such as diabetes, and a variety of medications such as anti-hypertensive medications can cause depression. The medical history is important in determining the cause and type of depression.
- The therapist may need to speak to family members to get other views of the person's depression and functioning.
- The therapist should always be willing to consider different treatment approaches and be willing to discuss the reasons for proposing a particular treatment.
- The therapist should clarify the type of depression, educate the person seeking treatment about the treatment plan and expected outcome, and provide steps to recovery with some general timelines. A therapist functions as consultant and coach in the process of helping a person heal from depression and feel terrific.

With proper evaluation and treatment, over 90 percent of those suffering from depression will get well and recover. In spite of that, only 10 percent of those suffering from depression ever seek help (Gold 1987).

Theories of causation of depression

There is no single cause for depression; there are many possibilities. Several theories have been proposed to explain the causes of depression. Over the last century, the best known are the psychoanalytic, behavioral, biological, social, and cognitive theories.

Sigmund Freud's psychoanalytic theory suggests that depression is caused by feelings of anger that the individual is unable to accept or express. This anger becomes unconsciously internalized, and the person develops depression. Treatment of depression in the psychoanalytic approach involves the process of uncovering and working through the internalized anger in what is called psychoanalytic therapy.

The behavioral theory as suggested by Martin Seligman Ph.D. (1992) states that depression is caused by a pattern of "learned helplessness." The person learns from role models that his or her behavioral actions are ineffective or "helpless," no matter how they are carried out. The knowledge that these actions are futile causes the person to give up and feel depressed. For example, a person with an extremely stressful job is forced to meet unreasonable deadlines and is faced with an unreasonable boss. The person attempts to speak with the boss, attempts to rearrange his/her schedule, and struggles to meet the deadlines. For a variety of reasons, he or she is unable to change jobs, to quit the job, or even take a vacation. At this point, the person is likely to believe that nothing he or she attempts to do will help change the situation. As a result, he or she gives up, feeling helpless, hopeless, and depressed. Treatment involves behavioral therapy, where the person seeks out situations in which he or she can test behaviors and experience success. Thus, the person re-learns by experiencing success from the new experience.

A third theory of causation of depression is the biological explanation. Within this perspective, depression is seen as a chemical imbalance occurring within the nervous system. Treatment within this approach involves medications, electroconvulsive therapy (ECT), or light therapy.

The social interpersonal theory is based on the work of Dr. Harry Stack Sullivan and contends that depression occurs in an interpersonal context (Sullivan 1953). Depression occurs secondarily to the real or perceived loss of a close relationship. The interventions used in interpersonal psychotherapy are directed at resolving the interpersonal conflicts and improving interpersonal relations, communication, and social functioning.

The cognitive theory of depression was developed by Dr. Aaron Beck. His theory states that depressed moods are caused by negative or "faulty" thinking (Beck et al. 1979). When a stressful or negative event happens to us, we might assume that the event itself causes our feelings of depression, anger, or guilt. However, Dr. Beck's theory states that our feelings are the result of our thoughts about the event. Cognitive theory maintains that depressed persons can help themselves by recognizing and changing their negative thoughts. This may in turn alter their feelings of depression.

All of these theories approach the understanding and explanation of depression from the perspective of a causative agent external to the person's mood. For instance, cognitive therapy assumes that the depressed mood is caused by negative thoughts. Interpersonal psychotherapy states that depression is caused by conflicts in interpersonal relations. The behavioral model of depression attributes the causation of the depressed mood to a learned style of helplessness. Finally, the biological theory of depression states that depression is caused by a chemical imbalance.

In this book, we will present an understanding of and an approach to the treatment of depression based on a completely different set of assumptions. What we present is based on our clinical experience and research findings reported in the literature in the area of mood regulation. Rather than attributing depression to an "external" causative agent such as a relationship or missing chemical, we understand depression to be a disorder that is caused by a malfunction or disruption in mood regulation.

Current approaches to treating depression

The treatment of depression has traditionally followed the orientation of the therapist or psychiatrist treating the depressed person. TABLE 4 highlights key practitioners and writers in the field.

Therapists who follow a psychoanalytic orientation are called psychoanalysts and treat depression through the process of psychoanalysis, which involves unveiling the unconscious drives and motivations behind the depression. There are many forms of psychoanalytic therapy. They are usually long term in duration.

Therapists of a strictly biological orientation use biological means to treat depression because they believe that the primary causative agent is a defect in the person's chemistry or biology. Accordingly, the primary—or only—mode of treatment will be medications, hormones, electroconvulsive therapy, light therapy, or other biological means of intervention that the biological therapist or physician believes is the way to treat depression.

Cognitive therapists use cognitive therapy for the treatment of depression. This includes a structured process of learning how to identify negative thoughts and then challenging them in a healthy manner in order to change them. This change in turn will lead to relief from the depression.

Interpersonal psychotherapy assumes that the major cause of depression is conflict within a relationship. Consequently the focus of the therapy is on identifying and repairing the relationship conflicts, which leads to the resolution of the depression.

Pastoral counselors treat a depressed person with spiritual counseling that is aimed at strengthening a person's faith and belief, which brings relief from the depression.

Behaviorists who base their theory of depression on learned helplessness or mis-cued behaviors use behavioral interventions to help the depressed person learn new ways of acting and relating to relieve the sense of helplessness and in turn relieve the depression.

School	Major USA Writers	Remarks
Biological	*Kety* *Winokur*	Derived from nineteenth-century Continental schools of psychiatry
Psychodynamic	*Erikson* *Kohut*	Strongly influenced by Freudian psychoanalysis but modified by the American experience, particularly with ego psychology and self-psychology
Social	*Meyer* *Redlich*	Leaning heavily on sociology, anthropology, and other social sciences
Interpersonal	*Sullivan* *Fromm-Reichmann* *Arieti*	Applied to family therapy and psychotherapy with ambulatory patients but also with schizophrenia, depression, and other conditions
Behavioral	*Skinner* *Lesisohn*	Mainly involving behavior treatment
Cognitive	*Beck*	Mainly involving cognitive treatment

TABLE 4. PRACTITIONERS AND WRITERS. THESE ARE THE MOST PROMINENT SCHOOLS OF THOUGHT IN PSYCHIATRY IN THE LAST CENTURY; EACH DEFINED DEPRESSION FROM ITS OWN PERSPECTIVE (KLERMAN 1983).

In addition to these modalities, there are many more approaches to the treatment of depression too numerous to discuss in this book. There are as many therapies for the treatment of depression as there are therapists willing to come forward with new theories because none have been able to adequately or completely explain the causes of depression and none have been effective across the board. That is why the majority of therapists use a combination of interventions, or in the vernacular of the day, whatever works.

All of the aforementioned modalities for treatment have been developed primarily for major depression. The strength of each of these treatment approaches is that each on its own can bring about a temporary change in mood and improvement, or what is called a "response to treatment" or partial remission. This response is primarily a lessening of the intensity of the symptoms of depression, not lasting change. Their collective weakness is that none works across the board for all types of depression or for all depressed individuals of one type. Some people will respond to behavioral therapy, others to cognitive therapy, and so on. In everyday clinical practice, each modality is applied by the therapist or psychiatrist using only a single theory of causation approach. So a behavioral therapist usually treats only with behavioral therapy, a psychoanalyst using only psychoanalysis, and so on.

This is a myopic and limited view of the causality of depression, which is probably why the suicide rate has remained unchanged in the last fifty years in spite of all the advancements in treatment, and why studies have shown that 70 percent of outpatients who have been treated for depression were back seeking treatment one year later (Weissman and Kasl 1976). We believe that as long as the therapist views a unitary etiology, such as negative thoughts, misbehavior, or repressed feeling as the cause of depression, then the treatment will be limited in scope and outcome.

> *When thinking about the causation of depression, our thinking should start with examining the big picture of mood dysregulation, and then move from there to the details of the four dimensions (biological, cognitive, social, spiritual) and not the other way around.*—Namir Damluji, M.D.

A mood dysregulation
perspective for understanding depression

Researchers have found depression to be associated with dysregulation of the body's normal circadian rhythm cycles. These rhythms include the sleep-wake cycle, body temperature regulation, appetite regulation, hormonal secretion, energy, and cognitive ability cycles, among others. As psychiatrist Dr. David

Jarrett (1989) states: "Notwithstanding, it is becoming clear that some if not all patients with a major depressive illness have a reversible disruption in the physiological regulation of the sleep-wake cycle and reductions in the amplitude of the body temperature rhythm and circadian neuroendocrine secretory profile. It can therefore be postulated that a depressive illness is frequently associated with a pathophysiological disturbance in the regulation of circadian biological rhythms."

Dr. Timothy Strauman (1999) wrote a commentary review to Depue and Collins' article (1999) where he related Depue-Collins' neurobehavioral model of extraversion to the construct of self regulation and how the two concepts can be applied together to better understand depression as a brain-behavior disorder. Drawing upon the theories of self regulation and applying the observations from the Depue-Collins model, Dr. Strauman proposed the causation of depression to be from a breakdown in the behavioral and neurophysiological self regulation functions.

These observations are consistent with observations of other researchers who proposed depression to result from cognitive, behavioral, or biological dysfunction (Costello 1973; Meehl 1975). More recently, self regulation theorists such as Cicchetti and Tucker (1994) and Derryberry and Reed (1994) showed how poor socialization and problems with biological development in the nervous system make a person vulnerable to developing a mood disorder such as depression. Dr. Strauman's conceptualization of depression as a breakdown in brain-behavior self regulation takes an integrated view of the above earlier work. He notes that this self-regulatory approach "allows us to consider simultaneously—at appropriate levels of analysis, from cellular to societal—how the human organism pursues positive outcomes and how normally adaptive processes can go awry at any level."

He further adds that this conceptualization of depression as a breakdown in self regulation "forces us to consider depression hierarchically so that (for instance) both biological and cognitive theories of loss of approach motivation might be valid, even within the same depressed person." In other words, this allows us to conceptualize depression as multi-factorial in causation and that several causative factors could be interacting and at play when a person becomes depressed, without any singular method of explanation. Dr. Strauman notes that if we view depression as a disorder of self regulation, then simply treating the symptoms of depression is not sufficient to lower the risk of relapse or recurrence of further depressive episodes. Accordingly, the treatment of depression should not be based on symptom reduction alone, as that leads only to a partial remission and not full recovery from depression.

Our own conceptualization of depression and its treatment with MRT is a further extension of the above observations. Indeed, we see depression as a disorder of mood self regulation that results from a breakdown in biological, cognitive, social, or spiritual dimensions of the self. We also agree with Dr. Strauman that the proper treatment of depression is not simply alleviating the symptoms of depression or reducing the intensity or frequency of depressive episodes but rather helping the person to return to a balanced and well "self-regulated" mood state that is under the control of the individual. It is only through the attainment of that personal self regulation of one's mood that one recovers fully from depression and feels terrific. The importance of that is when a person has attained the state of feeling terrific, he or she feels at their best, functions at an optimal level, and has decreased the risk of relapse and recurrence.

Depression as a mood regulation disorder: A paradigm shift

Our approach is to conceptualize depression as a mood regulation disorder. This represents a shift in how depression is viewed and how it should and could be effectively treated. Viewing depression as a deficit in the stability of the body's mood regulatory system does not negate or contradict the previous theories. On the contrary, our approach makes allowances for all the previously mentioned theories into one comprehensive mode of explanation that is scientifically based and research evident. The generalities of our method of persuasion using that approach do not contradict the specifics (that depression may be caused by a biochemical imbalance or cognitive deficit). Our approach is truly a synthesis of all the parts and allows the practitioner to better view the bigger picture of depression as it truly is—a central regulatory dysfunction that is affected by multiple factors. This perspective allows us to reformulate views about the causation and treatment of depression from a new angle, that of mood regulation, which is an emerging and well-researched field.

Our need for finding a new method of explanation arose from our own clinical experience and research in the field of depression. Our personal experience in treating depression using any one mode of explanation at a time paralleled current literature reports which find that, with the advent of newer antidepressants and cognitive and interpersonal therapies, the outcome of treatment has remained basically the same. For instance, the suicide rate with depression remains unchanged at 15 percent. The recovery rate from major depression remains the same—around 67 percent with any one antidepressant—with similar rates for cognitive therapy.

The fault is not in the therapeutic methods themselves but rather in their application and in the myopic view that therapists have been taught about depression. The conceptualization of depression as simply a distorted thought or missing chemical is an oversimplification and shows a lack of true understanding as to what occurs when a person gets depressed. Breaking down depression into a chemical or psychological problem has led to one of the major faults that have the field at a standstill and have caused recovery rates to be limited and suicide rates to remain unchanged. Then, too, most therapists and psychiatrists have a limited understanding of the process and in turn explain it to their patients and treat it in a narrow, restricted manner. As we mentioned earlier, most of what therapists and psychiatrists do is symptom reduction (response), at best achieving remission (few symptoms of depression, needing continuing treatment, with high chances of relapse).

It is this view of depression that led us to look further. Our aim through MRT is feeling terrific, which we define as a state of being symptom free, functioning at the highest potential one is able to, having a healthy set of anti-depressive behaviors and tools to use if symptoms ever recur, having a low chance of relapse, and most importantly, being at a point where one does not need ongoing treatment to stay there.

In our experience using MRT, we have witnessed very low rates of relapse. Our patients achieve feeling terrific as the outcome of treatment, which is a major change from the current practice and outcomes.

Feeling terrific with MRT

We use the term *feeling terrific* to describe a collective state of physical, psychological, and spiritual well-being. In this collective state of well-being, an individual can feel validated from his or her own core experience of who he or she is as a person. The feeling-terrific state offers the person an opportunity for self-definition that leads to clarity and meaning in his or her life. The person feels centered and has a sense of contentment, serenity, and tranquility.

The feeling-terrific state may be elusive to define. It denotes the absence of negative feelings and thoughts such as depression, anger, anxiety, or despair. At the same time, feeling terrific conveys a positive emotional state, with prevailing good feelings such as hope, contentment, and good self-esteem. The absence of negative emotions and the presence of positive emotions are associated with an assured sense of self. This intact sense of self is at the center of feeling terrific.

In 1890 William James wrote that "how to gain, how to keep, how to recover happiness is in fact for most men at all times the secret motive of all they do." Feeling terrific is not synonymous with happiness. Happiness may be part of it but not all of it. The philosopher Immanuel Kant described happiness as the satisfaction of one's desires. Freud regarded happiness as the gratification of one's drives. Feeling terrific is not limited to the satisfaction of one's drives, desires, or needs; it includes the person's ability to attain a state of psychological, physical, and spiritual well-being. Feeling terrific involves developing that sense of well-being, with feelings of contentment and quietude. Feeling terrific is a collective experience of the person, not limited to a drive or desire but to an experience of the person as a whole—in body, mind, and spirit. It seeks to gratify the mind and spirit primarily and the senses secondarily. When a person feels terrific, he is able to endure life's ambiguities, frustrations, and misfortunes. In this state the person is able to rise above the nuances of daily living and to participate in life with meaning and purpose. The feeling-terrific state is attained through MRT.

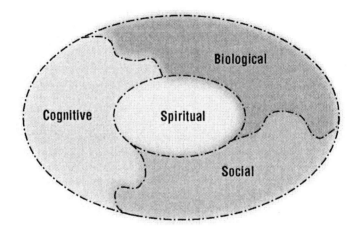

FIGURE 7. THE FOUR DIMENSIONS OF MOOD REGULATION. ALL OF THE DIMENSIONS OF MOOD REGULATION ARE CONTINUOUSLY INTERACTIVE AND CONSTITUTE THE WHOLE OF THE PERSON.

As we can see in FIGURE 7, mood is the outcome of the biological, cognitive, social, and spiritual aspects of our lives. In other words, we experience our moods and emotions as the result of biological, cognitive, social, and spiritual interactive processes. These processes are fluid, each affecting and affected by the other. The MRT continuum allows us to see the big picture and particulars that are the focus of mood regulation therapy. In MRT, the therapist or person using MRT is always aware of how the four dimensions of the self are collectively interacting to regulate mood and keep it stable while paying attention to each dimension by itself.

In summary, our view of depression starts with the understanding that depression as a mood disorder occurs over a spectrum. The second and more important consideration is our view that the change in mood seen in depression is the fundamental cause of the depression and is caused by a breakdown in the mood regulating system. The treatment of depression of any type in our opinion is only considered successful when the person doesn't simply feel less depressed but when he experiences a new state of well-being, which we refer to as feeling terrific. That is accomplished through our approach—MRT.

Mood regulation therapy is inclusive of other therapies such as cognitive behavioral therapy (CBT) and interpersonal psychotherapy (IPT) and does not attempt to replace them. MRT is the final common pathway for the scientifically validated treatment of depression and presents this treatment in a comprehensive and integrated framework. In the next chapter we will discuss the details of mood regulation therapy and how understanding and working with each of the four dimensions can lead to mood stabilization and feeling terrific.

CHAPTER 3
Mood Regulation Therapy

Defining Mood Regulation Therapy

Mood regulation therapy (MRT) refers to the self-generated actions that we undertake to evaluate, modify, and then monitor our emotions in order to attain a certain desired mood state, which is the feeling-terrific state. To do this, we examine and work on one or more of the four mood-regulating dimensions, aiming to shift from one set of dimensions to the other in order to maintain homeostasis. In accordance with the theory of emotion regulation proposed by Gross and Munoz (1995), MRT does not aim to control one's emotion but rather to allow the person to influence what type of emotion he has and how he experiences and expresses the emotion.

Therapy has always been presented as a well-defined set of interventions which, when applied appropriately, will help a person who is depressed to achieve a much better endpoint than where he or she started. Our experience has indicated that the currently established and validated therapies for depression (including cognitive, interpersonal, and medication, among others) all aspire to achieve an endpoint called remission, which is the remittance of the acute distressing symptoms of depression and no more. These therapies in our experience do little beyond offering symptomatic relief through the reduction of the intensity and frequency of the depressive symptoms. These methodologies are effective in symptom reduction as long as they are being actively used, as with medications, for example. Once stopped, relapse is high. None of these therapies offers methods of explanation or has as a goal the endpoint that we refer to as feeling terrific. Feeling terrific is an outcome of treatment where the person is not only fully recovered but has acquired skills to be at a better feeling place than before he got depressed and where the relapse rate has been reduced to the minimum.

Research protocols and academic centers commonly accept a 50 percent reduction in score on the Hamilton Depression Scale as an indication of treatment success when using medications to treat a person with clinical depression. The Hamilton Depression Scale is a standardized instrument for the assessment of depression. The psychiatrist or clinician rates depressive symptom severity with a 17-item questionnaire regarding mood, anxiety, sleep, and appetite. Each item on the questionnaire is scored from 0 to 4; the individual scores are then added together for a total score. The higher the score, the more severe the depression. Individuals with scores of 10–13 have mild depression, while those with scores of 14–17 have mild to moderate depression, and scores over 17 indicate moderate to severe depression. The scale is used in clinical trials to test the efficacy of medications but can also be used to test the effectiveness of other therapeutic modalities. It is administered before treatment for a baseline and then scored periodically during treatment. "Response" to medications is said to occur when there is a 50 percent reduction of symptoms (as evidenced by a 50 percent reduction of Hamilton Depression score). Remission, which is defined as the full resolution of depression, is said to occur when the score is 7 or less. Therefore, if the score before initiating treatment was 26 on the Hamilton Depression scale, and it went down to 13 after starting treatment with an antidepressant drug, then it is proclaimed that the drug is an effective antidepressant and that treatment has been successful.

Accordingly, at best, the treatment of depression has been defined by achieving a point (a score on the Hamilton Depression Scale) and not an endpoint (which MRT defines as resolution of symptoms, improvement in overall functioning, and feeling terrific). Mood regulation therapy goes beyond the achievement of a particular point on a scale in that it gives the person a host of strategies that allow him or her to regulate mood within a certain range and on an ongoing basis, not simply as a one-time intervention.

The approach to change with MRT

Change occurs with MRT because we examine and work on basic assumptions about depression and our mood, not simply the signs and symptoms of depression. The following example clarifies what we mean.

John has become depressed because he has ended his relationship with a woman he dated for a few years. His friends try to cheer him up to get him out of the depression and arrange for him to meet new women, socialize, or go out with the guys, but John does not respond and remains depressed. He then tries to cheer himself up. He does all of the things that used to work, but still he remains depressed. Having failed himself, his family, and his friends, John now starts feeling guilty. He feels he has become a burden, and his depression enters a more sinister stage. John's depression has been worsened because he failed to respond to the well-intended solutions applied by family, friends, and himself. If

John goes to a therapist who treats his depression using mood regulation therapy, the focus of treatment should be on how his mood is dysregulated and what needs to be done to help him feel better and improve his functioning. Mood regulation therapy approaches treatment with a focus on the acute depression that John is feeling now, which is exacerbated by the guilt, sense of failure, and letting down of friends and family. This should be the immediate focus of treatment, addressing first the current state of John's mood, how to regulate it, and thus change it to a better mood state. The MRT therapist will start from the first session to teach John how to measure and graph his mood and how to be aware of fluctuations in mood. The therapist will help John to look at what's going on with himself biologically, cognitively, socially in his relationships, and spiritually, and then learn the skills necessary to stabilize his mood and feel terrific.

Most clinicians, when treating a depressed person, immediately try to get to the reasons, origins, and basis for the depression by asking, "Why are you depressed?" and "Who contributed to this?" This obsessive search for causes and contributors occurs spontaneously and without any second thought on the part of the therapist, as most depressed persons and their therapists want to know *why*.

Pursuit of the *why* and *who* (causes and culprits) reflects a single-mindedness in search of one explanatory answer which will explain all and thus provide an answer to cure everything. More often than not, this approach is a fallacy, as the search for causes is circular; patient and therapist turn out empty-handed. The question "Why?" offers us insight, but insight does not treat depression and it does not allow the person to feel terrific. *Who* offers us blame, shame, or guilt—shame and guilt are well known as precursors of depression; blame creates a sense of victimization, of which depression is a hallmark and becomes a badge to bear. None of these answers help resolve or treat the depression. Our human curiosity is always evoked by the question "Why?" but it is rarely satisfied by an answer. After every question is asked, we will only ask "Why?" again.

Even when our curiosity is satisfied, research has proved that the answers are not capable of transforming a person from being depressed to feeling good. By the time most patients come to see a therapist or psychiatrist, they have figured out why in part or whole they are depressed and who, if anyone, is responsible for their predicament. If they spend the next two years in therapy clarifying or validating that *why* and *who* alone, it will not lead to the resolution of depression. As Ludwig Wittgenstein (1958) stated, "It often happens that we only become aware of the important facts if we suppress the question 'why,' and then in the course of our investigations these facts lead us to an answer."

When we ask the question "Why?" we deal with causes; if we ask "What?" we deal with effects. With causes, we wonder, "Why did this happen?" With effects, we want to concentrate on "What's happening now." With *why*, treatment is sought from within the box. *What* requires thinking outside of the box.

Dealing with *why* and *who* is self reflective and accusatory and attempts to solve the problem of depression in a tortuous, paradoxical manner that leads to worsening of the depression. Intuitively, patients use *why* and *who* on their own before they come to therapy and end up deadlocked. When offered the *what* and *how* approach, patients may be lifted away from the paradox traps created by negative loops of self-reflection and finger-pointing. MRT approaches the treatment of depression in terms of its present structure, status, and consequences by asking the questions "What?" and "How?"

The *what* and *how* in MRT are the basis for observation, analysis, and therapeutic action. The *what* includes:

- What is going on in the biological, cognitive, social, and spiritual dimensions that may be contributing to the onset or maintenance of the depression?
- What can be done to regulate mood and feel terrific by using mood-regulating strategies?

The answers to these questions allow us to understand depression in terms of its presentation and consequences. *How* addresses the mood-regulating steps that need to be taken to bring about change from the state of depression to a state of feeling terrific. The main question to answer at this point is, "How do I become un-depressed and feel terrific?"

What and *how* allow us to describe a set of operational criteria, establish clear goals and objectives, and decide how to attain them within a given timeline. The *what* and *how* concept refers to here and now and deals with core assumptions about the mood-dysregulated depressive process.

To use an analogy, if someone pinches me, I immediately ask, "Why did you pinch me?" However, knowing why doesn't change what happened. The more relevant question is, "How should I respond?" In MRT, we don't want to focus on why the depression occurred or who caused it. We want to focus on what keeps us depressed and how we can climb out of the depressed state in order to be a better version of our previous self and feel terrific. It is not important to focus all of the therapy sessions on how a depression-causing event occurred but what will change the result of that event. Like a scientist or mathematician, we ask, "What do you have to do to solve this problem?"

Mood regulation is achieved by addressing what's going on with a person's mood within the four dimensions and how to use mood-regulating strategies to regulate the person's mood. This line of inquiry is at the heart of MRT—allowing the depressed person to ask the right questions so he or she can learn how to use the four MRT strategies and feel terrific.

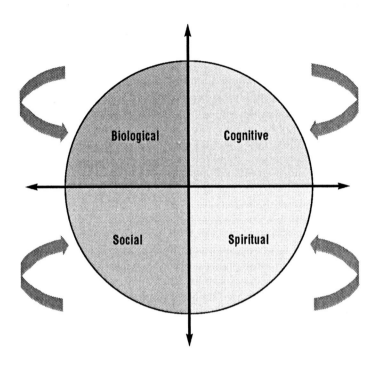

FIGURE 8. THE FOUR PROCESSES OF MOOD REGULATION. THE FOUR PROCESSES ARE INTERCONNECTED, IMPACT EACH OTHER, AND LEAD TO MOOD REGULATION.

The four goals of MRT

Depression is conceptualized as a disorder involving the biological, cognitive, social, and spiritual dimensions of a person's life. MRT targets each one of these dimensions to effect change and feel terrific, using an integrative approach that allows for multiple modes of intervention. Determining which dimension to work on depends on the dimension(s) that are dysregulated. In MRT we emphasize that each of the four dimensions must be understood and addressed individually, despite the fact that they interface with one another. We need to understand how each dimension impacts and regulates mood.

Individuals with depression have difficulty understanding their emotions and are often unable to change them. Understanding the four dimensions of mood regulation and how they interact with each other will allow the depressed person to develop skills to regulate his mood and change it in the direction he wishes.

As we discussed earlier, homeostasis makes it possible for the body to organize the mood regulating system to ensure that mood states are held between appropriate upper and lower limits. This range of stability that we call "normal" is attained through complex chemical and electrical reactions in a region of the brain we call the mood center. This biological function, like heart rate regulation, occurs involuntarily and away from a person's immediate consciousness. It does not act alone, however, to maintain a person's equilibrium; it functions with cognitive, social, and spiritual influences acting as regulators.

The basic matrix of the mood center includes biological processes in the brain as represented by the brain structure, neuro-chemicals, and electrical signals. At a basic biological level, the mood center operates to regulate mood. A person's spirituality, attachment behavior, and cognition are all mediated through the limbic system in the mood center. These other influences cause the biological system to shift from one set point to another in an attempt to self regulate. Research has shown that connections exist among the four influences and that they interact constantly. Research has also demonstrated that these interactions cause detectable changes in limbic system activity and function that contribute jointly to a specific mood state. This relationship goes two ways, where thoughts can change moods and moods can change thoughts.

Our thoughts play a big role in determining our moods; negative thoughts cause dysregulation, while positive or neutral thoughts play a regulatory function. The social environment that we immerse ourselves in and the relationships we engage in also have a direct impact on our mood regulation; healthy supportive relationships exert a stabilizing effect, while negative personal interactions have a destabilizing effect and cause depression. Spirituality also plays a major role in regulating our mood; several studies have demonstrated the protective effect that faith provides from the development of depression.

All of these processes interact constantly with each other to maintain our mood. For instance, if we wake up feeling down due to a biological disturbance such as being sleep-deprived or having nightmares the previous night, we can compensate for that by engaging in an "anti-depressive" behavior such as meditation, being with someone we like, or engaging in an enjoyable activity that is distracting. All of these activities may change our mood. If we are unable to engage in an anti-depressive strategy and correct the negative mood state, the mood may further deteriorate, leading to depression.

Depression is the result of failure in the mood regulating system that results from biological, cognitive, social, and spiritual irregularities and their interactions over time. Individuals with depression usually have the following characteristics with regard to their emotions:

• They pay more attention to negative emotions than positive emotions.

- They experience their emotions as intense events and they fear them.
- They have great difficulty regulating their moods when they experience negative emotions.
- They have great difficulty identifying and describing their emotions.
- They have great difficulty understanding their emotional experiences, differentiating various emotions, and clarifying what information the emotion may be conveying to them.
- They have difficulty accepting their emotional experience.
- They exert a lot of effort trying to control negative emotions through ineffective strategies such as worrying, ruminating, or suppressing emotions.
- They lack proper understanding of how their moods affect interpersonal relations and how interpersonal relations affect their moods.
- They feel comfortable and seek companionship of people who match their negative mood state.
- Individuals who are depressed are more likely to recall an unhappy and deprived childhood.
- They seek out people who criticize and find fault in them, while avoiding people who give them favorable and positive opinions of them.

We all have the capacity to employ anti-depressive strategies, if we know how and when. People who become depressed either don't know how to employ the anti-depressive strategies or are unable to. Most if not all people are deficient in skills and knowledge of using anti-depressive mood regulation strategies when they get down.

What we try to understand in MRT are the specific biological, cognitive, social, and spiritual influences that can affect mood regulation or cause dysregulation. Not all biological processes, for instance, have an impact on mood regulation, nor do all environmental or social changes have a significant impact on mood. This book outlines all the influences that have been found and validated through clinical and experimental research findings and what has been found in our own work to affect mood regulation. In addition to understanding the specific mood influences in a given person, in MRT we attempt to ascertain how one mode affects the other. For instance, does praying lead to less negative thinking?

Mood is an integrated response that represents the outcome of all these influences or processes at work. This work is integrated and automatic in mood regulation. There is a continuous feedback loop where mood not only is the outcome of the four processes, but in return it impacts these processes and changes them. For instance, a positive thought may lead to a positive mood. This positive mood state in return leads to more positive thoughts. In MRT we consider that no single one of these four dimensions is more important or influential than the other in mood regulation or dysregulation. What matters for the MRT therapist is not why a person is depressed, but what anti-depressive strategies the person needs to learn and employ to get out of the depressed state. Accordingly, we have to pay attention to all four dimensions equally in order to develop a sense of well-being and feeling terrific.

Feeling terrific

The goal of MRT is the establishment of a well-regulated mood state known as the feeling-terrific state. With feeling terrific there is a clear, cohesive, and assured sense of self. This content and intact sense of self is at the center of the feeling-terrific state. MRT accomplishes this by teaching the person about the four dimensions and processes that contribute to mood regulation. Contentment or feeling terrific is then attained as you learn the strategies to understand these four dimensions and develop the skills to regulate your mood on an ongoing basis.

The phases of MRT

Depression in all its forms may be a serious and disabling condition. It affects a large part of the population, and no one is immune from getting depressed. Dr. Mark Gold (1987) states in his book, *The Good News about Depression,* that "only ten percent of the millions of people estimated to be biologically depressed in this country ever seek help." Even though a small number of people with depression receive treatment, one study found that 70 percent of outpatients treated for depression were back seeking treatment one year later (Weissman and Kasl 1976).

This finding has been consistent with our experience. We have observed the treatment of individuals when they enter the mental health system and what outcomes ensue from their treatments. Many individuals who have come to our office say, "I've tried so many different medications and different styles of treatment, and I am still depressed." Explanation of the high rate of relapse may be due to the fact that many clinicians focus on only one particular dimension of depression, ignoring the big picture of mood regulation and the other three dimensions. This can be attributed to the fact that clinicians who are trained in the biological perspective see depression primarily as a biochemical imbalance. Those trained in the behavioral perspective explain depression as a maladaptive behavior, and so on. This view of depression and treatment will at best lead to a partial treatment and partial response. The other reason may be that many clinicians will aim for a response as an endpoint for their treatment. MRT aims at feeling terrific (response, remission, and beyond).

Another important variable that affects treatment outcome in depression is the interface between the beliefs that individuals bring into treatment and the rationale that the treating therapist or psychiatrist offers them to explain the cause and rationale of their treatment approach (McLean and Hakstian 1979). It stands to reason, therefore, that therapists and psychiatrists who do not have a coherent theory of explanation or one that the individual is able to understand will undoubtedly be unable to get good treatment outcomes and can't keep people in treatment for long.

The goals of mood regulation therapy are illustrated in TABLE 5 and FIGURE 9, which show how a person who is depressed can work on the four dimensions and move through the various phases till he or she reaches the feeling-terrific state.

Feeling Terrific	Improved functioning with a renewed outlook on mood and self. Sense of emotional well-being and contentment. Enriched capacity to experience happiness and joy. Sense of mastery over life. Heightened awareness and improved state of functioning in all four dimensions.
Recovery	Getting back to baseline, before the condition began. Sustained period of remission for 6 months or more.
Remission	Greater improvement than response. Minimal symptoms for at least 3 weeks.
Response	A partial improvement in symptoms, up to halfway better than when treatment started.

TABLE 5. POSSIBLE OUTCOMES OF TREATMENT OF DEPRESSION. FEELING TERRIFIC IS THE TARGET OF TREATMENT WITH MOOD REGULATION THERAPY (MRT).

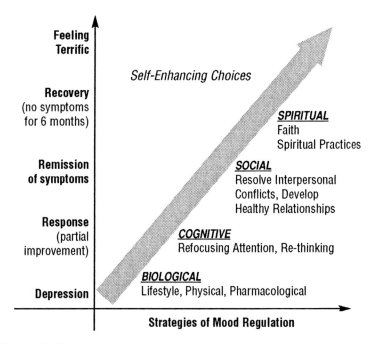

FIGURE 9. THE STRATEGIES AND GOALS OF MOOD REGULATION THERAPY.
FEELING TERRIFIC OCCURS WHEN WE WORK ON ALL FOUR DIMENSIONS.

Generally speaking, the treatment of depression aims to relieve the depressed person from the low mood state and associated symptoms. As FIGURE 9 shows, the initial phase is what we call a response, which is defined by a partial improvement in how the person feels (or an improvement of around 50 percent in Hamilton Depression Scale score from pre-treatment levels). Remission is defined as having few remaining symptoms of the depression for at least three months. Recovery is when the person returns to baseline and has no symptoms of depression for six months and is basically in a sustained period of remission. This is the point where most therapies end. Feeling terrific is a step beyond recovery, a step beyond where the person with depression may have been before getting depressed. It is a state that is marked by an emotional and physical sense of wellness, well-being, and spiritual fulfillment.

MRT departs from all other forms of therapy in that the goal is not merely the reduction of symptoms or partial response to treatment; the goal is for the individual to develop and appreciate all dimensions of self, learn the self-enhancing strategies, and feel terrific.

Moving from depression to feeling terrific

Depression permeates every cell of the body and gradually impairs the functions of several body organs. Reality as you know it changes and you start seeing life through a dark set of lenses. As you are pulled down, you start detaching and isolating from the world around you. You slowly sink into a dark and lonely abyss. All alone, wherever you turn, there are dark shadows, and beyond, even darker shadows. It feels like there is no escape, that your only choice seems to be to close your eyes and wish you never wake up to the same reality. You look at yourself and ask, "Why me?" and "Where am I going?"

Left to your own resolutions, you may be stuck in darkness. But if you enter into a process of self-inquiry—even better if you take that journey with an MRT therapist—the road will lead to a response, then remission from the depression, then recovery, and then on to feeling terrific. Depression can be seen as an opportunity for self-discovery, self-knowledge, and journeying on a path that leads to a serene state and contentment. Depression becomes the gate that leads to feeling terrific. If guided correctly, you can get to know yourself better and change by finding meaning, purpose, and joy in your existence. Discovering and learning about yourself is a rewarding and fulfilling experience. An undiscovered self is a forgotten self, an abandoned self. Anybody who feels depressed can feel terrific as long as there is a willingness to learn and a readiness to change.

So, while remission and recovery can be defined as the absence of symptoms of depression, feeling terrific is the presence of a new and improved state of functioning. Unlike other emotional states, the feeling-terrific state has few outward manifestations. The feeling-terrific state includes contented, centered, purposeful living with a sense of well-being. When people feel angry, they may raise their voice, throw a temper tantrum, or sulk. When someone is embarrassed, he or she blushes or pulls away. When anxious, most people get fidgety or restless. When someone feels terrific, however, there is serenity and tranquility within. There is an absence of negative feelings and thoughts such as depression, anger, anxiety, or despair. At the same time this state conveys a positive emotional state, with "good" feelings prevailing as hope, contentment, and a sense of good self-esteem. In that state the person achieves harmony between reason and emotion (Gross 1998).

Tools for feeling terrific

Before embarking on the process of mood regulation and exploring the four dimensions, the first step is to properly identify and recognize what mood state you are in—feeling depressed, feeling terrific, or anything in between. The details of how to identify and label specific feelings will be discussed in the chapter on cognitive strategies.

The Daily Mood Scale

The Daily Mood Scale (DMS) is a measurement tool and graph that allows you to be aware of your moods on a daily basis. The first step is to label your mood, which may be, for example, "I'm feeling depressed today," followed by the next step—rating it. Using the Daily Mood Scale's numeric system (See FIGURE 10), where 0 represents a very severely depressed mood with suicidal thoughts or intent and 6 represents feeling terrific or your best mood state, you will rate your mood. The third step is to plot your daily moods on the Daily Mood Graph. This graph leads you to awareness of your mood on a daily and weekly basis so that you can recognize patterns and cycles.

After you have plotted your daily moods on the DMS graph for a period of time, you will be ready to take the next step. The fourth step calls for taking an inventory using The Mood Regulation Strategies Inventory, which will allow you to indicate strategies you usually use to regulate your mood state (SEE FIGURES 13-1 AND 13-2). When you have finished the inventory, you will profile these strategies and skills. Then you will be ready to work on specific MRT strategies derived from the four dimensions.

Daily Mood Scale Rating Values

6 • *I feel terrific, at my absolute best*

5 • *I feel OK, "just fine"*

4 • *I feel neutral*

3 • *I feel slightly depressed*

2 • *I feel moderately depressed*

1 • *I feel severely depressed*

0 • *I feel very severely depressed, suicidal*

FIGURE 10. DAILY MOOD SCALE. THIS SCALE HELPS YOU RATE YOUR MOOD ON A DAILY BASIS SO THAT IT CAN BE RECORDED ON THE DAILY MOOD GRAPH.

The Daily Mood Graph

Use the Daily Mood Graph (FIGURE 11) to chart your daily moods. Rating and charting your moods on a daily basis will help you to detect the upward and downward shifts in mood that you experience as a result of the multitude of influences on your life.

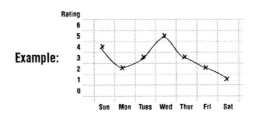

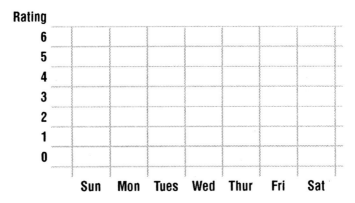

FIGURE 11. DAILY MOOD GRAPH. ONCE THE NUMERIC VALUE FROM THE DAILY MOOD SCALE IS MARKED ON THE GRID, A GRAPH CAN BE DRAWN TO SHOW A PERSON'S WEEKLY MOOD FLUCTUATION AND PATTERN.

The Depression Questionnaire

The Depression Questionnaire (FIGURE 12) provides a means of establishing a baseline of your mood and level of depression before you embark on learning the MRT strategies and completing the exercises presented in this book. The questionnaire includes twenty questions to help you to determine what your mood is like. The questions cover various functions and activities of your daily life and how you feel. When you have answered all of the questions and added the numeric scores, you will get a sum total that represents an approximate range of where your mood is.

Please complete the questionnaire by circling the number which best corresponds to how you have been feeling for the past thirty days, including today. The time period may be varied, according to the timeline you wish to measure your mood for. Circle 0 if you do not feel that way at all, 5 if you feel that way to a great extreme, or any number in between that best corresponds to the way you feel about the statement given.

	NOT AT ALL	MINIMALLY	MILDLY	MODERATELY	SEVERELY	EXTREMELY SO
1. I feel sad, blue, down, or depressed.	0	1	2	3	4	5
2. I believe I am a failure.	0	1	2	3	4	5
3. I feel hopeless about the future.	0	1	2	3	4	5
4. I do not enjoy the things I used to enjoy.	0	1	2	3	4	5
5. I feel guilty.	0	1	2	3	4	5
6. I feel dissatisfied.	0	1	2	3	4	5
7. I have lost interest in people and in my surroundings.	0	1	2	3	4	5
8. I have trouble with my sleep.	0	1	2	3	4	5
9. My energy level has decreased.	0	1	2	3	4	5
10. I am hard on myself.	0	1	2	3	4	5
11. I break into tears easily.	0	1	2	3	4	5
12. My interest in sex has decreased.	0	1	2	3	4	5
13. I have difficulty concentrating.	0	1	2	3	4	5
14. I have difficulty making decisions.	0	1	2	3	4	5
15. I am more irritable than usual.	0	1	2	3	4	5
16. I have difficulty getting started on a task.	0	1	2	3	4	5
17. I feel physically tired.	0	1	2	3	4	5
18. I have experienced an increase or decrease in my appetite.	0	1	2	3	4	5
19. I have trouble with my memory.	0	1	2	3	4	5
20. I am worried about my health.	0	1	2	3	4	5

Add the numbers you have circled for each of the 20 questions.

TOTAL: _____

FIGURE 12. THE DEPRESSION QUESTIONNAIRE. THIS LIST OF QUESTIONS ALLOWS YOU TO ACCURATELY MEASURE YOUR MOOD AT ANY GIVEN TIME.

The total you obtain after adding the scores of the twenty questions is a GENERAL estimate of your level of depression. Write your score in the space below.

Self rated depression score: _____

Today's date: _____

A score of 15 to 30 signifies you may be slightly depressed

A score of 30 to 55 signifies you may be moderately depressed

A score of 55 to 70 signifies you may be moderately to severely depressed

A score of 70 to 85 signifies you may be severely depressed

A score of 85 to 100 signifies you may be very severely depressed

The Mood Regulation Strategies Inventory

The Mood Regulation Strategies Inventory is a tool that we have found most helpful in determining which strategies to use to change your mood when you are depressed. The inventory, presented in FIGURES 13-1 AND 13-2, is a list of thirty-two items that you can rate according to how often you use that strategy to change your mood when you are depressed. The results are then plotted on a graph to help determine the strategies that you use and don't use for mood regulation and which strategies you may need to learn to increase your repertoire of mood-regulating ways to feel terrific. A person who has the skills and ability to utilize the majority of the strategies can feel terrific and maintain that state on an ongoing basis.

On the line next to each strategy in the inventory, place the letter I, S, or F to reflect the frequency with which you use the strategy when you are depressed to try to change your mood. Ranking should be made according to the following scale: I represents infrequent usage, S represents sometimes or occasional usage, and F represents frequent usage.

In front of each mood regulation strategy below, write the letter that indicates the frequency with which you use it when you are depressed. **I** *- Infrequently;* **S** *- Sometimes;* **F** *- Frequently*

A. Biological
___ Rest, take a nap, close your eyes, sleep
___ Take a bath or shower, Jacuzzi, splash water on your face
___ Eat something
___ Exercise/participate in sports activities
___ Have sex
___ Smoke cigarettes/drink coffee
___ Drink alcohol
___ Take drugs or medication

B. Cognitive
___ Evaluate the situation
___ Try to put feelings into perspective
___ Control your thoughts (calm yourself or try to not
think about it)
___ Reframe the way you view the situation
___ Tend to chores (housework, homework, gardening, etc.)
___ Engage in hobby
___ Engage in stress management activities (organizing, planning)
___ Read or write

C. Social
___ Be with family
___ Talk it out with someone
___ Spend time with friends
___ Play with a pet
___ Go to a support group
___ Engage in activity with friend (go for a walk)
___ Go to a public place (coffee shop, mall)
___ Chat on the Internet

FIGURE 13-1. MOOD REGULATION STRATEGIES INVENTORY. THIS SURVEY ALLOWS YOU TO SEE WHICH STRATEGIES YOU USE WHEN YOU ARE DEPRESSED TO REGULATE YOUR MOOD. (CONTINUED ON NEXT PAGE)

D. Spiritual
___ Pray
___ Meditate
___ Talk to spiritual advisor
___ Read spiritual literature (Bible, Koran, Torah, Kabbalah)
___ Engage in a spiritual/religious activity
___ Rituals (fasting, chanting, etc.)
___ Go to church, mosque, or temple services
___ Listen to inspirational speakers/tapes

Write the total number of strategies that you marked in each group in the blanks below.

A. Biological _____   **C. Social** _____
B. Cognitive _____   **D. Spiritual** _____

FIGURE 13-2. MOOD REGULATION STRATEGIES INVENTORY. (CONTINUED FROM PREVIOUS PAGE)

Once you have added the total strategies in each dimension, plot them on the graph in FIGURE 14 and determine your current MRT strategy profile. (The sample graph illustrates how someone else's profile might look if they rely heavily on biological and social strategies to regulate mood.) This allows you to see the dimensions you are currently addressing and the mood regulating strategies you currently rely on. Within each dimension, you may notice that you use some strategies more often than others. Once you start using the MRT strategies, you can then focus on the areas that need to be strengthened as indicated by your Mood Regulation Strategies Profile. Repeating the graph at the beginning, during, and at the end of treatment will allow you to see the progress you attain.

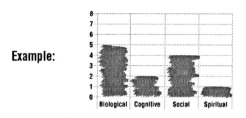

Example:

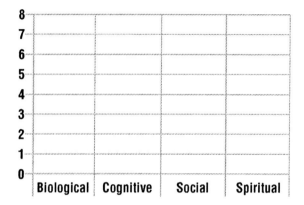

Biological   Cognitive   Social   Spiritual

FIGURE 14. MOOD REGULATION STRATEGIES PROFILE. BY TAKING THE RESULTS FROM THE MOOD REGULATION STRATEGIES INVENTORY AND PLOTTING THEM ON THE GRID, A GRAPH EMERGES WHICH SHOWS WHICH STRATEGIES YOU RELY ON AND HOW THEY RELATE TO THE OTHER STRATEGIES. THE SMALL SAMPLE GRAPH IS A GUIDE TO HELP YOU COMPLETE YOUR PERSONAL GRAPH.

The journey begins

In summary, depression is the result of failure in mood regulation processes. The mood thermostat is not broken, but it needs calibration. MRT teaches you how to restore your equilibrium and regulate your mood. This is done through learning skills and strategies that will lead to mood regulation and feeling terrific. When people are depressed, they try to regulate their moods in ineffective ways by withdrawing, oversleeping, or drinking alcohol, for example, with no resolution.

Like temperature and heart regulation, mood regulation is a process that is ongoing within us in wakefulness and sleep, consciousness and unconsciousness. This regulation occurs through the coordinating functions of the biological mood regulatory system, cognitive and social functions, and our spirituality. Our experience with MRT in the treatment of depression is that when a person is suffering from depression, all of the mood regulatory dimensions are affected to one degree or another. Therefore, looking at their collective effect on mood regulation and correcting what is needed are crucial to attaining full recovery and feeling terrific.

The process of MRT is designed so that you are able to see the whole from the parts while still working minute by minute, session by session, step by step on the individual components with new interventions and tools. As such, MRT is an inclusive perspective that does not favor one component more than the other. Nor does it consider one over the other. It is a perspective that is dependent on the functioning and well-being of all the components—biological, cognitive, social, and spiritual.

It is important to note that we do recognize that each of the dimensions can lead to mood changes independently. MRT emphasizes, however, that mood regulation is the medium that interactively binds and integrates these phenomena together. This integration is vital. In discussing the role of emotion regulation in anxiety Dr. Douglas Mennin eloquently stated, "In fact, the ultimate goal of an integrated treatment should be an integrated mind that is able to effectively process all levels of information (including both cognitive and emotional data) and act adaptively as a result" (Mennin et al. 2002). Mood regulation therapy involves a process of change in four categories, listed here and described in FIGURE 15:

Biological Strategies
- Lifestyle changes
- Physical interventions
- Pharmacological interventions

Cognitive Strategies
- Refocusing attention
- Re-thinking

Social Strategies
- Resolve interpersonal conflicts
- Develop healthy relationships

Spiritual Strategies
- Faith
- Spiritual practices

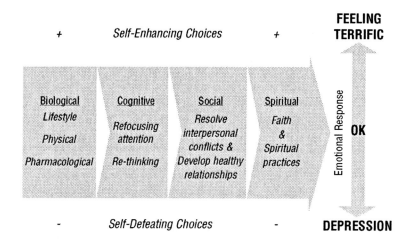

FIGURE 15. THE PROCESS OF MOOD REGULATION THERAPY. THIS DIAGRAM DEPICTS THE BIG PICTURE AND PROCESS OF MOOD REGULATION THERAPY (MRT) AND HOW IT LEADS TO FEELING TERRIFIC (ADAPTED FROM GROSS 2001).

MRT helps the person feel terrific by helping him or her develop strategies that
- Relieve the depressive symptoms
- Improve cognitive skills, decision making, and judgment
- Deal more effectively with relationship conflicts and create better capacity for a variety of mutually fulfilling and lasting relationships
- Create meaning in life, a sense of belonging, mastery, purpose, and hope.

MRT involves four steps to learn and use to feel terrific all of the time:
- Awareness of your mood: how to identify and label feelings and emotion
- Measure and evaluate your mood and mood-regulating strategies: identify and graph the dimensions you are using
- Utilize mood regulation strategies: make change in mood when warranted in order to feel terrific
- Maintenance: monitoring your feeling-terrific state. Maintenance allows you to continue discovering the influence on your mood and how to regulate mood promptly to remain feeling terrific. This allows detection of any backsliding to correct it immediately and allows you to maintain the feeling-terrific state while acquiring new skills in mood regulation.

The process of mood regulation therapy that we have examined in this chapter explains the big picture, the four influences on mood regulation, and the four strategies that are derived from them. In Chapters 4, 5, 6, and 7, we will be discussing each of the strategies in detail and presenting the skills that need to be acquired to effect a mood change. Each strategy has its own set of premises and facts and its own method of treatment in how it changes a mood state. Even though we discuss each dimension separately, we want to emphasize that the linkages between all four are continuous and dynamic, as each dimension affects the others and is affected by it. The strategies should also be seen as interlinking interventions. Before long, you will start appreciating how and when each one affects your mood and to what extent it is effective in changing it. At different times you will have to employ different strategies, depending on what's going on and how to best change it. Good luck!

CHAPTER 4
Biological Strategies

The word *biology* as it is used here refers to the "hardware" of the body, which is made up of cells, tissues, and organs. It is a physical matrix that comprises the various body systems—the nervous system, cardiovascular system, and endocrine system, among others. These systems of the body are dependent on each other for proper functioning. They affect each other through a complex network of enzymes, hormones, nerves, and other intricate biological pathways. For instance, the thyroid hormone affects heart function, the nervous system affects the gastrointestinal system, and so on.

Our moods are regulated in part by our biological processes. The emotion center in the brain helps in regulating our emotions and therefore our mood twenty-four hours a day to keep it in a steady biological state. We use the term *mood center* interchangeably with *emotion center* to describe this intricate set of regulatory activity. The mood center operates through chemical and electrical charges that regulate our moods through an intricate pathway of nerve circuitry. The mood center works like a thermostat. Its function is to regulate a person's mood within a set range so the mood doesn't go too high or too low. If that regulatory function is working well, a person's mood is good and stable. If the thermostat stops functioning or malfunctions, then the person feels depressed.

Biological stability exists when the regulatory function of the mood center is in its normal homeostatic state. If it is malfunctioning, biological stability is lost. Mood regulation requires the restoration of the biological stability state, which can be accomplished through several approaches, such as using antidepressant medications, exercise, diet management, and light therapy, among others.

Biological stability is one of the prerequisites for feeling terrific. In depression the mood center is malfunctioning and needs to be restored to its normal regulatory function. The biological therapies that will be discussed in this chapter are remedies that help in this restoration process. Once the mood center is functioning normally, we can feel terrific.

Achieving biological stability is accomplished by first identifying what is malfunctioning within the body and then correcting it. In depression any of several changes can take place in the body. In this chapter we will deal with biological therapies that are safe and of proven efficacy in the treatment of depression. All of these therapies assist in mood regulation. The antidepressant medications are the best studied of these biological therapies and have been shown to play a major and unequivocal role in the treatment of depression.

One of the things that a person learns in the process of achieving biological stability is how to listen to the body and respond to it. For instance, a headache is sometimes a sign of stress and inner tension. Listening to the body means knowing when it needs to rest, when it's ready for action, how the body reacts to the environment around it, and how it deals with stress.

Many people don't listen to their body and are not aware of its distress signs. We only pay attention to it when it stops functioning or is in pain. For instance, if we have a recurring headache, we take aspirin and stay in the same stressful environment. We often disregard the fact that our body is fatigued or that we need to avoid the high level of stress we are under.

We must learn how to listen to our bodies and respond accordingly. We must know our body's signals, its symptoms, and what it is communicating to us. For example, if we have a weight problem, we must learn to recognize the feelings of hunger and satiety. If we feel frustrated but we are not hungry, we need to understand how to nurture the body instead of stuffing it with food. We need to know our biological drives, how to enjoy them, and how to curb them, if necessary. The goal in MRT is to understand how the body works, recognize when it doesn't work well, learn how to nurture it, and learn how to properly care for it.

The process of learning about one's body, healing it, or attending to its needs will bring about a lifestyle change. This lifestyle change may include a diet change, exercise, yoga, attention to biological rhythms, or other adjustments. All of these things can heighten awareness about our physical presence in the world and give us the opportunity to connect to things around us with greater awareness. Once we learn how to effectively stabilize our body, we can integrate it with our mind and spirit in our quest for becoming a fully integrated person who is going to feel terrific. Biology cannot be separated from the psyche or the spirit. Our journey to feeling terrific is a process of healing and integration of the mind, body, and spirit. In this process of integration, a person's biology serves as the landscape upon which the mind and spirit exist.

The biology of mood

In order to understand the underpinnings of depression, it is important to understand how the brain functions normally in transmitting information from one cell to another. The brain is made up of neurons and glial cells. There are about 100 billion neurons in the brain. Neurons are brain nerve cells; they communicate with each other by sending and receiving electro-chemical signals. The glial cells provide physical and nutritional support for the neurons.

Each neuron is made up of a cell body and projections called the axon and the dendrite. Dendrites bring information into the cell body, and axons take information away from the cell. The connecting point between one neuron and another is the synapse, a gap that connects the axon of the transmitting neuron with the dendrite of the receiving neuron. The neurons are interconnected into specific functional circuits that are important for processing sensory input information; these circuits also affect motor output and are responsible for connecting and processing emotions and cognitions.

Information is carried in the brain through chemicals called neurotransmitters. These neurotransmitters are made either in the nerve cell itself from amino acids or they are absorbed from a fluid outside the cell called the extracellular fluid. Once the neurotransmitters are in the nerve cell, they are stored in granules called storage vesicles. When a nerve cell is stimulated, an electrochemical current is carried through the nerve cell by the exchange of sodium and potassium electrolytes that are present in the membrane of the nerve cell. Minerals, hormones, and other chemicals assist in this process of transmission of electrochemical impulse. When the nerve cell is stimulated, the resulting electrical impulse causes the release of neurotransmitters from the storage vesicle.

The normal processes of neurotransmitter release and transmission of the electrochemical impulse occur in stages, as illustrated in FIGURES 16A-C. FIGURES 16D and 16E illustrate how this process is affected in a person who is depressed.

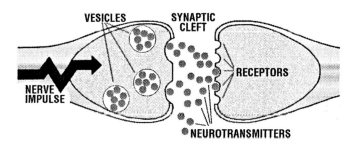

FIGURE 16A. NORMALLY, NEUROTRANSMITTERS ARE RELEASED FROM THE TRANSMITTING NERVE CELLS SO THEY MAY CARRY THE NERVE IMPULSE ACROSS THE SYNAPTIC CLEFT TO THE RECEIVING NERVE CELL.

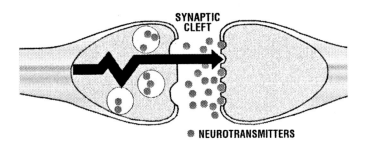

FIGURE 16B. WHEN THERE ARE PLENTY OF NEUROTRANSMITTERS, THE IMPULSE IS PASSED ACROSS THE SYNAPTIC CLEFT EASILY AND EFFICIENTLY.

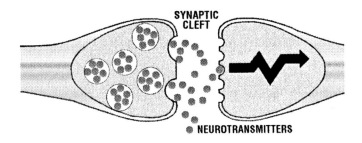

FIGURE 16C. AFTER THE IMPULSE HAS BEEN PASSED ACROSS THE SYNAPTIC CLEFT, THE NEUROTRANSMITTERS THAT REMAIN IN THE SYNAPTIC CLEFT ARE "RECYCLED" BACK INTO THE TRANSMITTING CELL (THIS PROCESS IS CALLED "RE-UPTAKE") TO BE RECYCLED OR DESTROYED. MEANWHILE, NEW NEUROTRANSMITTERS ARE ALREADY BEING MADE AND STORED IN THE VESICLES. THE TRANSMITTING CELL IS THEN READY TO SEND ITS NEXT IMPULSE.

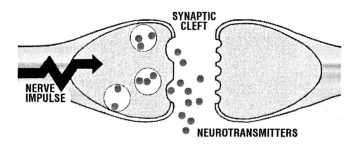

FIGURE 16D. IN DEPRESSION, THE LEVEL OF NEUROTRANSMITTERS MAY BE LOW; NOT ENOUGH ARE AVAILABLE TO CARRY THE NERVE IMPULSE TO THE RECEIVING NERVE CELL.

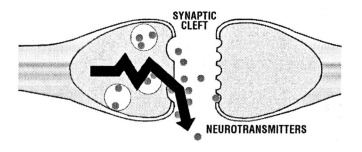

FIGURE 16E. BECAUSE THERE ARE TOO FEW NEUROTRANSMITTERS, THE NERVE IMPULSE CANNOT BE TRANSMITTED.

One of the causes of clinical depression has been thought to be an insufficient number or an imbalance of neurotransmitters made or released in the transmitting nerve cells. There are many theories as to what the imbalance or malfunction may be, but no conclusive evidence has yet been found. Many neurotransmitters have been the focus of research, but the ones most closely studied and related to clinical depression are called the biogenic amines. These neurotransmitters are norepinephrine, epinephrine, dopamine, and serotonin.

Neurotransmitters are important components that regulate our emotions. They work in conjunction with other systems and substances in our body such as the endocrine system, which regulates hormones, or the autonomic nervous system, which regulates our "fight-or-flight" response. Many psychiatric disorders exhibit abnormalities in the emotional realms described in FIGURE 17, so you can see how important neurotransmitters are in our behavior.

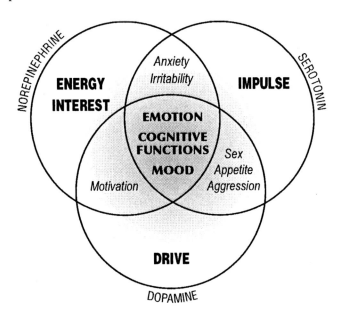

FIGURE 17. NEUROTRANSMITTERS AND THEIR EFFECTS. DIFFERENT TYPES OF NEUROTRANSMITTERS CAN HAVE DIFFERENT EFFECTS ON THE BRAIN AND BEHAVIOR.

Most psychiatric medications re-balance or modulate the balance of neurotransmitter activity and receptor sensitivity. Some medications work to block receptor sites in the receiving neuron, while others work to inhibit the re-uptake of neurotransmitters from the sending neuron. In either case, the result is more neurotransmitter substance available to the cells.

In summary, some key neurotransmitters are involved in our emotions and our behavior. We also have psychological and psychiatric symptoms that respond to medications that target the neurons in specific ways in order to alter, block, inhibit, moderate, regulate, or stimulate chemical neurotransmission.

The introduction of antidepressants

According to a December 2004 article in the *Washington Post*, one in ten women in America takes an antidepressant, and in the last 10 years the use of antidepressants has nearly tripled (Vedantam 2004). The discovery of antidepressants is considered a remarkable achievement in medicine because it confirmed the role that biology plays in determining our moods. Antidepressants have been considered a "pharmacological bridge" between the brain and the mind (Mandell 1980). Acting as a bridge for the depressed person, these medications provide a missing link that allows for the coordination and harmonization of thoughts, feelings, and other biological functions controlled by the brain.

The first antidepressant compounds discovered were the monoamine oxidase inhibitors, or MAOIs. Marsilid was the first MAOI introduced; it was initially used in the treatment of tuberculosis. Patients on Marsilid for the treatment of tuberculosis noted that their moods were elevated. Those that were depressed started to feel better as their depression lifted. It was then concluded that Marsilid had antidepressant properties and could be used in the treatment of depression. Marsilid actually proved to be quite effective in the treatment of severe depression. Reports of liver damage and toxicity due to interactions with certain food substances led to the withdrawal of Marsilid from the marketplace in the United States. Other MAOIs have since made their way to the market, but they haven't been as popular or as widely used as other available antidepressants mainly because of their safety profile when compared to newer antidepressants and the precautions needed with diet.

While the discovery of Marsilid's antidepressant properties was taking place, Dr. Roland Kuhn, a Swiss physician, was searching for a medication to help with sleep. The prevailing theory at the time was that most psychiatric illnesses could be successfully treated with sleep therapy. In his search for a sleeping medication, he came across a compound that was energizing instead of sedating. He started working on that compound to refine it and improve it. In his efforts, he discovered that the compound had antidepressant effects. That compound was called Imipramine. The discovery of Imipramine took place in 1954, and it was announced five months after the antidepressant effects of Marsilid were first reported (Kline 1974). Imipramine was the first of a class of tricyclic antidepressants to enter the market. The tricyclics, which constitute one class of antidepressants, are called tricyclics because of their chemical structure—the compound is made of three chemical rings connected to each other.

Dr. Kuhn's discovery changed the lives of millions in a dramatic way. Antidepressant medications have enabled people to live free of depression and free of the risk of suicide. No longer is depression an untreatable ailment, and no longer do we have to watch people suffer. We can correct the biological imbalance caused by depression and allow people to feel terrific again (or for the first time). Antidepressants can heal the body and form a bridge between the brain and the mind by reestablishing the mood center's normal regulatory function of mood stabilization. People can live a normal life, thanks to these compounds and the stability they bring about. With the discovery and use of antidepressants, medicine has in essence conquered the disease called clinical depression and made it possible to prevent its horrible complications.

There are many antidepressants on the market today in the United States. Many more exist on the markets of Europe and the rest of the world. Numerous other antidepressants are in various stages of research and development worldwide. Since 1954 the search for the perfect antidepressant has not stopped.

A new class of antidepressants called the selective serotonin re-uptake inhibitors, or SSRIs, which has entered the market in the past two decades, has rivaled the popularity of the tricyclic antidepressants. Other classes have been added since. They are listed in TABLE 6.

Types of antidepressants

Antidepressants available in the United States are divided into five classes. The different types of antidepressants reflect differences in chemical structure, mechanisms of action, and biochemical pathways. One reason we have so many antidepressants is the fact that there is no single antidepressant that works for everybody.

People vary in their biochemical and biological makeup, and each person has his or her individualized pattern of absorbing, metabolizing, utilizing, and eliminating a medicine. We each have individual and unique biochemical characteristics, as much as we have our own physical characteristics, our own personalities, and our unique fingerprints. Accordingly, we may respond very well to one antidepressant and not respond at all to another. Additionally, each antidepressant group works on its own biochemical pathways or neurotransmitter system. The antidepressant that may work wonders for one person may not work at all for another. There are no "good" and "bad" antidepressants. What makes the difference between them is that one person may respond to one but not to another. Or one person may have side effects with one but not with another. We still can't account for these individual differences or predict them. With the numerous antidepressants on the market, therapists and doctors eventually find one that works best for the individual.

This phenomenon of people responding to one medicine but not another is not uncommon; variable response occurs with other medications, as well. For instance, not everybody tolerates or responds to aspirin when they have a headache. Some do well with aspirin, while others prefer Tylenol; still others only respond to Advil. The same is true with the antidepressants: what may work for one person may not work for someone else. We have a large selection to choose from, and more are on the way. Ninety percent of the people with clinical depression will respond to an antidepressant in one of the groups or to a combination of antidepressant with other medications.

All of the antidepressants are equally effective. As a general rule, any one of the antidepressants is effective in two thirds of the people who take it. So if any of the above-mentioned antidepressants is given to one hundred people with clinical depression, around 66 percent will respond well to it. However, the 66 percent that may respond to one antidepressant may not be the same 66 percent that may respond to another. That is why we have so many antidepressants, and why we can switch from one to another if a person is not responding. For instance, a person may be a non-responder for Prozac, but when he's put on Wellbutrin he may be in the 66 percent responder group. Currently, there is no definitive way to determine who will respond to what, but there are some general guidelines and principles. A person's presentation, symptoms, medical history, family history, type of depression, and allergies are some of the important factors that help the psychiatrist decide which antidepressant to choose.

TABLE 6 lists the usual adult dosages of various antidepressants. Every person has his own optimal dose. During different episodes, however, the same person may respond to different dosages. For instance, a person may have required 100 mg of Zoloft to recover from depression he experienced at the age of twenty-nine. Eight years later, he experiences a second bout of depression but this time he needs 200 mg of the same medication to achieve the same response. Or he may need less medication this time.

One of the myths about antidepressants is that the amount of medication a person needs is correlated with the degree of the depression. This is not true. Dosage is not dependent on degree of depression but on the person's metabolism and degree of tolerance to medications. Some people know that they respond to small doses of any medicine and are quite sensitive to medications and side effects. Others know that they need high doses to get any effect from a medicine and aren't readily bothered by side effects.

GENERIC *(TRADE)* NAME | USUAL ADULT DOSE *(MG/DAY)*

I. TRICYCLICS

Amitriptyline *(Elavil, Endep)*	75–300
Doxepin *(Adapin, Sinequan)*	75–300
Desipramine *(Norpramine, Pertofrane)*	75–300
Imipramine *(Tofranil, Janimine)*	75–300
Nortriptyline *(Pamelor, Aventyl)*	50–250
Protriptyline *(Vivactil)*	20–60
Trimipramine *(Surmontil)*	75–300
Clomipramine *(Anafranil)*	75–300

II. HETEROCYCLICS

Amoxapine *(Asendin)*	100–400
Maprotiline *(Ludiomil)*	75–200
Trazodone *(Desyrel)*	100–600
Bupropion *(Wellbutrin)*	150–450
Nefazadone *(Serzone)*	100–600

III. MONOAMINE OXIDASE INHIBITORS (MAOIs)

Isocarboxazid *(Marplan)*	30–50
Tranylcypromine *(Parnate)*	10–60
Phenelzine *(Nardil)*	15–90

IV. SELECTIVE SEROTONIN REUPTAKE INHIBITORS (SSRIs)

Fluoxetine *(Prozac)*	10–80
Paroxetine *(Paxil)*	10–50
Fluvoxamine *(Luvox)*	50–300
Sertraline *(Zoloft)*	50–200
Citalopram *(Celexa)*	20–60
e-Citalopram *(Lexapro)*	10–20

V. SELECTIVE SEROTONIN & NOREPINEPHRINE RE-UPTAKE INHIBITORS (SNRIs)

Venlafaxine *(Effexor)*	50–375
Duloxetine *(Cymbalta)*	30–60

TABLE 6. ANTIDEPRESSANT CATEGORIES AND DOSAGE RANGES OF COMMON ANTIDEPRESSANTS. DOSAGES ARE DETERMINED BY THE THERAPIST OR PHYSICIAN TREATING THE PERSON WITH DEPRESSION.

The amount of antidepressant medication needed to overcome depression is determined by individual differences such as age and biochemical makeup and the body's ability to absorb, metabolize, and eliminate the medicine. Other factors that determine dosage include other medications that the person is taking or the presence of other medical disorders such as diabetes. Another factor that helps determine dosage is the presence or absence of a "therapeutic window" effect. A therapeutic window is simply a range within which the antidepressant exerts the maximum antidepressant effect. Above that range or below it, the antidepressant is not that effective. Not all antidepressants have such a therapeutic window.

The best-known antidepressant to have a therapeutic window is the tricyclic antidepressant nortriptyline. The therapeutic window of nortriptyline is measured by how much of it is present in the blood. For nortriptyline the therapeutic window is between 50 to 150 ng/ml. If the amount of medication in the blood falls below 50 ng/ml or goes above 150 ng/ml, the medicine loses its effectiveness. This therapeutic window serves as a guide for the treating psychiatrist to maintain the blood level in the therapeutic range to get the best antidepressant effect.

Differences in the body's ability to absorb and metabolize medications have been studied extensively with antidepressants. It was found that the blood level of an antidepressant medication may vary thirty times from one person to another for the same dose given. This variation is caused by individual differences in biochemistry. The conclusion we derive from this information is that what counts when taking an antidepressant is not how much medication is taken but how much is actually absorbed, metabolized, and getting into the system. As for some people, not all that they take gets into the blood or gets metabolized and used. That is why an increased dosage should not be interpreted as "getting worse."

Other antidepressants have been found to have therapeutic ranges rather than therapeutic windows. A therapeutic range is a level, indicated by a numeric value, beyond which an antidepressant becomes toxic and starts exerting severe and toxic side effects. Once the antidepressant goes over its therapeutic range, it goes into its toxic range. All antidepressants become toxic at a certain range, which is called the toxic range. Antidepressant levels enter the toxic range when they are taken in dosages greater than the ones recommended in the previous table. There are few instances when they need to be given in higher amounts than the dosages listed, but that is only done when toxicity is carefully monitored by the psychiatrist.

How antidepressants work

The exact manner in which antidepressants work is unknown. It has been suggested that, with the exception of the MAOIs, antidepressants may work by inhibiting the re-uptake of the neurotransmitter from the synapse. This allows for an increased concentration of the neurotransmitter at the receptor site. Depression is assumed to be the result of a deficiency of neurotransmitter (for example, serotonin or norepinephrine) availability in the brain and a change in the sensitivity and response of the receptor sites in the nerve cells. That means that in clinical depression there is a biochemical imbalance that causes malfunction and dysregulation in the mood center. When the mood center becomes dysregulated, it loses its ability to keep a person's mood stable. The mood center, as you will recall from our previous discussion, works like a thermostat to regulate a person's mood state. As such, the mood center ensures that a person's mood does not go too high or too low.

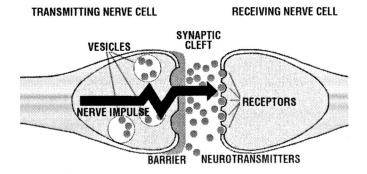

FIGURE 18. HOW AN ANTIDEPRESSANT WORKS. ANTIDEPRESSANT MEDICA-TION FORMS A BARRIER AT THE END OF THE TRANSMITTING NERVE CELL THAT INHIBITS THE RE-UPTAKE OF NEUROTRANSMITTERS. THIS ACTION INCREASES THE CONCENTRATION OF NEUROTRANSMITTERS IN THE SYNAPTIC CLEFT, CREATING A LEVEL HIGH ENOUGH TO ENSURE THE PROPER CONDUCTION OF THE NERVE IMPULSE.

When a depressed person is started on an antidepressant, it increases the supply of neurotransmitter at the receptor site, thus correcting the biochemical imbalance (See FIGURE 18). When that is corrected, the mood center regains its regulatory functions. A normally functioning mood center leads to feeling terrific.

The MAOIs act by inhibiting a nervous system enzyme called monoamine oxidase. This enzyme is responsible for metabolizing and breaking down serotonin and norepinephrine. As their concentration is increased, there are more of these neurotransmitters for the proper functioning of the nerve cell, which reverses the depression.

Unlike precautions with other antidepressants, a person who is taking an MAOI antidepressant has to avoid certain foods that contain tyramine. This is because monoamine oxidase is an enzyme that normally metabolizes tyramine, and it is inhibited and blocked from working by the MAOI. Failure to avoid eating foods that contain tyramine can lead to severe complications. The MAOIs are the only antidepressants that have a dietary restriction.

The above explanations about the mechanisms of action of antidepressants are still considered theoretical. We know beyond any shadow of a doubt that these medications alleviate depression through their biochemical action. Scientific trials and studies have been conducted on these antidepressants prior to their release. One of the conditions for their approval for release to the market by the Food and Drug Administration is being able to prove their efficacy. What that means is proving unequivocally that they are more potent than placebos in the treatment of depression. Every antidepressant has to go through that process prior to its approval and release.

These antidepressant medications don't work through the "power of suggestion," as some people think, but through their action on biochemical pathways in the nervous system. Their function is simply to regulate the mood center in the brain. They provide the missing chemicals that the brain needs for normal functioning but can't produce. What is actually remarkable about these compounds is that they only work in people who are clinically depressed—that is, those with a definite biochemical imbalance and a dysregulated emotion center. If a person does not have a biochemical imbalance or a dysregulated mood center problem that is causing the clinical depression, then the antidepressant will not work. They have no antidepressant effect on a person who is not chemically depressed.

Antidepressants are meant to take a person from a feeling-depressed state to a non-depressed state. They work on people with clinical depression. They are not drugs of abuse, and they are not habit forming. The feeling-good sensation these medications bring about in a depressed person is not an artificial one or drug-induced one as, say, having a drink of alcohol and feeling tipsy and giggly. The changes in mood that they bring about are a state of feeling good, not an artificial euphoric state. These antidepressants give the person the good mood he would have had if he hadn't been depressed. They restore an abnormal mood state to a normal mood state through biochemical regulation of a dysregulated mood center. In certain individuals who are predisposed to mania, antidepressants may "switch" the depression, causing a manic episode.

How antidepressants are prescribed

Prescribing antidepressants is both an art and a science. Unlike the prescribing of many other medications such as antibiotics, determining which antidepressant to use, how much to start with, how frequently to adjust the dosage, and how to adjust the dosage are not formulaic but are skills that are learned and acquired through experience and knowledge. Every physician can start a patient on an antidepressant, but not every physician can get the antidepressant response. The know-how is not in writing the prescription but in getting the medicine to do what it's supposed to do—make the person overcome depression and feel better. People who have "bad" experiences or lack of response with antidepressants are those that are usually treated by physicians who have inadequate training or knowledge in the treatment of depression.

Persons who have experienced recovery from depression through treatment by antidepressants have found them to be life-saving medications. Antidepressants are capable of taking a person from the depths of depression to the realm of normalcy. All this is accomplished without the risk of addiction, dependence, or major discomfort.

For antidepressants to work optimally, two conditions should be met: First, the medication should be prescribed correctly by the psychiatrist, and secondly, the person taking them regularly has to be willing to allow them to work. To prescribe them correctly, the psychiatrist should know the differences between the antidepressants and how to match the person with the proper one. He or she has to be trained and have experience in knowing what dose to start on, how to adjust the dosage, how to minimize side effects, what the differences are between generic and brand-name medications, and so on. Each antidepressant has its own individual profile. What we mean by that is that each medication has its own way of acting, its own side effects profile, and other individual characteristics that differentiate it from the rest. The psychiatrist learns about these individual characteristics and differences through specialized training and experience and utilizes this knowledge to match the right medicine for each person with depression he treats.

For the person taking these medications, there has to be an acceptance and willingness to allow them to work by participating actively in treatment. That means the person has to be willing to give the medications four weeks or more to work because these medications don't work instantly. He has to keep all his appointments so the psychiatrist can monitor his response and make adjustments. He has to be willing to take the medications as prescribed and with all the precautions given (for instance, no alcohol). He has to be willing to be educated about these medicines, ask questions when in doubt, learn about the side effects that may occur with the particular medicine he is taking, and report the side effects in a timely manner to the doctor. It is also important not to stop taking the medication suddenly or make any changes in the dosage without discussing it first with the psychiatrist. This is an active participation process that ensures compliance, a good response rate, and recovery from depression. Anything short of that is passive treatment, where the person pops a pill and hopes for miracles!

Once the psychiatrist chooses the correct antidepressant, he has to determine the dosage and time of day when the medicine should be taken. It is usually best to start with a low dosage and increase it gradually if it is well tolerated. The time of taking the medication depends on the medicine's energizing or sedating properties. If the medicine is energizing, then it is given in the morning; if it is sedating, it is given at bedtime to help with sleep. The process of adjusting the dosage is called titration. With titration the psychiatrist monitors the response of the person and makes judicious adjustments to maximize the beneficial effects and minimize unwanted side effects.

These medications require close monitoring, especially in the first eight weeks of treatment, to get them to work the way they are supposed to. They are not like an antibiotic for a urinary tract infection, where the doctor says as he is handing you the script, "Take one four times a day for ten days and call me if you are not better." Poor monitoring by the psychiatrist only leads to a poor response.

Antidepressants need to be tried for at least three or four weeks on an adequate dosage before declaring them ineffective. Many people who are started on these medicines are not told that by the treating psychiatrist, so they quit taking them after only a few days because they have seen no change or have uncomfortable side effects. It is the responsibility of the psychiatrist to provide this vital piece of information. Some antidepressants are very slow in their onset of action. It takes them a few weeks to form a therapeutic blood level, get into the right neurotransmitter sites, and start regulating the mood center's functioning. Accordingly, patience is very important on the part of the person taking them and the psychiatrist prescribing them. It is not uncommon to see people previously treated for depression with antidepressants whose treating physician kept switching them every several days from one medicine to the other when they failed to show a favorable response. The only reasons to quit an antidepressant early in treatment include severe side effects or an allergic reaction.

Side effects of antidepressants

Side effects are defined as the unpleasant, unwanted effects of a medicine. They are usually not serious or life threatening but are a nuisance and are uncomfortable. All medicines have the ability to produce side effects, but not everybody who takes a medicine gets side effects. People vary in their reactions to medications, especially their sensitivity to side effects. Around 50 percent of people starting on an antidepressant will experience a side effect in the first few weeks of treatment. The majority of side effects are minor and can be controlled by adjusting the dosage or the timing of the dose. A smaller number of people have severe or serious side effects, which necessitates discontinuation of the antidepressant.

Side effects occur for many reasons. The U.S. Department of Health and Human Services (1993) has identified several key reasons. First is the person's unique body chemistry and sensitivity or tolerance to medications in general. Every person has his or her individual characteristics and sensitivity pattern. Some people are very sensitive to taking medications and respond to or are bothered by very small dosages of medicines. Other people are very tolerant and need to take high dosages to get any response. Most people are somewhere in between.

The second factor is the type of antidepressant taken. Some antidepressants cause more side effects than others in one area or another. For instance, some antidepressants, like Elavil, are known to cause sedation in most people, while others, like Prozac, can cause irritability and agitation.

The third factor is the dose taken. Most antidepressants cause side effects at higher dosages. If the dose is lowered, the side effects diminish or dissipate.

The fourth factor is whether the person is taking any other medicines in addition to the antidepressant. Some non-psychiatric medicines such as cardiac medications or medications related to HIV treatment increase the level of the antidepressant in the blood or interact negatively with the antidepressant, causing severe side effects. Before prescribing an antidepressant, the psychiatrist should always ask what other medicines the person is taking. He should warn the person taking antidepressants about taking other medicines, especially over-the-counter medications, with antidepressants.

The fifth factor is the time of day the antidepressant is taken. For example, an antidepressant like Desyrel that causes sedation might be used if the person is having sleep difficulties, with instructions that it be taken at bedtime. This way we turn a side effect (sedation, in this case) into a beneficial effect—helping with sleep.

The sixth factor is age. Elderly people and children are more sensitive to side effects, and antidepressants need to be monitored closely for side effects and toxicity.

The last factor is how much of the medicine is taken at one time or how the medicine is taken. Some side effects can be reduced when the medication is given in divided doses or taken with food.

Most side effects of antidepressants abate after a few weeks of starting treatment. The most common side effects are listed here.

Dry mouth: It is helpful to chew on sugarless lemon drops, be hydrated, or use over-the-counter products such as Biotene.

Constipation: Add prunes, bran, or vegetables to your diet or use Metamucil.

Blurred vision: This occurs early in treatment and is usually temporary.

Dizziness: Occurs due to a drop in blood pressure when standing up suddenly. Standing up slowly may help.

Drowsiness: Some medications may cause sedation; they may be taken at bedtime, which minimizes the impact of drowsiness.

Increased heart rate: Pulse rate may be elevated with some antidepressants. Older patients should have an electrocardiogram (EKG) before beginning to take an antidepressant that may have an effect on cardiac function.

Sexual problems: Common with SSRIs. Lessening of dose or adding another medication may be helpful.

Headache: This will usually go away after a short time.

Nausea: Occurs with SSRIs and is mild and temporary.

Insomnia: Difficulty falling asleep or waking often during the night is seen with the more activating antidepressants (Effexor, Prozac). The medication can be taken in the morning or the dosage may be reduced to alleviate this problem.

Anxiety: Dosage reduction usually resolves this.

Antidepressants should not be mixed with other medications (over-the-counter or prescribed) or with herbal compounds without first discussing it with the prescribing doctor. Antidepressants can be potentiated by these other medications and lead to serious side effects. Alcohol and drugs can also cause serious and toxic reactions if combined with antidepressants. The antidepressants should not be discontinued suddenly because discontinuation symptoms or rebound depression may occur, which can be very uncomfortable. Your physician may give you a tapering schedule that allows you to go slowly off your medication without encountering any adverse effects.

Other medications that help with depression

In addition to antidepressants, a number of medications have been found to have antidepressant effects. These medications are not potent enough to treat depression on their own but are used as adjuncts in addition to the antidepressant to enhance their effect. The three most commonly used medicines in this regard are lithium, thyroid compounds, and stimulants. Antipsychotic medications are also used in the treatment of psychotic depression.

Lithium is a naturally occurring salt similar to sodium or potassium. Lithium is primarily used in the treatment of manic-depressive illness and is very effective in treating that disease. It is used to enhance the effect of antidepressants in people who don't respond adequately to the antidepressant alone. It is usually given in small amounts, and it exerts an effect in a few days. Lithium requires monitoring in the form of blood tests (a lithium blood level) to ensure that it is in a therapeutic range and not in a toxic range.

The common side effects of lithium include feeling thirsty, increased urination, a metallic taste in the mouth, stomach upset, diarrhea, hand tremor, water retention, increased appetite, and weight gain. Lithium may also affect short-term memory. That effect is reversible if lithium is discontinued. A small number of people taking lithium may experience slowness in the activity of their thyroid gland after being on it for some time. That effect can be remedied with a thyroid supplement to restore the activity of the gland. In another small group of people, lithium may affect the kidney's ability to concentrate urine and may affect kidney function. Periodic monitoring of the lithium blood level and thyroid and kidney functioning is necessary if a person taking lithium is to avoid complications in these organs.

Thyroid hormone has been shown to be effective in the treatment of depression if given as a supplement with the antidepressant. It enhances the effect of the antidepressant in certain people who may otherwise be unresponsive or only partially responsive to the antidepressant. A thyroid hormone called T3 is usually used in doses of 25 ug/day.

Stimulants that are used in the treatment of depression are the amphetamines (Dexedrine and Adderall) and methylphenidate (Ritalin). Their use is usually restricted to persons that fail to respond to any of the standard antidepressant medicines. Their use needs to be closely monitored due to the risks associated with the use of this group of medications.

Stimulants are usually energizing in adults and are very helpful if the person is having a depressive episode with a low energy level. They have a potential of abuse, and people may become dependent on them. Side effects need to be closely monitored because these medications, especially the amphetamines, may affect the cardiovascular system, raising blood pressure and the pulse rate. The stimulants have proven to be quite effective in the adjunctive treatment of depression when given with an antidepressant. They may turn a non-responder to a responder.

How hormones help

The hormonal system has direct and indirect effects on a person's mood and sense of well-being. Hormones may be implicated as a cause of clinical depression, for instance, in cases of hypothyroidism, Cushing's disease, postpartum depression, post-menopausal syndrome, and premenstrual dysphoric disorders. What is not clear is whether the hormonal changes are a cause or effect of clinical depression. Hormone replacement therapy in menopause has been shown to be a useful adjunct in correcting a depressive state. What is important is to make sure that the hormonal systems are working well, which can be verified by simple blood tests.

Lifestyle changes: Diet and exercise

The body is not separate from the mind. The body and mind are closely intertwined; they develop and function as one unit. Changes that take place in the body almost always affect a person's mood, and vice versa. For example, chronic anxiety and stress can lead to the development of an ulcer. People with low thyroid function may feel depressed; once their thyroid disorder is corrected, they usually feel better. Taking care of the body is conducive to feeling good. How you feel about your body and how well you take care of it have a direct relationship and influence on your mood and your ability to feel terrific.

Staying physically healthy is crucial to mood regulation and your sense of well-being. The Chinese have long known that fact and practice Tai Chi Chu'an every morning to center and balance the body and keep it healthy for the rest of the day. Practicing yoga does the same thing. Staying fit and caring for your body through eating well, exercising, taking part in a vigorous activity, and relaxation all contribute significantly to feeling good.

Because the body and mind are closely linked, what happens within the body affects the mood. An example is the relationship between the menstrual cycle and emotions. In the premenstrual phase of the menstrual cycle, many women feel irritable, anxious, or depressed. Another example is the relationship between the endocrine system and emotions as the mood change seen in people with low or high thyroid disorder. When someone has a strong emotion, they may express it with a physical response—for example, getting a headache when they are angry, hyperventilating if anxious, or getting flushed if embarrassed.

To feel terrific it is important that you get acquainted with your body and know how to keep it fit. Learning how to read your body's signals in health and disease is vital. Caring for the body is accomplished through a healthy diet; nutritional supplements; regular exercise; relaxation; avoidance of stimulants, irritants, and intoxicants; and being aware of one's genetic makeup and risk factors.

Depression exerts a direct effect on a person's appetite. Appetite is either increased with weight gain or decreased with resultant weight loss when a person is depressed. A well-balanced diet is important to stay healthy and helps give the person a sense of well-being. A healthy diet includes reducing the fat content, increasing the amount of fiber in the diet, and decreasing the amount of sugars. Fruits and vegetables are an important source of fiber and vitamins.

People often comment on the relationship between their moods and patterns of eating. When they feel anxious, they go on a binge or eat more. If depressed, they may eat more or they may eat less. If frustrated, they may binge on certain food items. When a person is depressed, their satiety center—the part of the brain that regulates appetite—may be dysregulated. As a person starts treatment to overcome the depression, it often helps to establish healthy eating habits. Paying attention to what one eats and how frequently one eats is important. One also needs to recognize and be aware of the sensations of hunger and fullness. It is important not to be fanatical about the diet and not to seek exotic dietary remedies or food types. Maintaining a balanced food diet is easy and inexpensive. According to recommendations by The Open University (1980), healthy eating habits include the following:

- Plan your meals and the times you want to eat.
- Resist the temptations to overeat and snack.
- Know the contents of your diet and keep it balanced between the four food groups (proteins, vegetables and fruits, dairy products, and carbohydrates).
- Reduce high-calorie foods to a minimum. Control the amount of sugars, sweets, desserts, chocolate, syrups, creams, butter, mayonnaise, chips, soft drinks, alcohol, and caffeine that you consume. Be liberal with your intake of fresh fruits, vegetables, greens, grains, yogurt, and especially water.
- Always be aware of the differences in the sensations of hunger and satiety.

There are no specific food items that make a person feel terrific. Some people notice that certain food items affect their mood adversely. For instance, some people note that a high intake of sugar slows them down or makes them jittery and anxious. Excessive intake of caffeine can cause irritability, anxiety, and mood changes. Identify any food items that you may be sensitive to or that may alter your mood and limit intake or eliminate them. The road to feeling terrific is about identifying what works or doesn't work for you and then making the necessary changes that will make a difference.

It is well known that even a moderate amount of exercise can improve sleep, decrease fatigue, increase overall well-being, and thus improve mood. Most studies have found psychological and physiologic benefits from exercise, with 90 percent of studies reporting antidepressant and anxiolytic (anti-anxiety) effects (Byrne and Byrne 1993). The Surgeon General (1996) reports that physical activity "reduces symptoms of anxiety and depression and fosters improvements in mood and feelings of well-being."

Drs. Gregg A. Tkachuk and Garry L. Martin (1999) reviewed studies since 1981 in which exercise was used as an intervention in treating individuals with the following clinically diagnosed psychiatric disorders: depression, anxiety, developmental disabilities, schizophrenia, psychosomatic disorders, and substance abuse. Their research concluded that regular exercise is a viable, cost-effective treatment for mild to moderate depression and may be useful in the comprehensive treatment of more severe episodes of the disorder.

How does exercise help depression?

Several theories explain how exercise helps the depressed person improve his or her mood and feel better. Physiologically, exercise has been thought to influence the metabolism and availability of neurotransmitters and increase brain serotonin levels (Lechin et al. 1995; Dunn and Dishman 1991; Chaouloff 1997).

Research shows increased levels of beta-endorphins—chemicals in the brain which can induce a sense of well-being and euphoria and have been linked to the "runner's high" after acute exercise—can help to elevate a person's depressed mood state (Carr et al. 1981; Lobstein et al. 1989). Psychological theories suggest that participation in exercise may enhance one's sense of mastery and self-esteem, which helps a great deal when a person is depressed and feels a loss of control over life. Exercise provides an avenue for refocusing attention and offers a therapeutic distraction from areas of worry, concern, and guilt (Weyerer and Kupfer 1994). Large muscle activity may help discharge feelings of pent-up frustration, anger, and hostility (Artal and Sherman 1998). No single theory has been accepted as explaining why exercise helps depression, and a combination of the above-mentioned factors may best explain the effects of exercise on improving mood and well-being.

It is recommended that exercise be done regularly and in moderation. There is no need for extremes. Moderate exercise improves mood; the goal should be to feel pleasantly tired, a normal feeling after any physical activity. Aerobic activities (brisk walking, jogging, swimming, and biking) and non-aerobic activities (stretching and weight training) are both beneficial. At any pace, walking, the most readily available exercise, is an excellent option.

Artal and Sherman (1998) recommend, "Be realistic, have a practical plan, and don't let exercise become a burden." Being aware of barriers is also helpful, they note. "Fatigue, lack of energy, hopelessness, and lack of motivation, which are all common symptoms of depression, may present as barriers."

Utilize what you learned about yourself in your Mood Regulation Strategies Inventory and Mood Regulation Strategies Profile. If you need to increase time with others, make exercise a social activity and join a gym or group of walkers. If you need to increase time for yourself away from work and family, walking can be a source of exercise and replenishment. Exercise is a very effective tool in mood regulation. Make a commitment to yourself to develop exercise as one of your biological MRT strategies.

Physical therapies

Physical therapy is another biological strategy that can make a difference in the way the body responds to depression.

Electroconvulsive therapy (ECT): This therapy has been in use for the treatment of depression for more than sixty years. Its use has been an ongoing controversy as a result of its misuse in the past and its negative portrayal in the media. ECT involves sending a small amount of electric current to the brain which in turn produces a seizure. The seizure leads to changes in the mood center, altering the brain's electrochemical processes and thus reducing depression. This therapy is effective in eight out of ten people who receive the full course. It is a safe medical treatment; the death rate is around 4.5 per 100,000, primarily from complications of anesthesia or heart disease. ECT is given three times a week for a total of eight to twelve treatments and can be given on an outpatient basis. The procedure takes ten to fifteen minutes and there is no pain during treatment. Improvement in mood occurs within two to three treatments with some people, while with others it may take the full course of twelve sessions.

The most frequent side effects of ECT are temporary confusion after the procedure and short-term memory loss. Some people feel confused after they awaken from the anesthesia. This usually clears up within an hour or two. The memory loss is for events occurring a few days or weeks around the time of treatment. ECT does not usually affect long-term memory and has no effect on intelligence.

When used properly, ECT is the most effective treatment of severe clinical depression. Its use, however, remains limited because of the stigma surrounding it. Today it is reserved for people with depression who failed to improve with medication or therapy or those who did well with ECT in the past.

Light therapy: This form of therapy involves exposure to light using either artificial light from a light box or natural light. Light therapy is used for the treatment of depression and some sleep disorders. The type of depression that is treated with light therapy is called Season Affective Disorder (SAD), which has a seasonal pattern, occurring mostly during fall and/or winter, although it may occur in individuals living in geographic areas where there is decreased sunlight or when days become shorter. It is thought to be caused when the brain receives a reduced amount of natural light.

The treatment requires very bright light from a light box that produces 10,000 lux (approximately eighteen times brighter than normal indoor light). The person has to sit twenty to twenty-four inches from the light source with their eyes open. The treatment is usually for twenty to thirty minutes per day, preferably in the morning.

The light entering the eyes goes to the retina, which transfers it to electrical impulses that are carried to the brain, stimulating the release of neurotransmitters involved in mood regulation. Light is necessary for the regulation of the internal body clock or circadian rhythm. Light therapy helps in regulating the circadian rhythm.

The main side effects of light therapy are irritability, headache, eyestrain, or difficulty sleeping. When these side effects are experienced, the person should decrease the amount of light therapy time, which resolves or eliminates these side effects.

Administering any biological treatment requires knowledge and experience and should be done under the supervision of a psychiatrist or therapist who is trained in these therapies. The tools may be used alone or in combination with each other. Treatment has to be individualized to the needs of the person. The person receiving treatment needs to be educated about the treatment and be actively involved in decisions.

Exercise: Biological Strategies

You may find this exercise helpful to assist you in evaluating your use of biological MRT strategies.

Assign a number from 0 (dissatisfied) to 10 (extremely satisfied) to rate how well you are doing with your self care in each of the following areas. You may also want to ask a close friend or family member to rate you and compare the results.

- Eating habits and food choices _____
- Exercise habits _____
- Sleep habits _____
- Attention to health care (taking vitamins or medications, seeing the doctor, chiropractor, dentist, etc.) _____
- Self care (taking showers, brushing teeth, care for hair, skin, fingernails, toenails) _____
- Time outdoors and in nature and sunlight _____

Results: Congratulate yourself on items for which you scored 6 or more. For each item for which you scored 5 or less, think of a strategy in each category that you could do to improve your score over the next month. Make a commitment to yourself to increase your score in each category over the next month. Write your goals in your calendar or diary and keep track of your progress. Then repeat this inventory in thirty days.

CHAPTER 5
Cognitive Strategies

Cognition and mood

Cognition or cognitive means *to know* or *to think*. The relationship between our thoughts and our feelings has been the subject of study and inquiry by philosophers and researchers for many centuries. Even though we still don't understand how thoughts influence feelings or how feelings influence thoughts, we know that they are interrelated and affect each other directly and indirectly.

Cognition and mood have long been viewed as distinct but closely interacting aspects of an individual's mental life. Researchers have demonstrated that emotional and cognitive functions are inseparable from the neural network aspect of the brain, and that not only do mood states regulate thoughts and behavior but cognitions also regulate moods (Gray and Braver 2002).

Animal research and neuroimaging studies have shown that there are specific circuits that connect the limbic system (mood center) with the cerebral cortex (thinking center). This anatomical circuit provides reciprocal, two-way interactions between emotions and cognitions. Dr. Helen Mayberg (1997) has proposed and described a cortical-limbic network model of depression and states: "Depression likely involves the disruption of a widely distributed and functionally interactive network of cortical-striatal and cortical-limbic pathways that is critical to the integrated regulation of mood and associated motor, cognitive, and somatic behaviors." In another study by Mayberg (2002) regarding the treatment of depression, she states that "the synchronized modulation of these dysfunctional cortical-limbic pathways is considered critical for illness remission, regardless of treatment modality." As Dr. Mayberg has documented in her research findings, it is clear that cognitive processes have a direct effect on mood and play a role in mood regulation.

Psychiatrist Aaron Beck (1979) developed cognitive therapy as a tool for treating depression. The basis of cognitive therapy is the belief that thoughts precede emotions and thus determine them. When a person has negative thoughts, he will have negative emotions and get depressed. Negative thinking is the hallmark of the person who does not feel good.

Cognitive therapy teaches the depressed person how to change negative thoughts and correct them; this process allows the negative mood to change to a better one. When a person does not feel good, he interprets everything going around him in a negative and distorted way. The negative thoughts are pessimistic, futile, and demoralizing, and they are self-directed and self-focused. The person is preoccupied with negative thoughts about himself, such as "I'm a failure, I'm no good," and similar ideas. These negative thoughts about oneself are not based in reality; they are a distortion of reality. However, these negative thoughts become part of the person's reality, and he believes them as fully valid and true. Negative thoughts feed on themselves and lead to more negative thoughts, where the person eventually becomes trapped in a maze of negativity that he finds hard to get out of.

The power of negative thinking exists in its ability to isolate the person from his immediate environment by creating a false reality that makes him misinterpret what's happening around him. When anything goes wrong in his life, he misinterprets it in a negative and self-directed way and gets stuck in a negative frame of mind. To get out of a depressed mood state, the person needs to change his negative style of thinking to a neutral or positive style.

Feeling good does not mean that a person has only positive thoughts. A person's thinking can contain positive or neutral thoughts. Positive thinking refers to thoughts that are optimistic, affirming, and hopeful; the person has a positive outlook. In a neutral thinking style, the thoughts are neither negative nor positive. They are realistic, factual, and non-judgmental. An example of a negative-thinking style is a person who thinks to himself, "I am a failure. I can't do anything right. Nobody likes me." Examples of positive thoughts are "I am going to be successful in whatever I do. I am going to make today a good day for me. I am a likeable person."

Negative and positive thoughts may be based in reality or have no connection to reality at all. That means that these kinds of thoughts may be true or false statements about the person.

An example of the neutral style of thinking is a person who thinks, "Even though I have a hard day ahead of me today, I will try to make it pleasant," or "I will learn from my mistakes with my children and try to be a better parent," or "I have some strengths and some weaknesses. I will continue to try and improve on my weak points." Neutral thoughts are reality based and are therefore more believable than negative or positive thoughts. Neutral thoughts constitute the basis of the thinking style of a person who feels good. They are more conducive to feeling good than positive thoughts because they are more realistic and more believable. A few positive thoughts are definitely conducive to feeling good, but the fundamental thinking style of the feeling-good person is that of neutral, realistic thinking.

The journey to feeling good is not about making positive statements and affirmations every morning, then hoping all will go well. It involves learning how to challenge and change distorted thoughts and replace them with neutral or positive thoughts. Cognitive therapy teaches the depressed person how to change negative thoughts and correct them; this process allows the negative mood to change to a better one. When we know how to understand and work with our thoughts, we have leverage over our mood, which helps us to change them in the direction we want. Thoughts or cognitions are powerful tools that can help us modify how we think and feel.

The broad usage of the phrase *cognitive functions* refers to thinking processes such as concentration, attention, memory, awareness, judgment, and intelligence. The cognitive strategies that we will discuss are related to the thinking processes of the brain. Two domains of cognitive function can impact mood and change it—attention and thinking. Attention and thinking are interrelated but separate functions of the brain (Posner and Petersen 1990). The two cognitive strategies we will focus on include:

- Attention regulation strategies, or "refocusing," which pertains to what we need to do to change our attention to improve our mood state from a depressed one to a feeling-terrific one.
- Thought regulation strategies, or "re-thinking," which pertains to what we need to do to change our negative thoughts, which can then lead to a positive change in mood and to feeling terrific.

Attention Regulation
Strategy: Attention and mood

Attention is a delicate mental function that denotes the individual's capacity to concentrate on a selected sensory stimulus and idea while keeping other stimuli away (Cohen 1997). It includes the activities of orienting, filtering, selecting information or stimuli, and getting the person prepared for action. This allows the person to maintain a stream of thought on a stimulus and activity on a specific goal.

Attention is a very important feature in everyday life; we need to pay attention while we drive to avoid an accident, while we are in the classroom in order to learn, and while others are talking to us so we can understand what they are saying. Our capacity for attention, however, is limited and we can only be aware of a few things at the same time. We usually pay attention to things that we value; otherwise we lose interest and disconnect from the situation.

The capacity to pay attention is influenced in great part by our emotional state and feelings. For instance, if you like a certain actor, you'll watch his or her program on television and get fully absorbed in it. If you don't like the actor, it is very hard to pay attention to the program, and you'll be flipping through channels until you find someone or a program you like.

There is a two-way relationship between our mood state and the direction of our attention. When we focus on something, it can trigger emotion in us, and when we experience a strong emotion, that emotion can divert our attention toward or away from the stimulus. When we are depressed, most of our thoughts and recollections are about negative and depressing events. A negative mood state brings with it negative thoughts and memories, which is where our attention is directed.

Emotions and feelings serve as informative signals and direct our attention to the topic or object of our feelings. For instance, if I'm working in my garden and I see a snake pass in front of me, I may jump in fear. The emotion of fear serves as a signal that there is danger and at the same time focuses all my attention on the snake to ensure that I get away from it. Accordingly, emotions direct our attention to specific objects. For example, when I feel angry, it is usually at a particular person or specific thing.

Researchers have proposed that strong emotions lead to what is known as "attentional funneling," which is the state where all of our attention is directed to the content of that emotion. The focus of attentional funneling can be on us, someone else, our memories, or something in our environment. For instance, when a person feels very depressed, all of his attention is funneled on himself in a negative self-focused state, and the person becomes filled with negative thoughts about himself such as, "I'm hopeless, I'm helpless, I'll never get better," and so on. This attentional funneling keeps our attention focused on the depressive thoughts which in turn intensify the depressive feelings. The persons starts ruminating on these negative thoughts and a negative loop cycle gets established; the negative loop cycle continues in a closed circle, escalating the depression to the point where a person may feel like harming himself (Clore and Gasper 2000).

Healthy forms of depression, like sadness, have attentional and motivational objectives and purposes. As a signal, depression serves to draw our attention to an internal change or malfunction that needs correction or repair. For instance, when we lose someone we care for, we feel sad. We are saddened by that loss. The sadness is a healthy form of depression and is a signal that we are hurting as we mourn our loss. This is a healthy human emotional response, integral to our experience as human beings. This sadness makes us reach out to others for consolation and support in that sad moment.

If depression is severe as is the case with major depression, the attention becomes unhealthy because it becomes self-focused and symptom-focused in a negative, analytic way. We become preoccupied with our symptoms, our shortcomings, our failures, and our low self-esteem, and all our attention is focused in a negative loop on our self-deficits. This ruminative, negative cycle increases and maintains the depression (Lam et al. 2003; Nix et al. 1995). Researchers have found that when a person is depressed, he or she engages in intense self-focused attention and experiences difficulty focusing on external events and cues.

Self-focused attention also leads to preoccupation with negative thoughts and feelings and interferes with functioning and interaction with one's environment. This selective negative self-focus is associated with hopelessness, loss, self-blame, a sense of failure, and reduction in social and occupational functioning. This self-preoccupation keeps the depressed person self-engrossed and always talking about himself and his depressive symptoms, which can compromise interpersonal relationships and friendships. When a person is depressed, the self-focus is almost exclusively on negative events and memories in one's life, with little attention to the positive side of one's life.

This self-focused rumination paralyzes us, and our attention is self directed to the exclusion of our external environment. This self-focused attention becomes a negative spiral that takes us down, further and further away from our reality, and detaches us from people and things around us. In its most severe form, it leads us to detach from everything around us by having suicidal thoughts and plans. When attention is self focused in a persistently negative way, an intervention is required, using a distraction strategy to refocus and repair attention to the positive inside and outside environment and away from the negative self-focus. This is accomplished through refocusing, which is defined as the steps we need to take to shift our attention from the depressive thinking to focus on neutral or positive things. This will lead to a positive change in our mood.

A man traveling across a field encountered a tiger. He fled while the tiger came after him. Coming to a precipice, he caught hold of the root of a wild vine and swung himself down over the edge. The tiger sniffed at him from above. Trembling, the man looked down to where, far below, two tigers were waiting to eat him. Only the vine sustained him. Two mice, one white and one black, little by little started to gnaw away at the vine. Turning his head sideways, the man saw a luscious strawberry near him. Grasping the vine with one hand, he plucked the strawberry with the other hand, popped it in his mouth, closed his eyes and thought, "Oh, how sweet and delicious it tastes!"—Paul Reps and Nyogen Senzaki

Refocusing

This parable told by Buddha highlights an important tool that we use to regulate and change our mood. Even though the man in the parable is facing certain death, he is able to refocus his attention for a few seconds and change his mood from fear to joy. He is able to stay in the moment. Dr. James Gross (1999) refers to this mental activity as "attentional deployment." Attentional deployment is a term used by many psychology researchers to describe how people re-direct their attention in a certain situation in order to change their emotions. We refer to it as "refocusing."

The aim of refocusing attention is to shift the focus from the negative self-focused state that the person is in when he or she is depressed. Refocusing involves learning how to direct attention away from depressing ruminations by focusing on positive or neutral thoughts, events, or issues. The mechanism that changes our attention is called distraction. We all use distraction as a strategy in our day-to-day life without being aware we are doing so. Distraction changes the depressed mood by shifting the attention to pleasant or neutral feelings or thoughts. Through this strategy, we disengage from the negative self-focus and symptom-focused thoughts, and we can think more clearly and feel better. Here are guidelines for using the refocusing strategies:

- Be aware of your mood. Are you depressed?
- What are you self-focused or ruminating on?
- Use distraction and/or concentration strategies to change your attention focus.
- How do you feel now? Did it work?

These four steps—defining the mood problem, listing the strategic solution, implementing it, then evaluating its effectiveness—are used with all of the strategies and will help you identify which strategy is the most effective.

Distraction

Distraction means that we switch our awareness to something completely different from what's consciously on our mind at the moment. By doing this, we divert our train of thought, and our mood changes. The common practice of distraction is used by mothers with their babies. Rather than engage in a battle of wills or a power struggle and saying "no," the mother can be more successful by using distraction to refocus the baby's attention. The baby forgets about the original struggle over the "no" and becomes interested in the next focus of attention. For instance, a baby wants to play with a shiny knife but obviously can't be allowed to do this. Mom distracts the baby with another safe, shiny, interesting object, which the baby grabs while letting go of the knife, thus redirecting interest and avoiding a temper tantrum. The shiny new toy does the trick, and the baby forgets quickly about the shiny knife.

Distraction has been found in studies to decrease levels of depression and reduce hopelessness (Lam et al. 2003). Distractions that will help to decrease the depression should be positive or neutral—engaging, entertaining, or pleasant. Distraction strategies are the thoughts and behaviors that allow you to take your mind off your depressive thoughts and preoccupations to think about these pleasant and rewarding thoughts or activities. An example is playing cards with a friend to distract yourself from a negative mood. When one is depressed, he or she needs to shift attention to an external, non-emotional-related thought or activity to help relieve the depressive mood.

Negative distracters are ineffective and may worsen depression and lead to more negative rumination and self-absorption. Examples of negative distracters are negatively producing activities and thoughts that are unpleasant or difficult.

The following are steps for refocusing and changing your moods (Domar and Dreher 1999): Focus on one thing at a time and turn your attention to pleasant and rewarding thoughts or activities. This way you break the rumination cycle of negative self-absorption.

Change your environment: Think of places or people who are not around you when you are depressed. Examples include calling a friend to play tennis with or going for a walk on the beach. The essence is choosing an environment that you know from past experience is pleasant and enjoyable.

Modify your existing environment: There are times when you can't change your physical setting, but you can make modifications to it. For instance, your office space at work may be dull and uninspiring and make you feel worse when you walk into it. You may not be able to change it, but you can make changes like putting flowers, changing the lighting, or adding music to distract you from the depressing mood it casts on you. Another method is to actually visualize through mental imagery the types of environments, situations, or creations that you consider happy, fun, or pleasant. You could visualize, for example:

- "I see myself working in the garden in my new house in the country."
- "I am traveling to my favorite country and enjoying the scenery."
- "I am meeting new people who are very excited to know me because of my talents and gifts."

Focus on physical activity: This refers to staying active when you feel depressed and tired. Examples include going for a walk, exercising in a gym, or organizing your garage. All these are distracting activities. The key is choosing one that you feel joy in doing. Another method involves physical activities such as looking at something that will remind you of being grateful for what you have—for example, looking at pictures of your child when she was younger and remembering how wonderful it is to have that relationship. Or maybe it will be old photographs of a favorite aunt or uncle, a happy summer on the lake in childhood, or a vacation with really good friends.

An old method was placing a rubber band around the wrist and snapping it whenever a negative, depressed, or repetitive thought appeared. The idea was that this would "snap" the person out of the thought. This may work for some but not for others.

Many times people will start cleaning, tell jokes, or move around simply to get their minds off the subject that seems to keep them stuck. Perhaps attending a play, opera, symphony, or sports event would be the activity to force your attention to something other than yourself and your depressed or negative thoughts.

Focus on mental exercises: This includes paying attention to things around you or in your mind. Examples of focusing on things around you include playing solitaire card games on the computer, studying details of a picture, or reading the newspaper. You may want to recite poetry from memory, plan a trip in your mind, or problem-solve a friend's dilemma.

Another strategy is to immediately visualize the words "STOP" or imagine a policeman saying "Halt" the minute a negative thought appears. Pick up the visualization by saying out loud, "No!" and then refocus your attention on the opposite of that negative thought.

Another strategy is to spend time visualizing a story that would be fun on an adventure type of outing. It could incorporate fantasy and excitement. For example, you could visualize the following:

- "I am seeing a beautiful healing white light encircle me as I go on a magic carpet ride to a beautiful forest location. I am safe and protected. This white light is growing larger and larger as I feel calmer and happier and more secure and loved than ever before."
- "I am pouring a green liquid, starting at the top of my head, to the bottom of my toes; this liquid has the powers of healing and energizing. After I have completed that, I see a waterfall of rainbow colors wash away all remnants of the tension I feel in my body. I feel light and joyful. I can see the colors glow from within my body and radiate around my body as I relax in my visualization."

Focus on colors and shapes: Get crayons or pastel colors and draw with them anything that comes to mind. Let your feelings flow freely as you color and draw. As an alternative, look at an artist's paintings and focus on the variations in colors and shapes that the artist drew.

Focus on smells: Find smells that you like, take a deep breath, and enjoy them. Examples are smells of the ocean's salty water, your cologne or perfume, cooking odors from the kitchen, or the smell of coffee. Alternately, you can buy various scented creams or liquid extracts, which could be flower scents or plant scents; by placing a drop on your skin, you can create the desired fragrance. Savor the fresh smells and note their effect on your mood.

Focus on sounds: Walk by the ocean and listen to the water breaking. Listen to birds chirping or a canary singing. You can buy tapes of pre-recorded nature or music sounds to listen to. Listen to your favorite musician or tunes. Classical music has been found particularly to have a positive mood-changing effect. White noise, music that is repetitive but calming, and the whirring of fans are also methods of refocusing that are frequently used strategies. Another method involves listening to some favorite music and really enjoying the variety and emphasis.

Focus on movement: Watch other people in motion while paying attention to a specific detail you choose, such as their clothes. Watch your pet as he or she moves, or watch the movements of children. Do body movements or stretching, neck rolls, or yoga postures to refocus. When stuck in a situation where it is not so easy to leave, an example of refocusing your attention could be repositioning the body or massaging the neck. If you are irritated with someone, you could say simple types of sayings or slogans such as "Let go and let God," "First things first," "How important is it?" or a prayer such as the Serenity Prayer. Perhaps a mantra or a calming type of affirmation will assist you to refocus, like "Be still...." or "Relax" or "Serenity."

Focus on sensations: Walk barefoot in the house and focus on the sensations in your feet. Take a shower and focus on the sensation of water on your body, the temperature change, or the pressure of the water.

Focus on the present moment: Find a comfortable, quiet place and sit in a relaxed position, fully relaxing into a state of presence, taking in all you see, hear, smell, touch, and feel. Close your eyes and take a few deep breaths and be aware of your breathing. Pay attention to whether your breathing is fast or slow and how your abdomen is expanding and contracting each time you inhale and exhale. As thoughts, feelings, and images intrude, watch them and let them go by. Don't hang onto them; just be mindful of them as a distant observer, noting the flow and movement of these thoughts and images. Focus on your breathing and let the thoughts slip into the background. Be aware of any sensations in your body and slowly return your awareness to your environment while stretching as you emerge from the meditation. Maintain the meditation for as long as it feels comfortable. Start with a few minutes each day and increase the length of time until you can do it up to twenty minutes a day. Observe how it changes your attention and mood. As you become aware of the present moment in your life, you disengage from the negative self-focused thoughts and feel a big positive change in your mood.

This comprehensive list of mental and physical activities can help you to change your focus of attention. Make a list of the ones that work for you and make you feel better. You will need to try a variety over a controlled period of time before you know what works best.

Guidelines for using distraction strategies

Distraction is not an escape or avoidance technique. It is a strategy to help you pull out of the ruminating and negative self-absorptive state of depression to a more positive state of mind. These guidelines will help you to understand and determine how to best use this strategy:

- Choose a distracting strategy that works best for you and the situation you are in. You will find the best distraction within your interests and preferences, and you can then tailor the distraction to work for you. If you are a swimmer, then swimming will work great for you. It is useless to use swimming, though, if you hate being in the water.
- Once you find a number of distractions that you like, personalize the techniques to meet your own needs. Be specific in your tasks and make sure they are effective in distracting you fully by engaging all of your attention.
- Develop a repertory of distracting strategies for different situations and practice them. Soon you will find yourself resorting to them automatically and unconsciously when you are down.
- Be aware of the influence the various strategies have on your mood. Rate them and use the strategies that elevate your mood the most. You may need to use several strategies in sequence or simultaneously to get the best results in changing your mood. For instance, if you like gardening, you may want to prune your roses while wearing a headset and listening to music at the same time. Whatever works, use it, and use it again.

If you have tried a number of these distraction strategies and they were not effective, it might be because:

- You have not chosen the best distraction that suits you or the situation you are in, or you have chosen a negative distraction instead of a positive distraction or neutral one. Think of others and try them.
- You have not had sufficient practice on perfecting a strategy. For instance, you may think you like classical music but you don't have enough experience and knowledge to know how to choose the right pieces that may help to relieve depression.

- Your depression is very severe and you require other interventions (such as biological intervention with medications) before this distraction strategy will work.

Exercise: Refocusing

Distraction techniques are very useful to change your mood. The following are sample exercises that can be used whenever your mood is depressed. The goal is to shift or refocus your attention in order to change your mood. Utilize any of the activities listed below for a few minutes or longer, until you become absorbed in the activity or thought. Note the result of the activity in the space provided.

Relaxation: Sit in a quiet room, close your eyes, and become aware of feelings and areas of tension in your body. Wherever you feel tension, concentrate on this area and release the tension. Then move to the next place where you feel tension.

Breathing: Concentrate on your breath and get into a regular rhythm (such as 1, 2, 3, IN and 1, 2, 3, OUT). Focus on your breathing and clear your mind.

Visual distraction: Choose an object in your environment. Study it in detail. Concentrate on it as long as you can. Note the shape, colors, and form. Note the intricacy, texture, and detail.

Positive imagery: Concentrate on a pleasant experience you remember from the past or visualize a beautiful, relaxing scene that you remember or create in your mind. Spend some time giving the scene details and colors, imagining your sensations as you see yourself in the scene.

Mental games: Do a crossword puzzle. Count backwards from 100. Read a book. Play relaxing or energizing music.

> *Two monks were once traveling together down a muddy road. A heavy rain was still falling. Coming around the bend, they met a lovely girl in a silk kimono and sash, unable to cross the intersection.*
>
> *"Come on, girl," said the first monk at once. Lifting her in his arms, he carried her over the mud pile to the other side.*
>
> *The other monk was noticeably upset by his brother's behavior and did not speak again until that night when they reached a lodging temple. Then he no longer could restrain himself and said in an angry and disappointed voice, "We monks don't go near females," he said, "especially not young and lovely ones. It is dangerous. Why did you do that?"*
>
> *"I left the girl back there," replied the first monk. "Are you still carrying her?"*—Paul Reps and Nyogen Senzaki

Thought Regulation Strategy: Re-thinking

Negative thoughts lead to negative mood states. The philosopher Epictetus said nearly two thousand years ago that "the thing that upsets people is not what happens but what they think it means." Cognitive therapy stipulates that our assumptions and beliefs about what is happening to us determine how we feel and act. When the beliefs and thoughts are irrational or negative, the ensuing mood is going to be negative and depressed.

Depressed individuals spend their time dwelling on negative thoughts, discarding any positive or neutral thoughts that may come along. According to cognitive theory, depressed people are constantly processing negative information, which colors their experiences, emotions, and behavior. Treatment with cognitive therapy focuses on identifying the negative thoughts, challenging them, and changing them, which leads to a corresponding improvement in mood. Dr. Beck noted that people who were depressed had errors in their thinking processes and attitudes. When these errors—what we refer to as dysfunctional thoughts—were corrected, their mood changed and the depression lifted.

What we will discuss in this section is a step-by-step approach to identifying negative thoughts, challenging them, and correcting them. This approach is drawn from cognitive behavioral therapy (CBT) concepts developed by Aaron Beck and David Burns; these concepts are based on the premise that negative thoughts lead to negative emotions, such as depression (Beck and Greenberg 1974; Beck et al. 1979; Burns 1981). CBT teaches you how to identify the negative thoughts, challenge them, and replace them with more accurate thoughts. This leads to a change in mood and lifting of the depression.

Some of the materials we will use have been adapted from *The Depression Treatment Workbook* (Damluji and Genett 1988). Our approach, which we call "re-thinking," is an adaptation of the CBT techniques we have been using with our patients for many years. Re-thinking is a method that teaches you how to alter your ways of thinking. It encompasses thoughts, beliefs, ideas, attitudes, and assumptions that are causing or maintaining your depressed mood state and teaches you how to convert them and feel terrific. The re-thinking process is comprised of five steps:

- Identify the negative feelings you have now and measure and rate your depression
- Search for the core negative thoughts behind the depression
- Identify the distortions the negative thoughts belong to
- Challenge the negative thoughts, formulate a corrective counterpart, and develop a new counterthought
- Identify how you feel after formulating a new thought.

Identifying feelings and measuring mood

One area with which people seem to have difficulty is the identification of feelings. Our language seems to be the culprit in this situation. We talk about feelings, thoughts, and beliefs as though they are interchangeable. Regardless of the source of the problem, it is important to be able to recognize the difference between a thought and a feeling.

When we begin a statement with the words, "I feel…," it doesn't mean that the words we use to complete the sentence represent a feeling. Consider this statement, for example: "I feel like I can't do anything right." Is this statement a thought or a feeling? It is a thought. There are no feelings present in this statement. So, the first step in becoming aware of whether you are expressing a thought or a feeling is to be careful when you use the words "I feel."

Feelings are essentially the same as events because they are facts. Feelings cannot be tested or disputed. If you say, "I'm sad," no one can argue that point with you. However, going back to our first example, someone can very easily argue with you if you say, "I feel like I can't do anything right." They can point out all the things you have done right. A helpful rule of thumb in cases of question is to substitute the words, "I am…" for "I feel…" If the end result is a statement that can be tested, then it is a thought (or a belief, which is a form of thought). If not, it is a feeling. For example, "I feel sad" switches to "I am sad." This cannot be tested or disputed. Here is another example: "I feel stupid" switches to "I am stupid." This can definitely be tested! Remember, feelings are neither good nor bad, and you do not need to justify them. Beliefs, on the other hand, are adopted concepts or thoughts, and we identify with and are influenced by our beliefs.

One final point about feelings: Feelings are usually discrete, in the sense that they occur all by themselves. Feelings do not usually lead to other feelings, but they may. Thoughts, on the other hand, usually do lead to feelings. If we feel sad and we think, "I am absolutely worthless," we are likely to end up feeling many more feelings such as angry, anxious, and depressed, in addition to sad. To review the topic of feelings then, remember the three most important guidelines:

- Be careful when you use the words, "I feel…"
- Feelings cannot be tested.
- Feelings do not usually lead to other feelings, but they may.

Feeling words describe physical sensations and emotions that we experience. There are many words to describe negative feelings. Below are some words that complete the sentence, "I feel…."

Afraid	Blue	Embarrassed
Angry	Bored	Enraged
Annoyed	Confused	Envious
Anxious	Depressed	Excited
Ashamed	Despondent	Fearful
Bitter	Disappointed	Frightened

Frustrated	Jealous	Resentful
Furious	Lonely	Sad
Happy	Miserable	Terrified
Hurt	Nervous	Tired
Irritated	Overwhelmed	

To make the process of identifying negative feelings easier, negative feelings have been divided into the four following types, each with several examples of words that indicate specific feelings.

Bad: ashamed, overwhelmed, humiliated

Mad: enraged, angry, furious, hostile, irritated

Sad: depressed, miserable, despondent, blue, hurt

Scared: anxious, frightened, nervous, terrified

To find a feeling word, you first select the type of feeling you are experiencing now, then try to find the right specific feeling word that describes your emotion at that moment.

Thought words describe the ideas that circulate in our head all the time. They are our opinions or observations. We may not be aware of them all, but they are there. Thoughts are what we say to ourselves. Our self-talk is made up of thoughts about people, about ourselves, and about the world. These are some of the thought words that occur in everyday speech:

Alone	Hopeless	Unimportant
Bad	Inadequate	Unloved
Deprived	Inferior	Useless
Disturbed	Stupid	Worthless
Helpless	Trapped	

The following states are often mistaken for feelings. Use these words with caution because they are not really feelings; they are also thoughts.

Abandoned	Dependent	Rejected
Alienated	Empty	Responsible
Betrayed	Guilty	
Defeated	Insecure	

A *belief* is a type of thought; it is a state of mind where we place strong confidence in a person, thing, or idea. A belief can be negative or positive, and it can be true or false. Examples are:

- "Making mistakes is unacceptable and intolerable to me."
- "There is no such thing as true love."
- "I am not good enough."
- "I can't trust anyone."
- "I am not smart enough."
- "I don't need anyone."
- "I shouldn't show emotions or cry in front of people."
- "I have to be the best at what I do in order to get the recognition I deserve."

Exercise: Thought Versus Feeling

For each statement in the list below, decide whether it is an example of a thought or a feeling based on the guidelines presented here. Circle your answer. The answers are listed at the end of this chapter.

1. "I feel hopeless."	Thought	Feeling
2. "I am afraid."	Thought	Feeling
3. "I feel sad."	Thought	Feeling
4. "I am inadequate."	Thought	Feeling
5. "I feel so stupid."	Thought	Feeling
6. "I am frustrated."	Thought	Feeling
7. "I feel so alone."	Thought	Feeling
8. "I feel unloved."	Thought	Feeling
9. "I feel confused."	Thought	Feeling
10. "I am angry."	Thought	Feeling
11. "I feel anxious."	Thought	Feeling
12. "I feel guilty."	Thought	Feeling
13. "I feel responsible."	Thought	Feeling
14. "I am very hurt."	Thought	Feeling

The Depression Questionnaire

Now that you know how to label feeling accurately, the next step is to identify and measure your mood. Look back at your score on the Depression Questionnaire (from Chapter Three). If it has been more than five days since you answered the questions and added up your score, you should take the time to fill out the questionnaire again. This score will give you a baseline before you begin to utilize the re-thinking strategies we are about to introduce. Please complete the questionnaire by circling the number which best corresponds to how you have been feeling for the past thirty days, including today. Circle 0 if you do not feel that way at all, 5 if you feel that way to a great extreme, or any number in between that best corresponds to the way you feel about the statement given.

	NOT AT ALL	MINIMALLY	MILDLY	MODERATELY	SEVERELY	EXTREMELY SO
1. I feel sad, blue, down, or depressed.	0	1	2	3	4	5
2. I believe I am a failure.	0	1	2	3	4	5
3. I feel hopeless about the future.	0	1	2	3	4	5
4. I do not enjoy the things I used to enjoy.	0	1	2	3	4	5
5. I feel guilty.	0	1	2	3	4	5
6. I feel dissatisfied.	0	1	2	3	4	5
7. I have lost interest in people and in my surroundings.	0	1	2	3	4	5
8. I have trouble with my sleep.	0	1	2	3	4	5
9. My energy level has decreased.	0	1	2	3	4	5
10. I am hard on myself.	0	1	2	3	4	5
11. I break into tears easily.	0	1	2	3	4	5
12. My interest in sex has decreased.	0	1	2	3	4	5
13. I have difficulty concentrating.	0	1	2	3	4	5
14. I have difficulty making decisions.	0	1	2	3	4	5
15. I am more irritable than usual.	0	1	2	3	4	5
16. I have difficulty getting started on a task.	0	1	2	3	4	5
17. I feel physically tired.	0	1	2	3	4	5
18. I have experienced an increase or decrease in my appetite.	0	1	2	3	4	5
19. I have trouble with my memory.	0	1	2	3	4	5
20. I am worried about my health.	0	1	2	3	4	5

Add the numbers you have circled for each of the 20 questions.

TOTAL: _____

FIGURE 19. THE DEPRESSION QUESTIONNAIRE. THIS LIST OF QUESTIONS ALLOWS YOU TO ACCURATELY MEASURE YOUR MOOD AT ANY GIVEN TIME.

The total you obtain after adding the scores of the twenty questions is a GENERAL estimate of your level of depression. Write your score in the space below.
Self-rated depression score: _____
Today's date: _____

A score of 15 to 30 signifies you may be slightly depressed
A score of 30 to 55 signifies you may be moderately depressed
A score of 55 to 70 signifies you may be moderately to severely depressed
A score of 70 to 85 signifies you may be severely depressed
A score of 85 to 100 signifies you may be very severely depressed

THE ABCs OF WHERE EMOTIONAL FEELINGS COME FROM

When you have an emotional feeling, you first **perceive** (taste, see, hear, physically feel, etc.) something. Next you **think** and **believe** something about your perceptions. Then you have an **emotional feeling**, triggered by your thoughts.

THE ABCs OF NEGATIVE EMOTIONAL FEELINGS

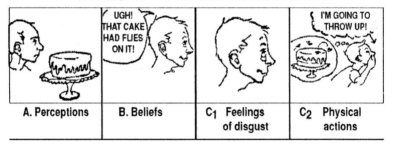

THE ABCs OF POSITIVE EMOTIONAL FEELINGS

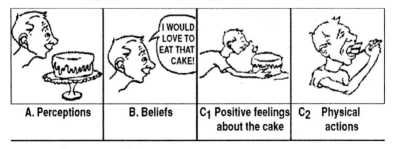

FIGURE 20-1. THE ABCs OF WHERE EMOTIONAL FEELINGS COME FROM (ADAPTED FROM MAULTSBY). (CONTINUED ON NEXT PAGE)

THE ABCs OF NEUTRAL EMOTIONAL FEELINGS

A. Perceptions	B. Beliefs	C_1 Calm feelings	C_2 Physical actions

FIGURE 20-2. THE ABCs OF WHERE EMOTIONAL FEELINGS COME FROM (ADAPTED FROM MAULTSBY). (CONTINUED FROM PREVIOUS PAGE)

The A-B-C-Ds of Re-thinking

Most people believe that an activating event causes us to feel certain emotional consequences. However, it is not the event that causes the feelings but our core beliefs and thoughts about the event that bring about the feelings. Accordingly, thoughts determine how and what we feel and they determine the way we react. When we face a stressful event, we usually feel appropriately sad, hurt, anxious, or something similar in response to the event. If, however, our thoughts consist of mostly irrational and negative beliefs, we will feel inappropriately depressed, anxious, or fearful in response to the event. Consider these two examples:

EXAMPLE 1

A1 (Activating Event): Spouse asks for separation
B1 (Core Belief/Thought): "This is very upsetting; things will be different without the person I've spent the last ten years of my life with."
C1 (Emotional Consequence/Feeling): Sad, Angry, Hurt
D1 (Action): Talk to someone, seek support, seek counseling

EXAMPLE 2

A2 (Activating Event): Spouse asks for separation
B2 (Core Belief/Thought): "This is awful. I can't go on with my life if I lose the only person that ever loved me. No one will ever love me again."
C2 (Emotional Consequence/Feeling): Depressed, Devastated, Anxious, Lonely, Fearful
D2 (Action): Try to hurt self, act out

Example 1 shows a belief system (B1) that is understandable and normal. In fact, it sounds very rational, and the resulting emotions will understandably be the emotions expressed—sad, hurt, and angry.

Example 2, however, shows an irrational belief system (B2) about the event. The resulting emotions are intense and negative, which in this instance include feeling depressed, devastated, anxious, lonely, and fearful. This emotional outcome would make sense if this belief system were true—that is, that no one will ever love this person again. However, it is obvious that this is not a rational thought and is it not likely that this person will never be loved again by anyone else.

These examples illustrate how our interpretations of our experiences have a tremendous impact on the emotional consequences of these experiences. It is not the activating event (A) by itself that determines how we will respond; our core belief system (B) and the way we feel emotionally (C) influence the action (D) we choose.

In this section we are going to analyze the way we develop dysfunctional thoughts and we will learn new skills that will help us to change and correct the way we think about certain events. In the Dysfunctional Thought Exercise presented later, we will identify our own A-B-C-Ds. You can lay the groundwork for this exercise by thinking of a recent event that you may have found upsetting in some way. There will be space in the exercise section to write down your A-B-C-Ds.

The Negative Thinking Triad

As we have discussed, thoughts influence feelings. When you are depressed, negative thoughts dominate your mind. We will now take a close look at the characteristics of the negative thoughts and beliefs one encounters in depression.

Dr. Beck found that people with depression have a consistent pattern in their negative thinking. This pattern consists of three elements that are always present. We call them "the negative thinking triad." This triad represents a stable cognitive pattern that causes a depressed person to regard himself or herself, his or her experiences, and his or her future in a dysfunctional manner. These three components include:

Negative view of self: Depressed people tend to view themselves as undesirable or worthless because of negatively perceived self-image. Such statements as "No one cares about me. I am worthless," and "I can't do anything right; I am such a failure" highlight the depressed person's negative view of himself or herself.

Negative interpretation of experience: Depressed people tend to see their actions as examples of defeat and/or deprivation. That is, rather than focusing on some positive aspect of an experience, depressed persons tend to overemphasize the negative. For example, if a person overcooks the vegetables in an otherwise delicious meal, he or she might think, "Everything I try to do turns out to be a disaster. I just can't seem to get any breaks in life."

Negative view of the future: Depressed people tend to expect continued failure and suffering throughout the rest of their lives. Such statements as "Things will never get better" and "I'll never be what I wanted to be" demonstrate this negative outlook on the future.

The depressed person, therefore, tends to expect and accept negativity as the major orientation of their life and to believe that it is futile to try to change things. Although it may seem futile to try to change, this is not really the case. This seeming futility is nothing more than another irrational belief. Actually, you can learn to help yourself. You can help yourself by learning to identify your dysfunctional thoughts and then replacing your dysfunctional thoughts with ones that are functional.

The first step is to identify your dysfunctional thought. It may be important to note here that the terms *dysfunctional* and *irrational* are used interchangeably, as are *thought* and *belief*, so don't let these terms confuse you. They have essentially the same meaning in cognitive therapy. Our thoughts are something we usually don't examine too closely, and it may seem a difficult task in the beginning to sort out which thoughts are rational and which are irrational. In cognitive therapy, however, it is our goal to closely examine our thinking patterns. As we do, we will learn how to identify the thoughts that are the most troublesome. Research by F. Reid Creech and our own development of cognitive exercises form the basis of the exercises you'll read in this section.

Characteristics of dysfunctional thoughts

A dysfunctional thought has four features. Any time we suspect that a thought is dysfunctional, we can check it against these characteristics to determine if it is:

Automatic: The thought pops into our head so quickly that we are unaware that we have thought it.

Negative: The thought is stated in a form that includes "can't," "shouldn't," "never," etc.

Self-focused: The thought makes a statement about the person thinking it; it is an "I" statement.

Inaccurate: The thought is false in some way.

A perceptive patient coined the acronym *ANSI* to help us remember the four characteristics of the dysfunctional thought. These thoughts usually result in our feeling just that!

We might ask ourselves at this point, "So what if these thoughts are Automatic, Negative, Self-focused and Inaccurate? What harm comes from thinking them? What makes these particular thoughts dysfunctional?" The fact is, dysfunctional thoughts are harmful in three ways:

They will not withstand reality testing. This means that we can look all around for objective proof to support our thoughts and we will not find it. We only think there is proof because we have never really looked closely at these thoughts.

Further, in operating under the assumption that the thoughts are correct, we are actually misperceiving reality. This misperception of reality is what makes these thoughts dysfunctional.

They lead to needlessly unpleasant emotional consequences. Rather than a natural emotional reaction to an event, these thoughts tend to result in extreme and overwhelming emotional reactions. From now on you will be asked to rate your feelings (which are triggered by the belief), on a scale of 1 to 10, with 1 meaning that you are minimally sad, depressed, angry, or anxious (or whatever the feeling may be), and 10 meaning that you are extremely sad, depressed, angry, or anxious (or whatever the feeling may be).

They interfere with our ability to cope with or change an Activating Event and may even make it worse. If our emotional response to an activating event is overwhelming, it will interfere with our ability to deal effectively with the event and make our experience of the event much more of a struggle than it needs to be.

As we can see, when we explore the nature of these thoughts more closely, we find that they are in fact dysfunctional. They are not based in reality, they are excessively upsetting, and they disrupt our coping strategies.

Now that we know how troublesome these thoughts are, we can redirect our attention to changing these dysfunctional thought patterns. Earlier in this chapter we asked you to lay the groundwork to explore the A-B-C-D's by recalling a recent event that was upsetting. Now we are ready to look a little more closely at the nature of our thoughts. We will look at the process of detecting dysfunctional thoughts and developing functional counterthoughts in stages so that the process is clear and understandable. The process will include exercises in identifying a dysfunctional thought, recognizing distortions, testing a thought, and developing a functional counterthought.

Exercise: Dysfunctional Thought
1. Please read the instructions for A, B, C, and D and write your answers in the spaces provided.
A (Activating Event): Think of a recent event that upset you. It may have been something you did or someone else did that resulted in a strong emotional reaction. Write a description of that event.

B (Core Belief/Thought): Think about what you said to yourself ABOUT YOURSELF at the time of the event. What kinds of NEGATIVE statements did you make to yourself?

C (Emotional Consequence/Feeling): What was your emotional response to the event? List the feelings you experienced AT THE TIME of the event.

D (Action): List the actions you took at the time.

2. Summarize in just a few words the A-B-C-Ds of this situation.
A (Activating Event):
B (Core Belief/Thought):
C (Emotional Consequence/Feeling):
D (Action):

3. Rate each emotional consequence/feeling in section C on a scale from 1–10, where 1 is a minimum intensity of feeling and 10 is high intensity of feeling, and write that number next to the feeling.
Feeling: _____ Rating: _____ /10
Feeling: _____ Rating: _____ /10
Feeling: _____ Rating: _____ /10

4. Now look more closely at your core belief/thought and check it against the ANSI characteristics. Is each belief/thought:

Automatic   Yes   No
Negative   Yes   No
Self-focused   Yes   No
Inaccurate   Yes   No

If you answered *Yes* to all of the characteristics above, your thoughts are dysfunctional. The next step is to change these thoughts into ones that are more accurate.

5. If you answered *Yes* to Inaccurate, state one way in which you believe each core belief/thought is inaccurate.

6. Do your thoughts have any characteristics of the Negative Thinking Triad (negative view of self, negative interpretation of experience, negative view of the future)? If so, identify these characteristics.

7. How are the thoughts you wrote down under B dysfunctional? State two ways in which these thoughts affect you most negatively.

Distortions

Dysfunctional thoughts are characterized by various distortions in thinking that cause us to maintain our belief in our dysfunctional thoughts despite evidence to the contrary. Any of these distortion types may be used to categorize dysfunctional thoughts:

Thinking in extremes: Refers to seeing things in extremes only, with no middle ground. Most often a depressed person will choose the extreme negative end of the scale. After making a simple mistake, for example, one might view oneself as a total failure rather than looking at the whole picture, including past accomplishments.

Overstatement: Involves a pattern of drawing a general conclusion on the basis of a few isolated incidents and applying this conclusion to all situations. Using the example above, this distortion would be evident if the person saw himself or herself as a failure in everything he or she attempts to do versus not being particularly talented in one specific area.

Negative deductions: Involves focusing and inflating the negative aspects of an event while ignoring the positive elements. For example, if you had a generally good day except for one minor incident but focused on that incident until your entire day seemed horrible, this distortion would apply.

Discounting: Overlooking or rejecting anything positive, such as not allowing ourselves to feel good or to have fun, is the distortion operating here. Often, we assume that something bad will come along and ruin anything positive we feel or experience. The result is bad feelings.

Selective forecasting: We see things as negative without any facts to support this notion. This process essentially involves forecasting negativity and failure for your future without entertaining the idea that neutral or positive things could occur. You predict you will fail at a task without allowing yourself the chance to try. For example, after exiting a job interview, you immediately predict that you will not get the job. You think: "I will never get hired because I don't interview well."

Wrack and ruin: Refers to our tendency to distort situations and always think of the worst expected outcomes. You always expect disasters, and a disaster means it's the end of the world. For example, you ask a friend out for a date and get turned down, which causes you to think: "I will never be in a relationship in my life. No one will ever want to go out with me." We are often quick to give others credit for their accomplishments and to overlook their mistakes, but when it comes to ourselves, we are relentless. No error is too tiny to beat ourselves with, and no success is so grand that it cannot be discounted.

Feelings are reality: Involves the assumption that because we feel badly, things are bad, without testing this assumption. It may be that things are going fine and we are feeling bad for other reasons.

Self-judging: "Should," "ought," and "must" are words we can identify as trouble words because they are self critical. These words often take our simple wants or desires and define them as needs or necessities. Statements such as, "I should understand this immediately," "I ought to do more than I do," or "I must get this done today" suggest that things in life should, ought, or must be different than they are. Restating these thoughts in terms of "I want" or "It would be nice" is more realistic.

Self-victimization: We think that we are externally controlled and see ourselves as helpless victims of fate. For example, Mary has no plans to go out with friends this weekend. She thinks: "No one likes me or cares for me. People always abandon me when I need them most."

Self-blaming: Refers to our tendency to blame ourselves for something we were not entirely responsible for or that was not under our control. For example, we may see ourselves as responsible for someone else's problem or as the sole cause of their problems.

Which of these distortions fits your dysfunctional thought patterns? Out of the ten distortions presented, which ones do you seem to use most? Are there some that you feel do NOT fit your thinking patterns?

Now that you know all ten cognitive distortions, keep on your guard to recognize them in your thoughts. If you catch a cognitive distortion, you know you also have a dysfunctional thought. To change cognitive distortions, we have to first recognize them and be aware when we are using them.

Exercise: Distorted Thought

1. Thinking back to the exercise you just completed, jot down in the spaces provided here a few words that describe the A-B-C-Ds of the situation. Your responses should be the same as the responses you provided in Question 2 of the Dysfunctional Thought exercise.

A (Activating Event):
B (Core Belief/Thought):
C (Emotional Consequence/Feeling):
D (Action):

2. Rate each emotional consequence/feeling in section C on a scale from 1–10, where 1 is a minimum intensity of feeling and 10 is high intensity of feeling, and write that number next to the feeling.

Feeling: _____ Rating: _____ /10
Feeling: _____ Rating: _____ /10
Feeling: _____ Rating: _____ /10

3. Check your dysfunctional thoughts against the ANSI characteristics. Are these beliefs/thoughts:

Automatic   Yes   No
Negative   Yes   No
Self-focused   Yes   No
Inaccurate   Yes   No

If the answers to the above questions are *Yes,* test your thought to see if it is inaccurate.

4. On a scale from 0% to 100%, how much do you believe your thought? _____%

5. Name the distortions in the thought you tested.

The following two exercises will help you understand further the concepts involved in thought distortion behavior. These exercises require concentration and focus in order for you to benefit fully by the learning experience.

Exercise: Distortions Go-Round Game

In this exercise, we will look at the way we use distorted thoughts during routine activities. Please select a name for the character that will experience the routine daily situations listed below. After you have selected a character name, read each one of the statements and fill in the blank with a distorted thought that your character might have. Use as many different types of distorted thoughts as you can think of. If you need help, look back in the Distortions section for ideas.

Select a name for the character in this scenario: _____.

1. _____ wakes up in the morning and thinks to him/herself, "*(Distorted thought)* _____
_____
_____ "

2. _____ slowly drags him/herself to the kitchen to make something to eat, burns the breakfast, and thinks, "*(Distorted thought)* _____
_____
_____ "

3. _____ scraps the breakfast and gets ready for work, muttering, "*(Distorted thought)* _____
_____
_____ "

4. On the way to work in morning rush-hour traffic, _____ gets lost in the following thought: "*(Distorted thought)* _____
_____
_____ "

5. Finally, _____ gets to work, plops down at a desk full of paperwork, and moans, "*(Distorted thought)* _____
_____
_____ "

Check the distorted thoughts your character has against the list of types of thoughts in the Distortions section you read previously. The purpose of this exercise is to become more aware of how often we use distortions without recognizing them as such, and to learn to laugh at ourselves, which is always therapeutic.

Exercise: Cognitive Distortions Review

To check your understanding of the ten cognitive distortions we have discussed, try to identify the distortion in each of the following scenarios. The answers to this review are at the end of this chapter.

1. You have recently moved away from your home state. After you have been there a short while, you find out that your parents are going to get a divorce. You

tell yourself, "I knew if I left this would happen. How selfish can I be? This is all my fault." *Type of distortion:* _____

_____

_____

2. You come home from work feeling tired and upset, even though you had a good day. You tell yourself, "Boy, this job must really get to me. It is probably just too stressful. I don't know if I can face another day there. Maybe I should look for another job." *Type of distortion:* _____

_____

_____

3. You throw a dinner party for a group of friends. Everything seems perfect. The meal is delicious and everyone raves about your cooking. You bring out the dessert, a masterpiece chocolate rum cake! As you start serving the dessert, one of your friends reminds you that she is allergic to chocolate. Your heart sinks because you had known about her allergy to chocolate but did not even think about it when you were planning the party meal. The rest of the evening you give yourself a hard time about this incident until, by the time the guests start leaving, you can't wait until they are all gone. You go to bed feeling miserable. *Type of distortion:* _____

_____

_____

4. On the way home from work, you stop at the store to buy some groceries. When you arrive at home, you realize that, with the groceries and the materials you brought home from work, you have a lot to carry but you decide to try to manage it all in one trip. As you are walking into the house, the grocery bag rips and the contents spill. You look at the mess of broken eggs and bruised fruit as you say to yourself, "What an idiot I am. I could have made two trips, but no, I am such a lazy slob I had to try to make it on one trip. Well, I got what I deserve!" *Type of distortion:* _____

_____

_____

5. You have been dating someone for a couple of months. You realize there are some things you do not care for in this person, although there are also qualities you do like. You tell yourself, "This person is not right for me. When will I meet

my Mr./Ms. Right? There's always some little thing that is wrong and then the whole relationship falls apart. I guess I am just not meant to be in a relationship." *Type of distortion:* _____

_____

_____

6. Your spouse comes home from work, walks directly into the bedroom, and closes the door. You think to yourself, "Gee, I wonder why she/he is so angry with me. She/He's probably sorry she/he ever married me. I just know that one of these days she/he will leave me." *Type of distortion:* _____

_____

_____

7. You enjoy a wonderful evening with your spouse. The dinner, dancing, and conversation are very enjoyable. Yet, all evening you think to yourself, "This is great, but it won't last. If we don't start fighting some time tonight, I'll be surprised." *Type of distortion:* _____

_____

_____

8. You were raised by parents who were seldom home. When they were home, they treated you very harshly. Even now, as an adult, the things they do and say are very upsetting to you. The times you feel upset with them, you say to yourself, "I am an adult. I shouldn't be reacting this way to them. Why can't I just drop the past? I should be above all this now." *Type of distortion:* _____

_____

_____

9. This is your second week on the new job. You decide you are ready to take on a project. As you get further involved in the project, you realize it is more difficult than you thought. To make matters worse, you find you can't seem to apply the new information you have learned on the job to the project. You tell yourself, "I'm no good at learning new things. Why did I set myself up for failure, just like I always seem to do? Now this entire project, not to mention my job, is a total disaster." *Type of distortion:* _____

_____

_____

10. You take a class with a friend. You and your friend are progressing in the class at about the same rate. An assignment is handed back. Although you did as well on the assignment as your friend, you say, "You are doing so well and I just can't seem to understand this stuff. I keep making all these stupid mistakes. You hardly made any mistakes at all. I wish I could learn as quickly as you do." *Type of distortion:* _____

_____

_____

In each of the examples above, one cognitive distortion is most obvious, although other distortions may be present as well. Most of the time our dysfunctional thoughts will involve several distortions because we start with one thought, which leads to a chain reaction of thoughts. The more we are able to detect the distortions present in our ways of thinking, the easier it will be for us to identify our dysfunctional thoughts.

From this point forward, labeling the cognitive distortions in your dysfunctional thoughts will be an important part of testing and disputing these thoughts. Look over the list of distortions again. Which are your favorites? Most of us have certain distortions we use more frequently than the others.

Challenging negative thoughts and formulating corrective counterthoughts

Now that we know how our dysfunctional thoughts get us into trouble, and we know how to identify our dysfunctional thoughts, the next step is to replace these thoughts with ones that are functional. Before we can do that, however, we need to know how to reality-test our dysfunctional thoughts. When we test these thoughts against reality, we find the inaccurate aspects of them and can change these aspects to make the thoughts more accurate.

The first step in thought testing is to fill in the A-B-C-Ds in order to find the thought we want to test. Look at this example about learning cognitive therapy:

A (Activating Event): Learning cognitive therapy
B (Core Belief/Thought): "I'll never learn this."
C (Emotional Consequences/Feeling and Rating): Frustrated, 8/10; Overwhelmed, 9/10
D (Action): "I'll give up."

In this example, the dysfunctional thought we will test is: "I'll never learn this!" The second step in testing a dysfunctional thought is to make sure it is dysfunctional by checking it with the ANSI characteristics. How does this thought—"I'll never learn this!"—correlate to the ANSI characteristics? Is this thought:

Automatic   *Answer:* Yes, it pops into our heads without us realizing it.

Negative   *Answer:* Yes, it suggests I will NEVER be able to learn this, no matter what.

Self-focused   *Answer:* Yes, it states that "I" will never learn this, not that other people in the group will never learn it.

Inaccurate   Let us test it and see.

The third step is to evaluate our belief in this thought. On a scale from 0% to 100%, how much do you believe your thought? _____%

Now that we have identified the thought and know it is dysfunctional, we are ready to test the thought. Beneath the thought we will set up two columns, a FACTS FOR column and a FACTS AGAINST column. In the FACTS FOR column we will write all the facts that prove our dysfunctional thought is true. In the FACTS AGAINST column we will write all the facts that prove our dysfunctional thought is false. The statements we write must be facts—statements that can be proven.

Thought to be tested: "I'll never learn this!"

FACTS FOR	FACTS AGAINST
I'm having trouble concentrating.	I have learned new things in the past.
I received poor grades in school.	I'm a fast learner.

If we are able to come up with at least one fact under the FACTS AGAINST column, we have proven that our dysfunctional thought is incorrect in some way and therefore is not totally based in reality. It does not matter how many TRUE facts we have in the FACTS FOR column; we only need one FALSE fact in the FACTS AGAINST column to show our thought is incorrect.

Developing a functional counterthought

Once we have reality-tested our thought, we are ready to use what we have found to develop a functional counterthought. A counterthought is developed by using the facts from both sides of our thought-testing exercise. Because we are using both true and false FACTS, the counterthought is indeed functional. This functional counterthought is then used to dispute our dysfunctional thought whenever it comes to mind. The counterthought begins with, "Even though…" and always uses FACTS from the two columns of the thought-testing exercise.

Continuing with the ("I'll never learn this!" we just tested, here's how our counterthought might sound: "Even though I'm having trouble concentrating, I have learned new things in the past" or "Even though I received poor grades in school, I am a fast learner."

In other words, even though some aspects of our dysfunctional thoughts are true, other aspects of these thoughts are false. It is the false aspects that get us into trouble. This is not the same thing as the power of positive thinking. Positive thinking that is not realistic or reality-based is just as irrational and dysfunctional as unrealistic negative thoughts. What we are promoting is rational and functional thinking.

Characteristics of a functional counterthought

In order for a counterthought to be an effective tool in disputing our dysfunctional thoughts, it must have three key characteristics. An easy way to remember these characteristics is with the acronym "APE." A functional counterthought must be:

Accurate: The functional counterthought must be true and correct. Because the counterthought is developed directly from the facts we used to show our belief had some true aspects and some false aspects, the counterthought will be accurate. Going back to our example, then, the counterthought is making the statement, "Even though (true fact) is true, (false fact) is also true."

Parallel: The counterthought must run parallel to the original dysfunctional thought. It is important that the counterthought is not based on positive thinking. Positive thinking only leads to further irrationality such as invalidating our feelings and being harsh and critical with ourselves. Positive thinking jumps to the positive side of dysfunctional thinking, whereas many of our dysfunctional thoughts fall on the negative side of dysfunctional thinking. Functional thinking, on the other hand, is somewhere in the middle of these two extremes. In the sense that our functional counterthought contains both the true and the false facts regarding our dysfunctional thought, it runs parallel to these thoughts.

Emotionally believable: The counterthought must be believable to us on an emotional level or we will not be able to use it effectively to dispute our dysfunctional thoughts. If it is believable, the severity of the feeling we initially identified will decrease on the rating scale when we rate it a second time. If the severity of the feeling does not come down, it may mean that the counterthought is not believable, in which case we will need to discard it and formulate a new one. Or it is likely that there are deeper dysfunctional beliefs that must be uncovered. To do this, it is sometimes helpful to take the belief that we tested and use it as the event, then determine what dysfunctional thoughts we have regarding this new event and test them.

The final step in this process is to use the counterthoughts we have developed to actively dispute our dysfunctional thoughts. It is important to work these thoughts out on paper because we can then refer back to our notes when we are feeling emotionally upset. We can even put our functional counterthoughts on note cards to carry with us. With readily available resources, we can easily disarm our dysfunctional thoughts at the time they occur.

Exercise: Step-By-Step Re-thinking

Here then is the complete process of identifying our dysfunctional thoughts, analyzing their distortions, testing them and developing functional counterthoughts (as adapted from Beck).

1. Identify the A-B-C-Ds of a situation.
A (Activating Event):
B (Core Belief/Thought):
C (Emotional Consequences/Feeling):
D (Action):

2. Rate each emotional consequence/feeling on a scale from 1–10.

Feeling: _____ Rating: _____ /10
Feeling: _____ Rating: _____ /10
Feeling: _____ Rating: _____ /10

3. Check your dysfunctional thought for ANSI characteristics. Is the thought:
Automatic   Yes   No
Negative   Yes   No
Self-focused   Yes   No
Inaccurate   Yes   No
If you answered *Yes* to all four ANSI characteristics, we can test the thought to see if it is Inaccurate.

4. On a scale from 0% to 100%, how much do you believe your thought? _____%

5. Test your thought.
        Thought to be tested: _____

<u>FACTS FOR</u>   <u>FACTS AGAINST</u>

6. Use the FACTS FOR and FACTS AGAINST your thought to develop functional counterthoughts.

"Even though _____"
"Even though _____"

7. Check your counterthought for APE characteristics:
Is the thought *Accurate*?
Is the thought *Parallel*?
Is the thought *Emotionally Believable* to you?

8. On a scale of 1 to 10, rate again the feelings you identified earlier:

Feeling: _____ Rating: _____ /10
Feeling: _____ Rating: _____ /10
Feeling: _____ Rating: _____ /10

9. On a scale from 0% to 100%, how much do you believe the thought you tested? _____%

10. Use your counterthoughts to dispute your dysfunctional thoughts! Take a moment to read the counterthought through two or three times. Does this more functional response cause you to feel less sad, depressed, angry, or frustrated? Remember, the goal of the counterthought is to reduce unpleasant feelings.

Summary: Step-By-Step Re-thinking

Aside from specific knowledge, we often need a sense of understanding about ourselves in order to use the knowledge we have acquired. To help us with this understanding, we can focus on three basic insights:
- Dysfunctional thoughts are related to understandable causes in our past. That is, these thoughts came from somewhere, and if we were to look hard enough we could probably find their source.
- Although these thoughts are related to the past, we have emotional trouble now because we keep using them over and over in the present.

- Because we have a role in our emotional difficulties through our dysfunctional ways of thinking, it is up to us to work at changing these patterns of thinking so that we can help ourselves to feel better.

Developing a step-by-step process simplifies and clarifies the learning process. This list may help you to remember the steps:

- Identify the A-B-C-Ds and pull out the dysfunctional thought you wish to test.
- Test your thought in order to gain a more objective and accurate perspective on your thought.
- Name the distortion in the thought you tested.
- Using the FACTS FOR and FACTS AGAINST your thought, you are in a position to challenge your dysfunctional thoughts and attitudes and develop a functional counterthought.

We have control over our dysfunctional thoughts. Recognizing our dysfunctional thoughts and attitudes and then challenging them with a believable functional counterthought may help us resolve our depressed feelings.

How do you feel now?

Now that you have learned how to correct your negative distorted thinking with accurate and realistic counterthoughts, it is important to check your mood and rate it. This is done by filling out the Depression Questionnaire and comparing it to the previous one. Extra copies of the questionnaire are located in the Appendix at the back of this book.

When you are depressed, you are a victim of erroneous thinking. The thinking process breaks the depression cycle by changing your negative thought and attitude. It may take many counterthoughts over a period of a few weeks before you feel full improvement. Thinking skills, like other newly acquired skills, take time to be mastered. They are strengthened through repetition and regular practice. Initially, it may feel awkward and slow to find and challenge your thoughts. In time and with practice, it will become automatic and the results then are felt instantly. By following the steps of the re-thinking process, old negative beliefs are challenged and changed, and the depression lifts, getting you on the way to feeling terrific.

Re-thinking Formula for Healthy Thinking
Catch it! Monitor your negative thoughts
Challenge it! Stop negative thoughts
Change it! Substitute the negative thoughts with healthy counterthoughts

Answers To Exercise: Thought versus Feeling
1. Thought
2. Feeling
3. Feeling
4. Thought
5. Thought
6. Feeling
7. Thought
8. Thought
9. Feeling
10. Feeling
11. Feeling
12. Thought
13. Thought
14. Feeling

Answers to Exercise: Cognitive Distortions Review
1. Self-blaming
2. Feelings are reality
3. Negative deductions
4. Overstatement
5. Thinking in extremes
6. Selective forecasting
7. Discounting
8. Self-judging
9. Overstatement
10. Wrack and ruin

CHAPTER 6
Social Strategies

Relationships and mood

The social environment refers to all individuals who can affect us and are affected by us. It includes family, friends, co-workers, and people who come into contact with us in daily life. We connect with the people in our social environment through relationships of varying kinds and intensities.

A relationship is a connection that forms between two people. This connection usually serves a purpose and meets a need for the people in the relationship. The purpose varies according to the type of relationship. In a mother-child relationship, the mother's purpose is nurturing and protecting the child. In a romantic relationship, the purpose is meeting the emotional needs of the two people in the relationship.

A flow and ebb of emotions, energy, and thoughts occurs in a relationship. Over time this process of exchanging and sharing thoughts and feelings leads to the development of a bond between the people involved in the relationship. This bonding process is called *attachment,* and it is an integral part of any healthy relationship. Research studies indicate that people are innately driven to form attachment bonds essential for survival and happiness (Bowlby 1969). Studies have also shown that failure to develop healthy attachment bonds in childhood or disruption of attachment bonds that are formed can lead to depression later in life.

When a relationship is disrupted or terminated—for example, when a person moves away or dies—the interruption in continuity is called *separation* or *loss.* Because every relationship starts with attachment and at some point undergoes separation or loss, loss is a natural occurrence in the course of many relationships. The processes of attachment and loss, their manifestations, and their consequences constitute the working dynamics of relationships.

Relationships impact our mood primarily through these processes of attachment and loss. A child cries, for example, when separated from its mother.

132

We feel happy when we are in the presence of our loved ones. An understanding of these processes is important to appreciate the impact of relationships on our moods.

Attachment is the process through which a link or bond is formed between two people in a relationship. This bond fulfills a purpose such as nurturing, support, safety, or companionship for the individuals in the relationship. Once this bond forms, people open up to each other, start communicating, and start affecting each other's lives in some way. Through this attachment bond, people experience intense emotions such as closeness, warmth, and caring for the other person. A healthy attachment is a necessary ingredient of any enduring relationship, whether it is between friends, child and parent, or spouses. The intensity of the attachment and accompanying feelings that come with it is dependent on the significance of the relationship. The closer the relationship, the stronger the attachment and feelings. An attachment is more meaningful to a parent, child, or spouse than to a boss, friend, or neighbor. The more intimate the relationship is between the two persons, the more "attaching" is apt to take place. For instance, in a relationship between husband and wife, there is mutual nurturing, support, and interdependency in more areas than, say, with a friend.

Attachments bring out the inner core of the psychological self to interact with others and make a meaningful connection. Attachments make the person aware of who he or she is and how he or she is viewed by others. In that sense, through the process of attachment, relationships allow us to see parts of ourselves as we are seen and experienced by others. An attachment to a friend makes us feel good as it conveys the message that another person is interested in us and that we may have something to offer in that relationship. An attachment also makes us feel good because through it we can receive from others what they have to offer us. An attachment bond allows us to mirror ourselves and find acceptance of that self. As the relationship grows, we use this attachment bond to improve ourselves and become more integrated. Anyone who is not capable of forming and enjoying relationships has great difficulty in feeling terrific.

Having the skills to form healthy attachments is important to our sense of feeling good. A person will feel good if he is able to get close to others and feel nurtured, cared for, and supported. Healthy relationships allow the self to feel accepted, validated, have a sense of belonging, and develop good self-esteem.

An Oriental saying states that, when a person reaches the senior years of his life and looks at what he has accomplished, he realizes that what counts is not the wealth he has accumulated or the knowledge he has acquired; what matters most are the lives he has touched along the way. Lives are touched through the attachments we form and maintain. These bonds are vital for our day-to-day functioning in society, and they are conducive to feeling terrific.

The other experience that occurs in the context of relationships that affects our mood state is separation or loss. Loss in one form or another is apt to occur in most relationships. Learning how to accept and adjust to the loss of a close person or significant relationship is a difficult and painful experience to endure or accept. Loss involves a disruption, with feelings of abandonment, anger, or rejection. The loss of a relationship may be partial or complete. A complete loss occurs when the whole relationship is terminated—for instance, by death, physical separation, or when one person ends the relationship. Partial loss occurs more frequently in relationships. It is experienced in the compromises that a person continuously makes in a relationship. This does not refer to the dissolution of a relationship but to the personal losses one incurs within the relationship. Examples are losing one's private space or losing the ability to make decisions alone when, for example, we get married. Through partial losses in such a relationship, one learns how to share and compromise, two elements that are ingredients of any healthy relationship.

The loss of a significant person can lead to the development of depression. Researchers in the field of psychology have found that children who lose their parents are at high risk for the development of depression in their adult life. The loss of a close friend, parent, or family member leads to grief. If the grief is not resolved, the person's mood becomes adversely affected. The ability to resolve and accept the loss is therefore important to prevent the development of a longstanding depression.

Understanding the process and emotions of loss is vital to feeling good. Loss is one experience that continuously occurs in our lives. At times it may be too subtle for us to notice. It seems to take away something from us that the attachment process gave us. If we don't reconcile with that loss and integrate it within us, it lingers on, pulling us down and preventing us from feeling terrific. Developing skills to deal with losses strengthens the sense of self and leads to feeling terrific.

Through learning about attachment and loss, we develop the ability to keep ourselves apprised of the role we are playing in significant relationships and how that role is serving our needs and the needs of the other person. The journey to feeling terrific entails understanding the processes of attachment and loss and developing relationship skills.

We live our lives within and through relationships. They can make us feel very good or very bad. What determines the outcome of a relationship is not only the other person but us, as well. How did we enter that relationship? How did we engage, and how did we disengage? Relationships have a big influence on our sense of self and our self-esteem. The persons with whom we engage in a relationship have great influence over our moods. Therefore, it is imperative to understand relationships and acquire the skills to deal with the conflicts that arise in them.

Our experiences in life occur in the context of relationships. Our ability to be emotionally present in those relationships and participate in them is crucial to feeling good. Relationships serve several functions, ranging from protection, role modeling, and nurturing by parents during childhood to support with friends, emotional fulfillment with spouses, and so on. Through relationships we build a support system, and we become part of a social network. Through relationships we are able to express who we are, and we feel appreciated and valued.

Relationships, especially close relationships, act as a mirror and reflect our inner needs, wishes, likes, and dislikes. We evaluate ourselves in contrast to our opinions of those we look up to. A low self-esteem in that context means that a person's opinion of himself is not as esteemed in comparison to his opinion of significant others in his life.

Harry Stack Sullivan's work (1953) highlighted the significance of relationships in our lives and the importance of relationships for our psychological well-being. His writings explain "how from birth onward, a very capable animal becomes a person, brought about, step by step, from very, very early in life, through the influence of other people, and solely for the purpose of living with other people in some sort of social organization." Dr. Sullivan goes on to state that "no matter what sort of social organization there is, everyone who is born into it will, in certain ways, be adapted or adjusted to living in it."

Dr. Carl Rogers was a psychologist who emphasized the role of relationships, self-concept, and self-esteem for the pursuit of well-being. Dr. Rogers stated that all people have a need for positive regard from significant others in their life. That need is thought to be pervasive and persistent. Positive regard means acceptance, validation, and respect by others. If a person has a positive regard experience from significant others in his life, then he is likely to develop a positive self-esteem and feel good. A low opinion and poor regard by others leads to a low self-esteem state (Corsini et al. 1984) and contributes to the development of depression.

If the relationships formed in early life with our parents and siblings were healthy, then we develop a clear sense of self and a good self-esteem, which contribute to a healthy and stable mood state. The ability to form and maintain newer relationships later on supports ongoing growth of that positive sense of self. Relationships therefore play a very important role in supporting and maintaining our sense of self, identity, and self-esteem. Conflicts in relationships may lead to disruption in our sense of self and to a lowering of our self-esteem. That in turn leads to a disruption in our sense of well-being. To feel terrific in this instance, we have to tackle the relationship issues first. If a person starts having difficulties in relationships and doesn't have the skills or abilities to deal with those difficulties, then depression may develop.

A form of therapy called interpersonal psychotherapy (IPT) was developed by a group of psychiatrists and therapists at Columbia University in New York. Interpersonal psychotherapy is used primarily for the treatment of depression. IPT has been proven in several scientific studies to be an effective treatment for depression and is one of the most studied and researched forms of therapy for the treatment of depression. It is directed at dealing with the relational problems between people that contribute to the development of depression. IPT is helpful in defining the relational problems of the depressed person and then providing that person with the appropriate skills to resolve these conflicts. The vehicle to building a healthy relationship is acquired through example and practice, that is, through the relationship the depressed person develops with the therapist. Skills are acquired in an experiential and participatory way for the short term. The counseling sessions of IPT are time limited. The entire counseling period lasts no more than twelve sessions.

The IPT therapist views depression as a consequence of and occurring in the context of one or several relationship conflicts. The techniques of IPT resolve the depression by working with the relationship problems and correcting them. As the relationship issues clear up, the depression lifts.

Let us focus on describing the types of conflicts that occur in relationships and the general way of solving these conflicts. From the IPT perspective, knowledge of the conflicts and the approach to treatment are important, for if you don't know where you are going, any road will get you there.

The first step in IPT is identifying the area in which the problems exist. The IPT theory states that people with depression have difficulty in the following relationship areas:
• Relationship conflicts
• Grief
• Role transition
• Social isolation

A person with depression can have a problem in one of the above-noted areas or in several areas at the same time, which is helpful in identifying the relational problems and determining the skills needed to correct them. The successful resolution of a relationship conflict is accompanied by an improvement in self-esteem, by yielding acceptance, and generating positive regard. An improvement in self-esteem is accompanied by feeling better and moving toward remission of the symptoms of depression.

Relationship conflicts

Every relationship goes through conflicts, disputes, and hardship. Communication is never perfect between two people, nor are expectations always met in relationships. People do well when they have established lines of communication with each other and have methods for resolving their conflicts. Those who do not have a way to resolve conflicts may get stuck or depressed. Relationship disputes have been found to be a common cause of depression. The presence or absence of methods of conflict resolution is what differentiates those that get depressed from those who don't. An important component in healthy relationships is the ability to resolve conflicts as they arise.

Relationships are important for us emotionally and for our social survival. Our cultural infrastructure and day-to-day lives are dependent on the availability of healthy relationships. For instance, we work with people with whom we have to be able to communicate and relate. We live in neighborhoods among people we have to relate to in a healthy way. We develop relationships with our spouses, parents, and children. Relationships not only serve as a format for our daily lives but also sustain us and nurture us. It is through relationships that our individual needs are met and fulfilled; we love and are loved back. In relationships we share, we give, we receive, and we gain acceptance.

There are four types of relationships that we engage in. These include love relationships, friendships, work relationships, and social relationships. In depression, the major disturbance occurs in the closest of relationships, those people who are in our inner circle and with whom we have the closest attachment bonds. This group includes immediate family, close friends, and people we are in frequent contact with at work or in the community. When there is a disturbance in one of these relationships, there can be a corresponding change in a person's mood. The reverse is also true—i.e., when a person gets depressed, the depression may impact his or her closest relationships. It is thus important to be aware of the conflicts that can occur in these relationships and have the skills to resolve them.

Conflicts in relationships are caused by any of the following factors: poor communication, emotional dependency, unrealistic expectations, unmet needs in relationships, lack of intimacy, irreconcilable differences, and hostility and resentments.

Poor communication

Poor communication is a frequent cause of conflicts and disputes. People often assume that what they say is automatically understood. However, the meaning of a certain communication may be very clear to the sender but not to the receiver. We all attach a hidden meaning to the messages we send and expect others to understand that meaning. When they don't, problems arise. Failure in communicating leads to misunderstanding, which leads to frustration and detachment from the relationship and eventually further miscommunication. The relationship then becomes a battleground, generating anger and resentment.

There are five faulty communication styles that depressed people use. These faulty styles contribute to the misunderstandings and frustrations in relationships.

Indirect and vague nonverbal communication: When people are depressed, they resort to nonverbal communication, expecting the other person to understand their intentions, needs, and desires. The cause is usually fear of verbal expression or discomfort with the expression of feelings and thoughts. Some people don't have the skills to express their feelings. An example is a husband who may get angry and start throwing things to express his frustration. Another example is someone who withdraws and pouts if upset or a person who makes suicidal threats in the middle of an argument instead of expressing their feelings honestly. Thoughts and feelings get acted out rather than expressed verbally. This is an unhealthy way of relating. Actions don't speak louder than words in this instance. Healthy relationships are based on the ability of the two people communicating to express verbally and honestly their thoughts, wishes, and feelings in an appropriate way. Messages communicated should be clear and overt. Hidden messages and covert agendas should be avoided. In a healthy communication, we should not only verbally express our true thoughts but check with the other person that they understood what was said and ask their opinion about it. A vague and indirect communication style almost always leads to problematic relationships that are short-lived and conflict-ridden.

Making the incorrect assumption that we have clearly expressed ourselves: When a person is depressed, he may express part of his message and expect that the other person sees the total picture. Thinking of something and expressing it clearly are two different things. The speaker assumes that the listener can mind-read and understand the whole message. When the listener does not understand what is being conveyed, the speaker gets frustrated and angry. Healthy communication is about being able to convey the whole message clearly and accurately. That message could be a wish, a desire, an opinion, or just an observation. People can't read minds. They can only interpret what they have been told. Otherwise they make assumptions, and most assumptions are inaccurate and lead to conflicts in the relationship.

Making incorrect assumptions that the person has understood us: Faulty communication occurs when the depressed person misses the message of the speaker and assumes incorrectly that he understood what was said. If the full meaning of the speaker's message is missed or misinterpreted, then the person will make incorrect conclusions and respond in a defensive or angry fashion. Healthy communication involves checking out the clarity of the message that was received.

Indirect or ambiguous communication: When we are depressed, we may have difficulty discussing our feelings and thoughts directly. We may talk around the point, use indirect inference, go into excessive detail and monologue and lose our listener. We may speak in too low a voice, mumble through the message, present vague messages, and/or assume that the listener understands what is being conveyed. This leads to miscommunication and/or a breakdown in communication.

Silence and withdrawal: Shutting down and withdrawing are also common in depression due to the negative feelings and thoughts associated with depression. We may withdraw and disconnect, failing to communicate anything except that we want to be left alone.

Poor communication: A solution

Resolving faulty communication is important to feeling good. The first step is to identify the type of faulty communication style and the underlying assumptions the person is making. Faulty communication leads to making wrong assumptions about the other person's wishes, thoughts, feelings, or needs, and sending the wrong messages to the listener. Learning how to express and listen correctly is important. It is equally important to properly decode what is being said in the communication. Listening is an art, and it is important to listen attentively and without interruption, and to understand what is being said. It is important to learn how to express our feelings, thoughts, and wishes directly, clearly, and effectively.

In therapy we examine our communication style and identify the faulty style we are using. We learn how to listen, decode, and respond by learning new communication skills. The goal is to achieve direct, clear, and honest verbal communication that reflects the true thoughts and feelings of the person.

Excessive emotional dependency

Some form of emotional dependency occurs in every close relationship. It becomes problematic, however, when it is unequal, and one person is overly dependent on the other. We may be overly demanding and possessive. We may be very fearful of emotional dependency and be distant and avoidant for fear of getting dependent. This unhealthy dependency eventually leads to a breakdown in the relationship. Healthy dependency is when two people can lean on each other equally, with an equal share of give and take.

Excessive emotional dependency: A solution

The therapy involves identifying the emotional needs of the dependent person and learning how to be self-sufficient in meeting those needs so that they don't stifle the other person.

Hidden and unrealistic expectations

We all have expectations of each other in relationships. Sometimes we express them; at other times we think others should be aware of them so we don't express them at all. When expectations are not fulfilled, disappointment follows. Disappointment in turn leads to conflict in the relationship and lowering of the person's self-esteem. Expectations may be unrealistic, where one person expects from the other what's beyond the person's ability or the scope of the relationship. An example is the overly dependent person who expects others to take care of him all the time and meet all his needs. That is unrealistic and will lead to conflicts and dissolution of the relationship.

Having our expectations met in relationships contributes to our well-being and feeling good. Many people, however, don't know what their expectations are of the people they interact with. This leads to confusion in the relationship and dissolution of the relationship. When expectations are repeatedly unmet in relationships, we get disappointed, frustrated, and depressed. Unmet expectations lead to a lowering of self-esteem. We feel discounted and misunderstood. The way to remedy that situation is to determine whether these expectations are realistic and whether they have been expressed or are hidden.

Hidden and unrealistic expectations: A solution

The therapist identifies the unrealistic or hidden expectations. The therapy focuses on helping us to identify our expectations and learn how to express them in a realistic way. The therapist also teaches us how to meet these expectations within and outside the relationship. When expectations are defined, expressed, and met, our self-esteem improves and our mood gets better.

Unmet needs in relationships

Disputes occur in relationships when a person's emotional, intellectual, and physical needs are not met. If we are too self-absorbed, we may be unaware of the other person's needs or wishes and be unable to meet them. Most people in relationships expect the other person to sense their needs and how and when to meet them.

A person who is depressed and with low self-esteem has difficulty in identifying needs. We develop the tendency to suppress these needs or deny them. This in turn worsens the depression and lowers self-esteem. It also makes it difficult for others to identify or meet our needs.

Unmet needs in relationships: A solution

In therapy, we learn to identify and express needs openly and comfortably. We ask ourselves, "What do I want from my spouse/partner in our relationship?" and "What does my spouse/partner want from me?" We learn to express our needs and wishes, as well as to ask about the other person's needs. Learning to properly define and express needs can lead to an improvement in self-esteem.

Lack of intimacy

Intimacy is important for forming bonds with others. Bonds provide nurturing and support. In close and significant relationships, a certain amount of intimacy and closeness is essential. Researchers in the United Kingdom have found that women who have intimate and confiding relationships with men had a low chance of getting depressed when under stress (Brown et al. 1977). Researchers have also found that medically ill men and women who didn't have an intimate and confiding relationship with their physician were more likely to get depressed and have psychological problems (Miller and Ingham 1976).

When we are depressed, we may be withdrawn and may be frightened of intimacy or attachment. This in turn leads to isolation and lowering of self-esteem, which leads to conflicts in the relationship. The importance of intimacy is that it provides nurturing and validation of one's sense of self-worth.

Lack of intimacy: A solution

The therapist helps the depressed person explore the reasons that make it difficult to develop closeness and intimacy. This may include past and traumatic experiences, fear of rejection, or the lack of skills. The therapist works to increase skills that involve learning how to get close to others, thereby removing the fear. Intimacy gives us support, nurturing, and a sense of belonging. This in turn lifts the depression as it elevates self-esteem.

Irreconcilable differences

If conflicts persist in close relationships (especially marital), they lead to irreconcilable differences. There are times in a relationship when differences can't be overcome because of vast differences of opinion, values, or varying interests. Whatever the cause, the presence of irreconcilable differences needs to be acknowledged and dealt with. For instance, trying to maintain a marriage when major disagreements and irreversible changes have taken place in the relationship is futile and leads to further damage in the relationship. There are times when a relationship can't be corrected, and there are times when certain disputes can't be resolved. At that point the relationship needs to be ended.

Differences may become irreconcilable if one of the above-mentioned factors such as an ongoing communication problem or unmet expectations is not resolved or dealt with for a long time. If these conflicts become chronic, then each person in the relationship becomes fixed in their positions and resentful of each other. What used to be a close relationship turns into a sour, ugly one. Trying to maintain a relationship that has irreconcilable differences is destructive, as people can hurt each other emotionally, intellectually, and spiritually. That damage leads to a loss of respect for the other person and damage to one's self-esteem.

Irreconcilable differences: A solution

Conflicts need to be acknowledged and dealt with as they arise. They can't be pushed aside or put on the back burner. The longer they are left unresolved, the more they are apt to become a permanent part of the relationship and lead to dissolution of the relationship. Recognizing that a relationship has run its course and is beyond repair is important. The therapist helps the person come to terms with the fact that the relationship is over and that it's time to move on. Once that is acknowledged and action is taken, the depression lifts.

Hostility and resentments

Hostility arises when communication breaks down, when needs are not met, and when people misunderstand each other's actions and intentions. Ongoing and unresolved anger that is mismanaged and misdirected almost always leads to hostility in a relationship. When hostility sets in, it indicates a breakdown in the bond that may have existed. Persistent anger within a close relationship is associated with depression.

Hostility and resentments: A solution

We must examine the situations where the hostile feelings arise. We may be responding to issues from the past that may have nothing to do with the current relationship. We must examine our responses of anger and loss of control. Dealing with the original source of anger becomes the focus of resolution. Once hostility is defined and understood, it can be resolved. We must learn controlled ways of expressing anger and frustrations.

Grief

Grief can be due to the loss of someone close or something meaningful to the person. It may be a person, pet, job, possession, or something else meaningful.

The normal mourning process leads to sadness and bereavement, not depression. Grief is a time-limited process and doesn't require therapy or treatment. The normal stages of grief that were described by Dr. Elisabeth Kubler-Ross are denial, anger, bargaining, depression, and acceptance.

If for any reason the person fails to go through the normal stages of grief after the loss of someone close, then the grief becomes chronic and unresolved and will lead to depression. People with unresolved grief can either have a delayed grief reaction or a distorted grief reaction. A delayed grief reaction is one that occurs many months or years after the loss. It is usually triggered by an unrelated or less significant event a long time after the loss took place. An example is someone who loses a parent from cancer and doesn't experience the grief after the loss. A few years may go by, and one day a friend at work may be diagnosed with cancer. Shortly after hearing the news, depressive feelings begin, and the signs of the grieving process emerge.

A distorted grief reaction is one where the person doesn't react with sadness but expresses his grief through other symptoms or behaviors. These symptoms may occur any time after the loss. For instance, after the loss the person starts having stomach problems, headaches, or general aches and pains for which no medical reason is found. Alternatively, a person starts "acting out" the grief through new behaviors he hadn't had before, like going on spending sprees, bouts of rage and anger, or shoplifting. If a distorted or delayed grief reaction sets in, depression follows, and intervention is required to resolve it.

Grief: A solution

The resolution of the depression is accomplished by "working through" the grief process, letting go, and establishing supports and relationships to help overcome the loss. As we express our thoughts and feelings about the loss, we are able to overcome the sadness and grief. We then are able to reestablish a supportive social network.

Role transitions

Role transitions can lead to depression when a person is forced to change roles but is not yet ready for the new role, or when a person experiences great difficulty with the transition from one role to another. Examples include retirement, divorce, becoming a parent, or any change imposed on a person through work, moving, change in economic status, illness, recovery, growing up or growing older, and so on. Some of these transitions are part of the life cycle, such as those we experience growing up, or when a woman becomes a mother; other transitions are traumatic, for example, in the case of illness or divorce.

The roles that are assigned to us in life or those that we carve out for ourselves are important in defining who we are and how we relate to others. If change is forced upon us too quickly, we may have difficulty adjusting to the new role. Difficulty in adapting to the new role is then perceived as failure by the person making the change, and that leads to depression. A person may either have difficulty with the new role or be unhappy with it. Either way, that leads to depression.

Some of the common role transitions are those associated with age. Adolescence, adulthood, childbirth, menopause, and retirement are part of the normal life cycle. If transition from one stage to another is hampered in the normal developmental process, then the person gets stuck and has difficulty coping. The difficulty is manifested by a change in mood or by depression. For instance, an 18-year-old adolescent who has difficulty with separating and individuating from his parents will be more clingy, dependent, withdrawn, and prone to depression. Treatment of his depression is through dealing with the individuation and separation process so he can move on.

Roles are important for us because they define for others and for us our social status, our career, our role within the family, and our identity. Our roles are not stagnant entities; they change constantly, and we need to adapt to the change. We don't stay kids forever. We move from being teenagers to responsible adults, to becoming parents, to the next stage of adult life. Our career roles change as well, from employee to employer, from active employment to retirement. All of these changes require adjustment; every new role imposes on us its new demands and takes away from us a previous level of familiarity and comfort. The change in role entails loss of the previous role. If we aren't prepared to accept the loss, then difficulty arises and depression sets in.

Role transitions always present a threat to our self-esteem by taking away the secure and familiar position we had and putting us in a new and untried situation. If there are difficulties in accepting and coping with the new role, then our self-esteem is injured, and depression follows. To make the changes, we usually need skills and guidance. If these are lacking, then we feel inadequate and unable to make the necessary changes. We are forced into the new role, where we become overwhelmed and unable to perform. We then withdraw and become depressed.

Role transitions: A solution

We relieve depression caused by a difficulty in coping with role transition in four steps. First, we identify the old role and work on letting it go. Second, we express the feelings associated with the loss of the old role and deal with anxieties of the new anticipated role. These feelings are usually fear, anxiety, anger, or guilt.

Thirdly, we acquire new skills that are needed for the new role. Fourthly, we develop new friendships and a new system of support. Once we go through these four stages, we are able to make the transition and feel terrific.

Social isolation

This refers to people who have difficulty in establishing and maintaining relationships, so they isolate and withdraw. The lack of close and nurturing relationships leads to depression. People usually become isolated due to the lack of social skills, anger at others, or other predominant negative feelings that lead to distancing and avoidance. People who socially isolate have a dysregulated mood and are depressed.

Social isolation: A solution

We must focus on past experiences and examine why we failed. One of the most significant relationships in our lives is the one we have with our parents, which has a great impact on one's sense of self and self-esteem. If the relationship was positive and rewarding, we move on to form healthy and lasting relationships with others. If the relationship was punitive, non-nurturing, or dysfunctional in any way, we learn to avoid people and see relationships as a source of trouble and pain. This leads to social isolation. In therapy, we explore the past relationships we had with our parents and try to "undo" the damage. We are taught new skills that become the foundation for new and lasting relationships. Negative feelings and fear are replaced with confidence. New communication skills are learned. The relationship with the therapist can become the learning vehicle and role model for healthy communication. It is through the relationship with the therapist that the skills are learned and practiced. In undoing the unhealthy fear, anger, and avoidance, new doors open, allowing us to get close to others, develop improved self-esteem, and move toward recovery from depression.

Relationships are important for our sense of well-being. Conflicts are common in all relationships. The closer the relationship, the higher the chances for conflicts. Having the skills to deal with these conflicts is essential to maintain a sense of connectedness and to feel terrific. MRT gives the person the skills and abilities to deal with conflicts in relationships. We must explore and define the problem, determine expectations of our relationships, and then explore the alternative ways of problem solving by learning new skills. In time we learn how to do this process on our own, and most if not all relational conflicts become easier to deal with.

General guidelines for
Interpersonal Psychotherapy (IPT)

Interpersonal psychotherapy (IPT) is a short-term focused approach to the treatment of depression that was pioneered by Drs. Klerman and Weissman. The therapy addresses difficulties in how depression affects key relationships in one's life and how these relationships affect and are affected by depression. Interpersonal therapy is done with a therapist who will help you look at the four areas that are usually involved in depression and find solutions on how to deal with relationship problems. The goal of IPT is the reduction of symptoms of depression and improvement in social and interpersonal functioning. The aims of the therapy are to help you to define and understand the significant relationships in your life, and to identify the problem as it relates to the depression. To do that, the following questions will be addressed:

- Who are the significant people in your life—your inner circle—and how do they affect you emotionally?
- What expectations do you and these people have for each other? Are they met and fulfilled?
- What image do you portray to others? How is that self-image related to your current problems and difficulties?
- How are the current conflicts you are having in relationships related to your significant relationships in childhood and adolescence?
- How is the relationship contributing to your overall feeling? Are you feeling good or feeling bad? Is it satisfying?
- What changes do you want in the relationships?
- What are the problems in the relationship relating to your depression?
- How can the problem be changed?

The therapist will then help you to reappraise your relationships and restructure them with the new knowledge acquired from the answers to these and other similar questions.

In MRT we use the IPT approach plus additional techniques that we have found helpful. The steps that you will work on with the therapist include:

- Completing the Relationship Inventory to find the areas of conflict
- Identifying and ranking the problem areas in interpersonal relationships
- Relating the depression to interpersonal conflict and context
- Exploring the relational problems in detail, as mentioned above
- Examining the expectations and perceptions of the relationships that you have and how you would like to resolve the problem
- Examining, reappraising, and restructuring the relationships and helping you with strategies in how to restructure and reappraise the relationship

• Implementing the change into the relationship.

Exercise: Relationship Inventory

Answer each of the questions to determine the areas of conflict in your life.

1. What was happening in your life (work, school, home life) when you started feeling depressed? Any conflicts or change?

2. Are there any events linked to the onset or maintenance of your depressed mood?

3. Any difficulties or changes with relationships with friends or social life?

4. Have you had less contact with people lately or have you been more socially isolated?

5. Do you feel lonely?

6. What do you like and not like in the key relationship in your life (parents, spouse, child, siblings, close friends)?

7. Any unmet expectations in your key relationships?

8. Have you recently lost someone close?

9. Who are the key people in your life?

10. Anything stressful in your life?

11. Would you like to have more friends and more supportive people in your life?

12. Any changes in your role at work, home, or socially?

13. Do you spend more time alone than you would like?

14. Is it hard to make friends?

15. Are you worried you may lose someone soon from serious illness?

16. If you lost someone recently, how do you feel now?

17. What are your perceptions of the cause of your problem in your relationships in your life at the present time?

Identify the key areas

After obtaining the answers from the Relationship Inventory, the next step is to see which are the key areas that you have indicated that have been a problem. Usually there are one or two key areas and these key areas can be derived from the questions on the inventory as the inventory covers all the four areas. After identifying these area(s), the next step is finding the answers to these questions:

- Who are the key people with whom you are having difficulty?
- What is the relational problem?
- What would you like to change in the relationship to resolve the problem?
- How would you approach solving the problem?

IPT is directed to specifically identify the problems and conflicts in the key relationships and correct them so that they are healthier and will lead not only to more satisfying relationships but to the resolution of depression. Interpersonal psychotherapy will not be discussed here in detail but we will go over the basic principles in the four areas.

If the problem is grief:
- Reconstruct the relationship.
- Describe sequences and consequences of events prior to, during, and after the loss.
- Review positive and negative feelings associated with the loss. Express your emotions.
- What are the feelings about the change? How is it changing you or your role?
- Explore new opportunities.
- Learn skills to develop new relationships, social support, and healthy attachments.

If the problem is relationship conflict:
- Identify the conflict.
- How does the conflict relate to the depression?
- What stage is the conflict?
  - —Impasse: The relationship has stalled.
  - —Renegotiation: Persons are aware of differences and are working on them.
  - —Dissolution: The relationship is irreconcilable.
- Understand the roles and expectations as they relate to the conflict.
  - —What are the issues being disputed?
  - —What are the differences in expectations?
  - —What are the options?
  - —What resources are available to bring about change in the relationship?
- Develop strategies to deal with conflict.

If the problem is social isolation:
- How is the depression related to your social isolation?
- What were past significant relationships in your life and the negative and positive effects?
- What patterns emerge from how these relationships end?
- Develop skills to start new relationships that are fulfilling and supportive.

If the problem is role transition:
- What was the role that was lost or changed?
- What did you like or not like about it?
- How does it feel to give up that role?
- How do you feel about the new role?
- What new skills do you need to develop for the new role?
- How can you establish new social supports in the new role?

The following exercise is one you can do to identify barriers to communication and conflict resolution.

Exercise: Communication and Conflict

Every relationship goes through conflicts, disputes, and hardship. Resolving disputes often depends upon communication skills and the ability to recognize blocks or barriers to healthy conflict resolution. Think of an occasion where you've had a conflict or dispute with someone you have more than just a casual relationship with (such as a loved one, friend, sponsor, family member who lives near or far, co-worker, or boss). Answer the following questions as quickly and honestly as you can.

1. I could tell that there were hidden messages, things not being said during the conflict/argument.   Yes   No

2. I made an incorrect assumption that I was expressing myself clearly and effectively.   Yes   No

3. The other person incorrectly assumed that I understood what he/she was communicating.   Yes   No

4. I was indirect and ambiguous. I didn't get to the point, didn't make my wishes clear.   Yes   No

5. The other person was indirect and ambiguous (didn't get to the point, didn't make his/her wishes clear).   Yes   No

6. I began to feel hostile and resentful, which shut down the communication. Yes   No

7. I could tell that the other person began to seem hostile and resentful, which shut down the communication.   Yes   No

8. One or the other of us shut down or decided to withdraw and end the communication.   Yes   No

9. If I had to rate how this conflict affected my mood, I would rate it *(Circle your answer)*:
None   Slightly   A little bit   Quite a bit   A great deal   Severely

Results: Review your *Yes* answers and list the top two or three that caused the most problems with communication and resolution. Consider the following actions:
- List three strategies that you can use to improve your ability to get your message across directly.
- List two ways to check out assumptions and/or clarity during a conversation or dispute.
- Ask the other person to fill out this inventory about the same dispute. Compare your answers and discuss ways to improve communication.

Exercise: Your Support Inventory

Having the skills to form healthy attachments, nurture these relationships, and maintain a support system is an important aspect of mood regulation. When we are feeling unsure, fragile, or depressed, or when a crisis occurs, we need to know who we can turn to and who we can rely on. We also need from time to time to take an inventory to determine whether we are spending time with those who support and nurture us, or are spending time with those who drain us and exhaust our energy. This exercise is designed to help you take a closer look at your support circle and examine your support network and relationships that may drain you or nurture you.

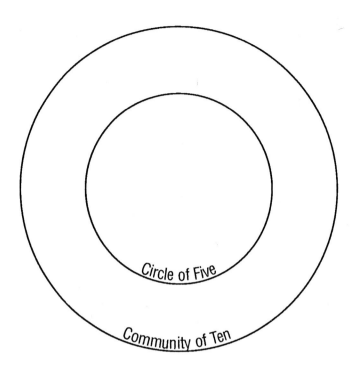

FIGURE 21. THE CIRCLE OF FIVE-COMMUNITY OF TEN CONCEPT. IT CAN
BE HELPFUL TO TAKE AN INVENTORY OF ONE'S PERSONAL SUPPORT SYSTEM.

- Think of the first five people you would call if you had the most wonderful news in your life. These might be family members, friends, or a boyfriend or girlfriend. Next, think of the first five people you would call if you were in a crisis or accident, frightened or hurt, or needed immediate help or good advice. Compare these lists and select the overall top five people that you would consider your circle of support. We will call these your "Circle of Five." Write these names in the inner circle in the diagram in FIGURE 21.
- Now, think of the next five people you would call, after you've tried to contact your Circle of Five. Write these names in the outer circle in the diagram. We will call the people in the inner and outer circle your "Community of Ten."
- Are there one or two more that must be listed? Feel free to add them (outside of the circles).
- Now, take a moment to look at your Community of Ten. Think about the last time you've seen or spoken to each of those people. What have you done lately to appreciate, honor, or acknowledge these important people in your

life? If you haven't done so recently, consider sending a card or making a call just to say hello and mention how important they are in your life. Make a note of those you want to call soon.

- Next, take a moment to think about the people you spend a lot of time with. Are they in your Community of Ten? Are they outside the circle? List the names that come to mind. Spend a few moments to think carefully about these relationships. Are they contributing to your growth, your happiness, your well-being? Or are these people who depend on you for their happiness and well-being? Are any of these relationships that you would like to nurture and move to a closer/deeper level? Are any of these relationships that you would like to consider spending less time with to make room for your own needs or make room for time with your Community of Ten?

This exercise is useful to do from time to time, especially when you feel alone or in need of a "tune-up" with someone we trust, or when we have a need to "tune in to" support. It helps us to identify those we can depend upon, those who we give our self and our time to, and to recognize the wealth (or the void) in our support system.

CHAPTER 7
Spiritual Strategies

When our days become dreary with low-hovering clouds and our nights become darker than a thousand midnights, let us remember that there is a great benign Power in the universe whose name is God, and He is able to make a way out of no way, and transform dark yesterdays into bright tomorrows. This is our hope for becoming better men. This is our mandate for seeking to make a better world.—Dr. Martin Luther King, Jr.

Defining spirituality

All humans have a spiritual dimension but not everyone is aware of it. Spirituality is the divinity that is expressed from within our soul. It lies at the core of each person's being and is the source of meaning and hope; it is an internal resource for coping. Spiritual coping is the term used to describe the extent to which a person with spiritual beliefs and practices relies on them to help him or her cope in daily life (Koenig et al. 1997). Spirituality is the belief in God and is expressed through spiritual and religious practice.

Spirituality and religion overlap in meaning as the expression of one's divinity in the search for meaning and transcendence in the realm of the sacred. We use the term spirituality throughout this book to express this experience of divinity.

Spirituality influences and finds expression in many activities of the mind and body. Khavari (1999) and Huddleston (1993) have summarized some of its fundamental themes:

- An awareness of a spiritual dimension to life and how it bonds us to others with respect and compassion and harmonious living
- A sense of the sacredness and interdependence of life
- The belief and acknowledgement that there is a creator
- A self-esteem and responsibility that comes from the belief that man is the highest form of life

• A recognition that the purpose of life is to nurture and develop our spirituality and to cultivate the humane righteous qualities of honesty, compassion, truthfulness, and other similar values.

Spiritual health describes that aspect of our well-being which helps define our values, organize our relationships, and find purpose and meaning in our lives (Seidl 1993). It plays an important role in our physical health and emotional well-being. Spirituality gives us a sense of meaning and direction in life and has a direct beneficial effect on physical and psychological health.

The field of psychology became increasingly secular in its orientation during the last century, neglecting the spiritual dimension and ignoring how spirituality affects a person's life, mood, thoughts, or behaviors. Some well-known psychiatrists even pathologized and belittled the human spiritual experience; one such example (Hassed 2000) is when Freud described religion as a "universal obsessional neurosis." Carl Jung, however, saw that man's search for his spirituality is the central theme of the human experience, even though it is often ignored or denied. He wrote, "People will do anything, no matter how absurd, in order to avoid facing their own souls" (Jung 1968). He used the term "soul sickness" to describe the lack of meaning in life. This lack of meaning is the hallmark of depression and contributes to helplessness and suicide.

Spirituality encompasses one's belief in God, the search for meaning, and a sense of purpose and connectedness to others in the universe. Spirituality is founded in our spiritual beliefs and expressed in our spiritual practices. Spiritual beliefs are concerned with:

• Faith
• Finding meaning
• Relationships with God.

Spiritual practices are comprised of:

• Prayer
• Worship and service attendance
• Reading religious material or books
• Spiritual discussions and activities with spiritual community members.

Spirituality and mood regulation

Neurotheology, which is also known as biotheology, is a new area of research where scientists try to pinpoint which regions of the brain are associated with subjective spiritual experiences. Certain areas of the brain and chemical brain functions, primarily in the limbic system, have been found to be associated with spiritual experiences. Several researchers (Rahwan 2000; Saver and Rabin 1997) have pinpointed the limbic system as the brain site where spiritual experiences are mediated or reflected. Dr. Andrew Newberg from the University of Pennsylvania did several brain imaging studies, measuring the blood flow of the brains of people while they were praying or meditating. He found that the more deeply people meditated and prayed, the more active their frontal lobes and limbic systems became, thus indicating that these were the areas involved in praying and meditating (Newberg and Iversen 2003; Newberg et al. 2003). Dr. Newberg and colleagues (2001) reported how electrical stimulation studies of the limbic system produce experiences similar to those experiences during spiritual practices, and Jacqueline Borg (2003) has proposed that the spiritual experience may be expressed biologically through the neurotransmitter serotonin in the limbic system. Saver (1997) notes how patients with Alzheimer's disease with damage in the limbic areas of their brain demonstrate loss of religious interest.

Dean Hamer, director of the Gene Structure and Regulation unit at the National Institutes of Health, compared 226 volunteers who were measured on a scale on the degree of their ability for self-transcendence. Transcendence is the ability to get out of one's self and become one with a higher power. Hamer (2004) compared their DNA samples and found that the more a person was able to spiritually self-transcend, the more likely they were to have and share a gene called VMAT2. This VMAT2 gene is a regulator that controls the amount of neurotransmitters dopamine, norepinephrine, and serotonin in the brain. These neurotransmitters regulate our mood in the mood center. Hamer's finding was that this gene was more prevalent in people who were spiritual. The fact that our spirituality is mediated by the same gene responsible for the production and regulation of mood-altering chemicals shows the close relationship between our spirituality and mood and how they may affect each other.

These studies point to the fact that our spiritual experiences are reflected in our brain's activity. This does not mean that our biological brain activity determines our spiritual experiences. It does point to the fact that we function in unison at all levels biologically, psychologically, and spiritually. It also shows that the connection between our spiritual experiences and our biology occurs in the mood center. Accordingly, spiritual experiences impact our mood center directly and cause changes in it, as Dr. Newberg's study showed. Given these pathways and connections between our spirituality and our mood center, it can be seen how our spirituality can have a direct mood-regulating effect, in that it can alter the brain chemistry and activity in the mood center.

In addition to the effect of spirituality on mood, spirituality has been shown in many studies to be associated with better health and better outcomes in recovery from illness. Doctors at the Mayo clinic conducted a study (Mueller et al. 2001) to examine the effects of faith on health. They reviewed 850 studies of mental health and 350 studies of physical health associated with spirituality. Religious involvement and spirituality were found to be associated with outcomes in recovery from illness, better health, greater longevity, coping skills, and health-related quality of life measures.

Spirituality and depression

McCullough and Larson (1999) reviewed eighty studies that examined the association of religious involvement with depression. They found that people who had a high level of general religious involvement and motivation were at lower risk for becoming depressed and having depressive symptoms. They concluded by suggesting that religious involvement may be protective against developing depression.

Spiritual well-being achieved through faith and spiritual practices has been found in studies to protect against depression and to have significant influence on psychological well-being. Levin (1994) reviewed hundreds of studies and found evidence to suggest that spirituality or religiosity influences physical health positively.

Spirituality and religious coping have been found to be associated with improvement in depression and regulation of the depressed mood. Individuals who are spiritually involved have been shown to have fewer depressive symptoms, a better sense of emotional well-being, and better functional ability (Payne et al. 1991; Idler 1987). Greater religious involvement has also been associated with less risk of suicide (Koenig 2001). Additionally, individuals who embrace spiritual beliefs and who express these beliefs through spiritual practices have been found to have a higher rate of recovery from illness compared to those who don't (Koenig 1997; Carter 1998). In *The Varieties of Religious Experience,* William James (1922) summarizes the healing process of spirituality and faith:

> We may now turn from these psychological generalities to those fruits of the religious state which form the special subject of our present lecture. The man who lives in his religious centre of personal energy, and is actuated by spiritual enthusiasms, differs from his previous carnal self in perfectly definite ways.
>
> The new ardor which burns in his breast consumes in its glow the lower "noes" which formerly beset him, and keeps him immune against infection from the entire groveling portion of his nature. Magnanimities once impossible are now easy; paltry conventionalities and mean incentives once tyrannical hold no sway. The stone wall inside of him has fallen, the hardness in his heart has broken down. The rest of us can, I think, imagine this by recalling our state of feeling in those temporary "melting moods" into which either the trials of real life, or the theatre, or a novel sometimes throws us. Especially if we weep! For it is

then as if our tears broke through an inveterate inner dam, and let all sorts of ancient peccancies and moral stagnancies drain away, leaving us now washed and soft of heart and open to every nobler leading.

James used the term religious melancholy to describe a passive loss of appetite for life's values. James stated that a depression state develops in the absence of meaning in a person's life, where there is self-doubt and fear in one's existence, with no one to turn to. It also occurs when a person struggles with his or her inner sense of value and righteousness, or lack of it, and finds no explanations or supports. Once this melancholia sets in, a person's sense of optimism and self-satisfaction gets "leveled with the dust."

D. Martyn Lloyd-Jones (1965) used the term "spiritual depression" to describe a person who is "dejected, disquieted, and miserable…unhappy and depressed and (it) always shows in his face. He looks troubled and he looks worried. You take one glance at him and you see his condition." He goes on to describe the spiritually depressed person: "He looks as if he is carrying the whole universe, as it were, upon his back. He is borne down, sad, troubled, perplexed. He is weeping and tearful, and all because he is in the state of perplexity and of fear…He cannot control his feelings…. It is even affecting his very appetite." Lloyd-Jones summarizes the "ultimate cause of all spiritual depression as unbelief." Unbelief is when the person forgets God, so his faith in God and God's power is weakened.

Religious melancholy and spiritual depression, then, become identical in describing a condition where a person has lost the core sense of meaning in life. The person sees no purpose, has lost all hope, and is struggling with and in a state of emotional and spiritual despair, distress, and emptiness. James and Lloyd-Jones remind us that depression and its symptoms have roots in the spiritual realm that are often neglected. These spiritual symptoms are called noogenic symptoms, which relate to the deeper issues of life meaning and one's existence and being. Richard Close (2000) states, "If the biological symptoms of major depressive disorders are a crisis of the body, and the psychogenic symptoms are a crisis of the mind, then the noogenic (life meaning) symptoms are a crisis of one's life purpose, a concern of the soul." Close continues the discussion of theories of depression by observing, "The main theories usually considered are psychological or neurobiological and genetic. However, in some cases at least, depression can not fully be explained by these theories, but may lie within the deeper issues of life meaning (noogenic) and being." It is well known that when someone is depressed, he or she questions the meaning of their existence, is preoccupied by feelings of worthlessness and lack of purpose, is hopeless and experiences a loss of core meaning, and lives with suffering.

These fundamental questions define the existential and spiritual dimensions of depression and cannot be explained simply by biological or cognitive processes (Juchli 1991). They can be better understood from a spiritual dimension, which is a source from which a person gets his sense of meaning, purpose, and hope in life. The spiritual dimension is a real manifestation of one's life and brings about a spiritual reality, which exerts as much influence as the biological and psychological reality of our life. When this spiritual reality is impaired, the person's existence is at stake, and life loses meaning.

Several studies have found that spirituality plays a major role in altering mood states. Low levels of spiritual coping and a loss of well-being are associated with depression. High levels of spiritual coping and improved well-being are associated with feelings of wellness, a positive mood state, and are protective against depression.

Lawler suggests that spiritual involvement increases the sense of coherence and strength of the individual (Lawler and Younger 2002). In turn, the person will have better resistance to stress and improved general health. He uses the term "hardiness" to describe those who are resistant to the effects of stress on their health. Hardy individuals have been shown to have strong commitment to their work and to themselves and they perceive life as meaningful and find purpose in what they do. A sense of coherence is seen in individuals who perceive the world as comprehensible and manageable. Spiritual beliefs and practices increase and strengthen the sense of coherence and the hardiness of the individual, which exert a strong positive regulatory effect on a person's mood. People with depression have major deficits in their level of hardiness and have a lack of coherence and clarity in their life. When depression gets severe, life becomes so meaningless that suicide is the only option.

By increasing hardiness in the depressed individual, spirituality may help lift the depression by giving the person a sense of control over his life with meaning, purpose, and hope. The depressed person becomes optimistic about the future, which in turn decreases negative thinking. The sense of coherence helps by making life comprehensible and manageable, which in turn relieves the hopelessness by giving the person a sense of control over his or her destiny.

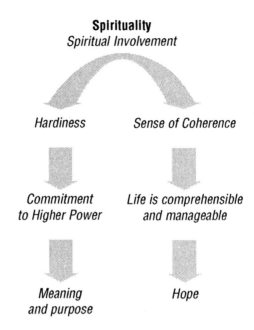

Spirituality
Spiritual Involvement

Hardiness   *Sense of Coherence*

*Commitment   Life is comprehensible
to Higher Power   and manageable*

*Meaning   Hope
and purpose*

FIGURE 22. MEANING, PURPOSE, AND HOPE AS THEY RELATE TO SPIRITUALITY. SPIRITUAL INVOLVEMENT CAN BE A CATALYST FOR ACHIEVING A GREATER LEVEL OF PURPOSE IN LIFE.

Those gracious influences which are the effects of the Spirit of God are altogether supernatural.... They are what no improvement, or composition of natural qualifications or principles will ever produce; because they not only differ from what is natural, and from everything that natural men experience in degree and circumstances, but also in kind, and are of a nature far more excellent.... There are new perceptions and sensations entirely different in their nature and kind from anything experienced.—Jonathan Edwards in *The Varieties of Religious Experience* by *William James*

Spiritual care

Spiritual consolation constituted the main approach to treating depressed individuals prior to the nineteenth century. The therapy drew heavily from the heavenly religions and was based on the person's faith and efforts to seek comfort in their relationship with God. This gave the depressed aid to prepare their mind for adversity and to accommodate the pain and suffering of their illness (Rippere 1980).

For many centuries spirituality was the only therapeutic tool available for those with depression. With the introduction of the psychological and biological therapies in the last century, spirituality was abandoned as a therapeutic tool. It has slowly returned to be part of the whole therapeutic armamentarium.

Depression is marked by hopelessness, helplessness, denial of the condition, withdrawal, and avoidance. The MRT steps to spiritual care include:

- Acceptance of the depression and recognition of the need for help
- Discovery
  —What do you really believe in? Look beyond the material things in your life; look to dimensions of the spirit.
  —Expand your awareness. Study religious teachings and turn to God for guidance. Find the sense of sacredness and interdependence of life.
  —Develop faith, belief in God, belief in the creator. Reflect and contemplate the deeper meanings of faith and the teachings of religion.
- Surrender and self-transcendence
- Find meaning in life and recognize that the purpose of life is to mature and develop the spiritual side of ourselves to cultivate the noble qualities of honesty, patience, and compassion.

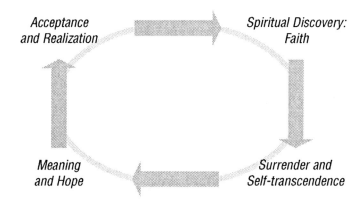

FIGURE 23. FOUR ELEMENTS OF SPIRITUAL CARE. THE ELEMENTS OF SPIRITUALITY ARE INTERCONNECTED.

Acceptance and realization

Acceptance is one of the key ingredients of meaningful living. The first step is about confronting our denial and admitting the negative impact that depression has on us. It is important to recognize and acknowledge our depression and the pain and suffering it inflicts on us and those around us. We may realize in the midst of our depression how helpless we are at controlling it. This may lead us to discover our soul and then reach out to a supreme power beyond us for help. This supreme power is God.

Writer Andrew Solomon, author of *The Noon Day Demon: An Atlas of Depression*, expressed this experience succinctly in his words: "It was also in depression that I learned my own acreage, the full extent of my soul." He goes on to say, "I do not love experiencing my depression, but I love the depression itself. I love who I am in the wake of it…I have discovered what I would have to call a soul, a part of myself I could never have imagined until one day, seven years ago, when hell came to pay me a surprise visit. It's a precious discovery."

Eddy Elmer (2003) is a psychology student in Canada who also wrote about his experience with depression, offering original ideas on what has helped him in his recovery. He wrote about coping with his depression, acknowledging that "paradoxically, transcendence seems possible only when we accept that which we don't want to transcend." He recounts how trying to "forget" or "dismiss the presence" of his depression or "just cope with it" only kept him depressed longer and sunk him deeper into depression. Still, he was able to accept it, give it a name, and then move beyond it.

Acceptance means embracing the reality and taking responsibility for our depression. Once we do this, we can look inward honestly and clearly and realize that we need to reach out for help beyond us. The pain of depression may be an opportunity to awaken our soul and allow us to reach beyond ourselves to God for help, solace and comfort. Dr. Elisabeth Kubler-Ross wrote in 1999 that pain and hardship in life (as in depression) are opportunities given to us for spiritual growth and maturity. She adds, "To grow is the sole purpose of existence on this planet Earth."

Realization means knowing that, if we can't change the depression, then we can change ourselves by reaching out to God. Then we may be empowered and healed. If we don't have the resources within to overcome the depression, we have the ability to reach to the divine power of God and find healing, serenity, and hope (Lloyd-Jones 1965).

So, if your depression won't leave you, you can leave it. Realizing that we have the option to overcome depression is powerful, especially when we are feeling helpless and hopeless. Knowing that there is a divine power that we can reach out to and be healed by is powerful. It brings hope and lasting recovery in a short period of time.

Exercise: Spiritual Involvement and Beliefs Scale

The Spiritual Involvement and Beliefs Scale was developed by Dr. Robert Hatch. The scale aims at measuring one's spiritual practices and beliefs. By answering the questions on the scale you can derive a total score, which can give you an impression of the degree of your spirituality. The higher the score, the more you are aware of your spiritual dimension, and the more spirituality plays a role in your daily life and is part of your belief and value system. We find the scale helpful; for the MRT therapist working with you, it can give him or her an idea of your spiritual beliefs, the degree faith plays in your life, and how involved you are in regular spiritual practices.

Spiritual Involvement and Beliefs Scale

Items 1-21: Read the statement in the left column and then circle in the right column the number that most closely reflects your feeling about the statement.

Item 22: Circle the number that most closely reflects your view of your own spirituality.

Items 23-26: Choose one answer (A, B, C, D, or E) that most closely reflects your actions.

	STRONGLY AGREE	AGREE	MILDLY AGREE	NEUTRAL	MILDLY DISAGREE	DISAGREE	STRONGLY DISAGREE
1. *I set aside time for praying and/or meditation.*	7	6	5	4	3	2	1
2. *I can find meaning in times of hardship.*	7	6	5	4	3	2	1
3. *I regularly interact with others for spiritual purposes.*	7	6	5	4	3	2	1
4. *I believe in an afterlife.*	7	6	5	4	3	2	1
5. *I have a relationship with someone I can turn to for spiritual guidance.*	7	6	5	4	3	2	1
6. *Spiritual writings enrich my life.*	7	6	5	4	3	2	1
7. *I have been through a time of great suffering that led to spiritual growth.*	7	6	5	4	3	2	1
8. *I have a personal relationship with a power greater than myself.*	7	6	5	4	3	2	1
9. *I have had a spiritual experience that greatly changed my life.*	7	6	5	4	3	2	1

FIGURE 24-1. THE SPIRITUAL INVOLVEMENT AND BELIEFS SCALE QUESTIONNAIRE. THE ANSWERS YOU PROVIDE TO THE QUESTIONS PRESENTED HERE CAN HELP YOU IDENTIFY QUALITIES OF YOUR OWN SPIRITUALITY (ADAPTED FROM HATCH ET AL. 1998).

10.	Some experiences can be understood only through one's spiritual beliefs.	7	6	5	4	3	2	1
11.	My spiritual life fulfills me in ways that material possessions do not.	7	6	5	4	3	2	1
12.	I have joy in my life because of my spirituality.	7	6	5	4	3	2	1
13.	A spiritual force influences the events in my life.	7	6	5	4	3	2	1
14.	In times of despair I can still find reason to hope.	7	6	5	4	3	2	1
15.	I have experienced healing after prayer.	7	6	5	4	3	2	1
16.	Everything happens for a greater purpose.	7	6	5	4	3	2	1
17.	My relationship with a higher power helps me love others more completely.	7	6	5	4	3	2	1
18.	Spiritual health contributes to physical health.	7	6	5	4	3	2	1
19.	I depend on a higher power.	7	6	5	4	3	2	1
20.	I solve my problems using spiritual resources.	7	6	5	4	3	2	1
21.	I examine my actions to see if they reflect my spiritual values.	7	6	5	4	3	2	1

22. I would rate my own level of spirituality (with 7 being the most spiritual and 1 being not spiritual) at (circle one):

7   6   5   4   3   2   1

23. During the last WEEK, I prayed....(check one)
_____ A. 10 or more times
_____ B. 7-9 times
_____ C. 4-6 times
_____ D. 1-3 times
_____ E. 0 times

FIGURE 24-2. THE SPIRITUAL INVOLVEMENT AND BELIEFS SCALE QUESTIONNAIRE (CONTINUED FROM PREVIOUS PAGE)

24. During the last WEEK, I meditated....(check one)
_____ A. 10 or more times
_____ B. 7-9 times
_____ C. 4-6 times
_____ D. 1-3 times
_____ E. 0 times

25. During the last MONTH, I read spiritual books....(check one)
_____ A. 10 or more times
_____ B. 7-9 times
_____ C. 4-6 times
_____ D. 1-3 times
_____ E. 0 times

26. Last MONTH, I participated in spiritual activities with at least one other person....(check one)
_____ A. more than 15 times
_____ B. 11-15 times
_____ C. 6-10 times
_____ D. 1-5 times
_____ E. 0 times

SCORING INSTRUCTIONS
For items 1-22: Your score value is the number you circled.
For items 23-26: A = 5   B = 4   C = 3   D = 2   E = 1

Add all of the score values to get your **TOTAL SCORE:** _____

RESULTS
Over 140: High degree of spirituality (strong beliefs and very involved in practices)
101-140: Moderate degree of spirituality (spiritually aware and moderately involved in practices)
61-100: Low degree of spirituality
60 and below: Little involvement with spirituality or non-spiritual person

FIGURE 24-3. THE SPIRITUAL INVOLVEMENT AND BELIEFS SCALE QUESTIONNAIRE (CONTINUED FROM PREVIOUS PAGE)

Discover the spirituality and deepen the faith

The next step is getting in touch with our spirituality and the awareness of the spiritual dimension of life. Ask yourself: "What do I really believe in?" Be open to inspiration. Be open to not knowing but to experiencing. Make time for reflection and reading spiritual material. Join a spiritual fellowship of those who are close to your values and beliefs so you can learn about and discover your spirituality. Read spiritual and religious literature, and pray and meditate. Spend time with nature and become aware of non-material aspects of life. Study religious teachings and turn to God for guidance. Find the sense of sacredness and interdependence of life. We deepen our faith through praying, reading holy books, and attending religious services.

These spiritual practices and discoveries will open up yearning and drive us to be spiritually connected, and through this connection the grip of depression on us is loosened, and light and hope come into our life. As faith comes in, we turn away from focusing on our negative feelings and symptoms. Lloyd-Jones advises when discussing the spiritual treatment of depression: "Avoid the mistake of concentrating overmuch upon your feelings. Above all, avoid the terrible error of making them central." Our emphasis should be on the search for the spiritual truth inside us through self-examination, self-inquiry, and searching our hearts. Only then do we get in touch with our soul, and truth and meaning do emerge. He concludes by saying, "And it is as we apprehend and submit ourselves to the truth that the feelings follow." That feeling is feeling terrific.

According to William James (1922), in seeking his spirituality Tolstoy deepened his faith and found that to believe in God is where his happiness and joy were:

> "I remember," he says, "one day in early spring, I was alone in the forest, lending my ear to its mysterious noises. I listened, and my thought went back to what for these three years it always was busy with—the quest of God. But the idea of him I said, how did I ever come by the idea?
>
> "And again there arose in me, with this thought, glad aspirations towards life. Everything in me awoke and received a meaning...Why do I look farther? A voice within me asked. He is there: he, without whom one cannot live. To acknowledge God and to live are one and the same thing. God is what life is. Well, then I live, seek God, and there will be no life without him...
>
> "After this, things cleared up within me and about me better than ever, and the light has never wholly died away. I was saved from suicide. Just how or when the change took place I cannot tell. But as insensibly and gradually as the force of life had been

annulled within me, and I had reached my moral death-bed, just as gradually and imperceptibly did the energy of life come back. And what was strange was that this energy that came back was nothing new. It was my ancient juvenile force of faith, the belief that the sole purpose of my life was to be better."

Faith is an oasis in the heart which will never be reached by the caravan of thinking.—Kahlil Gibran

Faith

Faith is the belief and trust in a divine power. Faith is the secure belief in God and the unquestioning acceptance of God's will. It changes our thoughts and emotions and moves us to action. Faith defines our principles and ideals regarding the fundamental matters of life.

Lloyd-Jones states that faith is an activity and not simply a feeling that comes on automatically at a whim. A person has to exercise his faith with action and behavior, for faith is a walk of life and not merely a thought or a feeling. As an activity, the walk of faith brings with it an awareness of our own sense of responsibility or what Dr. Victor Frankl (1984) called living with "responsibleness," which he claims is "as if you were living already for the second time and as if you had acted the first time as wrongly as you are about to act now." By adopting this attitude of responsibleness, the depressed person can access his faith and get out of the negative mood state by taking charge and changing or amending the past depressed state he has been stuck in to search beyond himself for solutions and solace. Dr. Frankl adds that "such a precept confronts him with life's finiteness as well as the finality of what he makes out of both his life and himself," which is the meaning he finds and develops for himself. This meaning is found in our relationship with God and through our faith.

James (1922) commented on Tolstoy's pursuit of his spiritual inquiry and his journey toward finding his faith:

"Since mankind has existed, wherever life had been, there has also been the faith that gave the possibility of living. Faith is the sense of life, that sense by virtue of which man does not destroy himself, but continues to live on. It is the force whereby we live. If Man did not believe that he must live for something, he would not live at all. The idea of an infinite God, of the divinity of the soul, of the union of men's actions with God—these are ideas elaborated in the infinite secret depth of human thought. They are ideas without which there would be no life, without which I myself," said Tolstoy, "would not exist. I began to see that I had no right to rely on my individual reasoning and neglect these answers given by faith, for they are the only answers to the question."

Faith involves cognitive and behavioral processes that are purposeful and goal oriented. As such, faith implies work, which entails being responsible to God, community, and self.

Meaningful living implies responsibility, and faith gives us the road map to fulfilling these responsibilities. Responsibility is to look and work beyond one's own sufferings and depression, knowing that through faith a person will get better as he or she reaches beyond the self to help and be with others and put meaning in life. When faith goes in, depression goes out. When we have deep faith, we are fully aware of our responsibilities in life. These duties and responsibilities are spelled out in the holy books.

Depression causes us to turn inward and disconnect from everyone and everything around us. Finding, renewing, and deepening one's faith in God are major sources of strength and comfort at a time when depression brings uncertainty, detachment, and helplessness. Faith gives the depressed person a flickering of light in an otherwise dark and hopeless situation.

Surrender and self-transcendence

Surrender is the defining character of faith and implies that the person surrenders himself and his will to God and then is able to experience God's serenity and peace (Mawdudi 1997). Surrender can be understood as a twofold discipline—one is an outward action aimed at a life of obedience to God's ordinance and teachings and remembrance of God; the second, an inward "single-minded devotion, purity of thought and absolute sincerity" for the purpose of devotion to God (Nygard 1996). Surrender then is the unity of meaning and action in a person's life that allows the person to reach out through his spirituality to God.

Surrender to God allows the depressed individual to get above depression, as the focus moves from one's self to God's divine power and presence. With surrender there is freedom from the harsh stronghold of depression. With surrender, there can be a feeling of unity and a sense of inner wholeness and being wholehearted (Tiebout 1953). The surrender of our will to God releases us from negative emotions and regulates our moods.

Through our deepened faith, we surrender to God and we transcend ourselves and our environment. Through that, we rise above our depression to find meaning beyond the dark clouds of sadness and despondency. James (1922) described the relationship of faith to self-surrender:

> So much for the human love aroused by the faith-state. Let me speak of the Equanimity, Resignation, Fortitude, and Patience which it brings. "A paradise of inward tranquility" seems to be faith's usual result; and it is easy, even without being religious one's self, to understand this. A moment back, in treating of the sense of God's presence, I spoke of the unaccountable feeling of safety which one may then have. And, indeed, how can it possibly fail to steady the nerves, to cool the fever, and appease the fret, if one be sensibly conscious that, no matter what one's difficulties for the moment may appear to be, one's life as a whole is in the keeping of a power whom one can absolutely trust? In deeply religious men the abandonment of self to this power is passionate. Whoever not only says but feels, "God's will be done," is mailed against every weakness; and the whole historic array of martyrs, missionaries, and religious reformers is there to prove the tranquil-mindedness, under naturally agitating or distressing circumstances, which self-surrender brings.

Self-transcendence connects us with a higher divine power and allows us to see our life with a larger purpose and serves as a basis for meaningful living. Dr. Paul T. Wong (2003a) states that "self-transcendence is essential to mental health and personal development." When we are depressed, we are self-engrossed and cannot see beyond our misery and negative thoughts and emotions. To get out of the depression, we need to recognize the immaterial, sacred, and transcendental dimension of our spirituality.

Dr. Wong defines transcendence as the opposite of being "stuck." More specifically, he states that transcendence "indicates the movement of one's soul towards a higher purpose, an ideal, which is far greater than one's self." He (1999) goes on to say that "transcendence offers hope when no hope can be found; it supplies illuminations where only darkness rules. It is the secret yearning of everyone who feels burdened or trapped."

The ability to self-transcend is a human capacity which is found in our spiritual nature. The path to self-transcendence is through our spiritual self-care practices, which are prayer, fellowship with those who share our beliefs, reading holy books, and attending services. These spiritual practices allow us to surrender to a higher divine power and transcend ourselves.

He who has a why to live for can bear almost any how.—Victor
Frankl paraphrasing a statement by Friedrich Nietzsche

Finding meaning and hope

We are meaning-seeking, meaning-making creatures who live in a world of
meanings (Wong 2000). Meaning is the effort we exert to understand our lives
and be able to answer the question, "What does my life mean?" Depression is
marked by loss of meaning and purpose and leads to withdrawal and isolation
from people and from God. If we are able to develop our faith in God, then the
search for meaning will be easy and productive.

Dr. Frankl (1984) wrote how the human spirit was resilient and defiant, and
even in the midst of suffering or adversities we can rise above them to tranquility
and calm. When we are depressed, we need to start by finding meaning in very
simple ways that fit our life at that moment.

No one is immune from getting depressed. Life is always a mixture of the
happy and the sad, and there is a diametric and dynamic relationship between
suffering and happiness in our lives (Wong 2003b). Feeling depressed and feeling
terrific are interconnected in a similar, complex, interactive way. Just as the moon
will eventually shine to brighten the darkest night, we can often find the feeling-
terrific state in the depths of the depression.

Depression is an experience devoid of meaning, and our faith helps to restore
true meaning and purpose to life. Human beings have an enduring spirit that can
go beyond the limitations of depression and can seek meaning. Dr. Wong (2000)
teaches us to listen with our soul when we are seeking spiritual guidance and
wisdom to grow and develop a deeper understanding of ourselves, our life
situation, the higher purpose in life, and discover new meanings and new
passions. This process allows us to "re-author" our story, which in turn allows us
to see things in a different light and recover with new self-understanding.

When a person is depressed, he feels that life is meaningless and that he is
drifting without purpose. If depression remains untreated, all meaning is lost,
and the depressed person contemplates suicide. The depressed person can be
helped if he strives to find meaning and purpose in life. We need to know that
life is meaningful and not in vain. That meaning is found in our faith and is lived
and experienced through our spiritual life.

To feel terrific the depressed person needs to seek meaning in his daily life and
find a role for expressing it. People may derive meaning from many areas of their
life, including relationships, work, and so on, but the most enduring sense of
meaning is that derived from one's spiritual life and through one's faith.

A person who feels terrific who would say, "My purpose in life is to serve
God," has not only defined his direction and purpose but also put meaning in his

life. Serving God becomes the meaning of his life. The service of God then gives the person reason and direction. When our lives have meaning and purpose, then we can break through the despair of depression. Meaning derived from one's faith removes the anguish of depression by giving the person direction in life. Meaning removes the inner struggle and gives us hope. With meaning one knows that his life is part of something greater than himself, that he belongs to it, and his life is not in vain.

According to a workshop exercise devised by Dr. Wong, meaning answers these fundamental questions:

- Why am I here?
- What is my role in life today and tomorrow?
- What is missing in my life?
- What do I really want?
- Is there a void in my life?
- How is the depression troubling me?
- What are the recurrent themes in my life that are connected to my depression?
- If I were to re-write my life story, what would it be?
- What is my calling and mission in life?
- What would I like to accomplish in my life to fulfill my calling?

The answers to some of these questions will allow us to start to find the meaning we are looking for and re-author our life story so we may change it from its depressive, dark course. Meaning gives us hope, momentum, and direction. Finding meaning in the service of others allows us not to get stuck in our needs and wants and to see that, in giving to others, there is a lot of receiving and fulfillment. That is one of the powers of faith—the ability to look beyond ourselves and find meaning in life in what we do for others whom we care about.

How does one find meaning?

Through faith the depressed person seeks to find meaning through the purpose he or she establishes. This purpose is to be found in the service of God, surrender to God's doctrine, and being available to help others. Meaning is derived day by day, moment by moment, in the little things that we do. Meaning is found in the commitment to the work that we do, no matter what that work is. The more "others-directed" that work is, the more meaningful it is. Faith teaches us to be dedicated to others and to be able to find purpose in the world around us. Faith opens our eyes to the living world around us and the wisdom in God's creation. Through faith we find a place for ourselves in the bigger picture of life, which lends further meaning to our presence.

Religion tells us that nothing in this world is created for its own purpose. Everything is created for the service of others around it. Plants serve as nutrition for insects, insects and plants serve as nutrition for animals. Animals serve as a source of food and transportation for man. Everything has a purpose.

Abraham Heschel was a Jewish theologian, philosopher, and professor of ethics and mysticism at the Jewish Theological Seminary of America from 1945–1972. Heschel's view of a meaningful life, described in a paper written at Tufts University (Marks 1972), was based on service: "For Abraham Heschel man experiences his life as meaningful when he lives in God's presence - not simply by encountering God in the world but primarily by serving God in everyday life, infusing every moment with the spirit of God, and by dedicating himself to ends outside himself."

Nothing is created to only serve itself, especially man. The path of faith teaches us how to find meaning in serving God and others. The lives of the prophets were all ideal roles for us to examine and follow. Their lives were based on the service of God and mankind. Their lives are great examples of what a meaningful life is about. They all lived to serve God and spread God's doctrine. That was their message. Their faith was through the submission to the will of God and God's discipline. They left us their teachings to learn from and their lives and deeds to be guided by. It becomes our duty then to study and examine their teachings and lives so we may learn and find meaning.

No one appreciates the importance of loss of meaning like the depressed person. In the weakest moments of despair, the depressed individual searches desperately for meaning. It is the complete loss of meaning and purpose that ultimately drives the depressed person to suicide. With the search for meaning, the depressed person is driven to search beyond himself. With spiritual practices and the deepening of one's belief, he finds it in his relationship with God—the Bible tells us, "Seek and you shall find." Maybe that is why grief and sadness are part of life. Depression drives us to search for meaning beyond ourselves and to find God. The faithful learns that man's purpose is not in himself alone. Man's purpose is in serving God first, and in serving others. The religions give guidelines on how to perform that service.

Man is created so that he may find and know God. Man then works to worship God and to follow God's teachings. The teachings direct us to care for others through charity, compassion, availability, kindness, and unselfish love. The teachings also direct us to care and be responsible for God's world and to ease the suffering and struggles of others. In doing this, we not only find meaning but we find out more about ourselves. We are given meaning as we give to those around us. In finding God and following God's doctrine, the depressed person finds meaning in being and discovers the purpose for being alive. As meaning enters his life, serenity sets in, and the person feels terrific.

Dr. Frankl has written extensively about his experiences in the concentration camp. He wrote that survival in the camps was dependent on the person's ability to have meaning beyond suffering and pain. Dr. Frankl notes that when people in the camps lost meaning and their sense of purpose, they lost the will to live and gradually deteriorated mentally and physically. He states (1984) that man "finds identity to the extent to which he commits himself to something beyond himself, to a cause greater than himself." That cause is the service of God. Having such a purpose prevents the person from becoming too self-focused and self-consumed and brings to him a new world to be part of.

Every life has purpose, and every life is meaningful. Every person has to be willing to search and define that purpose and then derive meaning from fulfilling it. In our work we help our patients to search and define the meaning that they identify, and then we set a plan of action on how to fulfill it. That plan of action includes setting goals, then outlining a specific strategy to meet them.

> *Every problem has a solution. Every dark cloud has a silver lining. Every dead end is a starting point. Every crisis is an opportunity. Every transition is a transformation. Every empty cup is time for a refill. Every person has the potential for positive change. Every weakness can become a strength. Every defeat is a stepping stone towards victory. Every pain is stimulus for growth. Every loss is an opening for grace. Every tragedy is a heroic journey.*—Paul T. Wong

Hope

Author George Iles wrote that "hope is faith holding out its hands in the dark." Faith offers us hope and allows us to endure what we are going through and look forward to what gives us comfort and joy. In the face of life's adversity and sad moments, hope and the ability to expect relief carry us through.

The loss of hope—hopelessness—is the leading cause of suicide in depression. Hopelessness means getting stuck and experiencing the expectation that nothing will improve. Hopelessness is accompanied by despair, despondency, and resignation. This is the core of the depressive experience. Hopelessness ultimately leads to loss of self-confidence and a low self-esteem. With hopelessness the person is unable to find a way out of his depression. Hopelessness eventually leads to self-destructive behavior, as the person becomes convinced that he is not going to get better. Reversing this hopelessness is vital to get out of the depression and feel terrific. Anything that brings hope helps a person feel better. Restoring hope comes from finding meaning through faith and seeing that life can be lived meaningfully.

Prayer gets the depressed person closer to God and gives him meaning. Prayer communicates and connects. Prayer opens doors to a new reality. Through praying the depressed person transcends his depression and gets reassurance and comfort. Prayer provides comfort in the knowledge that one is not alone, that God is with him or her at all times. Prayer disconnects the person temporarily from his depression and connects him to his creator so he can remember and be thankful. Through praying comes hope and a feeling that he is not alone.

When a depressed person starts to pray, he starts to change. He sees a light that touches, guides, and directs him. That light takes him from the depth of his darkness and despair to a better place, then to feeling terrific. Prayer has many healing powers. Praying opens the door to hope and to deeper levels of faith. It brings the faithful closer to God. Heschel expresses these words (Stahl 1998) about prayer:

Prayer is a ladder on which our thoughts mount to God.

Prayer takes our mind out of the narrowness of self-interest.

Prayer clarifies our hopes and our intentions.

Prayer, like a gulf stream, imparts warmth to all that is cold.

Prayer is a dialogue with God.

Prayer is an answer to God.

Prayer is an invitation to God to intervene in our lives.

Prayer is our desire to let God's will prevail in our affairs.

Prayer is opening our soul to God.

Prayer is our intention to make God the master of our soul.

Prayer is to sense God's presence.

Prayer is a gift to God. Amen.

The other way to find hope is through the remembrance of God. Remembrance of God is the practice of remembering and thanking God. We remember God by our tongues, in our deeds, and with our hearts. Remembrance is done through recitation of thanks to God verbally or through acts of remembrance. Remembrance is also done through meditation and contemplation.

For the depressed person, remembrance assures him that he is not alone. Remembrance keeps him in the company of God and brings comfort and faith. The depressed person needs to connect with God and remember. Through the practice of remembrance, the depressed person feels connected and knows that God is looking over him and after him. Remembrance awakens the soul and lifts up the depressed to feeling terrific.

Spirituality and feeling terrific

There is a complex and dynamic relationship between depression and feeling terrific. This relationship is best described by the term *noodynamic,* which Dr. Frankl describes as the dynamic of two opposite poles. From within the extremes of these two poles, one derives meaning, purpose, mental health, and well-being. It is this tension between depression and our desire to feel terrific that leads us to strive for meaning and to find a way to rise above the depression.

To feel terrific we need to learn how to let go and transcend the pain of depression. We do that by following the path of the human spirit, which is our healthy core. Dr. Wong (2001) writes, "Happiness is like a tapestry of many colors. What makes a particular tapestry a picture of mature happiness is not the overabundance of bright colors, but the contrast between darkness and light, which helps create a sense of hope and joy in the midst of sorrow." He states that the human spirit is always intact and never gets sick, but it may be blocked by biological or psychological illness in depression.

According to well-known logotherapist Joseph Fabry (1994), the human spirit contains the ability to find meaning, purpose, love, creativity, responsibility, and other similar qualities. Through spiritual care, we aim to access our spiritual self and through it grow and transcend the depression and feel terrific. The steps in spiritual care that help lift the depression can be summarized as:

- Accepting my depression as something happening to me not as a punishment but as a predicament in my life. I acknowledge the depression and take responsibility for it. If I can't change the depression, then I can change myself. I see life as a mixture of the sweet and sorrow and reach beyond me for help from God. I reach for God's power and discover my spirituality.
- As I seek through my spiritual journeying, my faith in God deepens.
- As my faith deepens, I surrender to God and self-transcend my sorrow and pain.
- As I am able to practice my faith and self-transcend, I search for meaning. I seek it and I create it through my faith. Meaning gives me hope, which relieves my hopelessness and frees me from the chains of my depression. As I infuse meaning in my life, I can re-author my story and change my course. This relieves me from my despair and allows me to endure the dark days if they recur. I know tomorrow will be brighter, that "Weeping may go on all night, but in the morning, there is joy" (Psalm 30:5).

The following exercise may be helpful to become more aware of your spiritual dimension.

Exercise: Spirituality

All humans have a spiritual dimension. Consider the idea that meaning is derived in the little things that we do and in our commitment to the work that we do. The more "others-directed" that work is, the more meaningful it becomes. To become aware of our spiritual dimension, it is helpful to be specific about what we believe. Please write down your answers to the following questions. Don't spend too much time thinking about each item. Write the first things that come to your mind. Try to complete this within the briefest period of time possible.

1. What are the first three things that come to your mind when you think of faith? What does faith mean to you? How would you define it?

2. Think of three occasions in your life when you can say you relied on faith to get you through a situation.

3. What three qualities or attributes would you use to describe your idea of God, a Higher Power, Universal Being or Source?

4. What religious beliefs or philosophy were you raised with and what would you describe as the three basic tenets of that religion or philosophy?

5. How happy are you with those beliefs or tenets on a 0 to 10 scale? (Zero equals very unhappy and 10 equals very happy)

0   1   2   3   4   5   6   7   8   9   10

6. What spiritual practices do you currently use in your life? List as many as you can think of. (Examples may range from singing hymns, chanting, dietary restrictions like no meat or pork, going to church, blessing the house with sage or holy water, using a God Box, going to confession, talking to a spiritual adviser, etc.)

7. What kind of things do you do to serve others? List all you can think of. (Some examples include volunteering at a hospital; sponsoring someone in a 12-step program; helping the homeless, runaways, or at-risk youth; donating time at a church or temple; assisting in a literary program for the underprivileged; serving at a soup kitchen; cleaning up trash in your community, etc.)

8. What would you say are the three most important things that bring meaning and purpose to your life? What keeps you going? How do you do the things you do?

9. Name three books or movies that you have read or seen that made a deep impact on you in a spiritual sense.

10. If you could add three new activities to your life that would bring meaning, increase your faith, or serve others, what would they be?

CHAPTER 8
Case Studies

All types of depression arise from mood dysregulation caused by a disturbance in one's biological, cognitive, social, or spiritual domain of life. A particular type of depression such as major depressive disorder may arise more from, say, biological influences than the other influences but no type of depression is all biological, all social, or all spiritual.

The final common pathway for the four influences is expressed through mood regulation. All four processes are usually affected in the various types of depression. Understanding these processes and their effects and developing strategies to correct the disturbances in each dimension leads to mood regulation and feeling terrific. The multiple roots of mood regulation mean that using multiple treatment approaches is the most effective way to treat depression and to feel terrific. These are the five steps of mood regulation therapy:

Step 1. Understanding mood regulation and the MRT process: How are moods regulated?
- Understand the fundamentals of mood regulation.
- Learn how your moods are normally regulated through the four dimensions of mood regulation.
- Understand what happens when your moods are dysregulated.
- Identify the relationship between mood dysregulation and depression.
- Determine the type of depression that's present and which of the four basic influences of mood regulation is primarily causing the mood dysregulation and depression.
- Learn how to define and be aware of mood states at all times by recording and monitoring mood on a daily basis with the MRT Daily Mood Scale and Graph.

Step 2. Biological strategies
- Make lifestyle changes with diet and exercise that can regulate and stabilize your mood.
- Develop a simple and consistent exercise program that involves walking, swimming, or aerobic activity four times a week to contribute to mood regulation.
- In terms of diet, the key is eating healthy portions and specific food items while reducing refined sugars and fats. That means your diet should include more grains, fresh fruits and vegetables, and fewer fat and protein sources. This will help you manage your weight and stabilize your mood.
- Medications may be an extremely helpful treatment tool in mood regulation and in alleviating the symptoms of depression. Learn which medication works best for you, recognize possible side effects, expectations, and length of recommended treatment.
- Consider other beneficial biological therapies such as light therapy or electroconvulsive therapy.

Step 3. Cognitive strategies
- Identify your negative thoughts, perceptions, and beliefs. These negative thoughts contribute to mood dysregulation.
- Use the re-thinking exercise to identify distorted thoughts and underlying assumptions behind your negative thoughts.
- Restructure the thoughts, which will lead to rational and realistic thoughts, observing that when your negative thoughts are neutralized, your mood gets regulated and the depression starts to lift.
- Refocus attention by shifting your attention and focusing on a pleasurable activity or thought. This regulates your mood by distracting you and dismantling your negative thoughts.

Step 4. Social strategies
- Identify how your personal relationships have contributed to or been affected by your mood dysregulation and depression.
- Learn communication skills to improve your ability to convey to others your ideas, feelings, and thoughts.
- Learn how to deal with the loss of a relationship, relationship conflicts, role transition, or social isolation.
- Learn skills to cope with your interpersonal vulnerabilities and shortcomings. This leads to regulation and stabilization of your mood.

Step 5. Spiritual strategies

- Identify religious observance, prayer, and other spiritual practices in which you are interested.
- Understand that spiritual strategies play a fundamental role in mood regulation and in promoting physical and psychological well-being.
- Exercise your spiritual beliefs and spiritual practices, which can lead to mood regulation and feeling terrific.

We present here seven case histories of patients whom we have treated with mood regulation therapy in clinical practice. These cases represent several types of depression and the challenges and difficulties that patients experience from them. The goals of MRT as presented in these case histories include making the proper assessment, formulating a coherent treatment plan, implementing it with the consensus of the patient, and monitoring the outcome. These cases show the MRT focus on the process of recovery and its outcome, which is feeling terrific. They also exemplify how we work within each of the four dimensions with every patient and how every dimension receives equal attention. We hope that these cases will help illustrate the MRT process.

Catherine

Background: Catherine was a 56-year-old woman living in San Diego who presented with a history of depression after her 83-year-old mother died eight months earlier. Catherine was very close to her mother; they had lived together for the last forty-six years. Catherine stated, "I can't imagine life after losing my mother. She was everything to me."

Following her mother's death, Catherine had been feeling depressed, sad, hopeless, and helpless. She was crying most of the day, unable to imagine waking up and not finding her mother at home with her. She had less pleasure in all things than she had experienced previously. Her husband tried to take her on vacation to help her to forget and to deal with her grief, but she had to cut the vacation short and come back because she was feeling sad and having a hard time imagining how life could go on without her mother.

Catherine felt trapped in her sadness and grief. She stated, "We were very close. After I lost my mother, I lost myself. How can I go on?" She started having physical symptoms, including stomach upsets, difficulty falling and staying asleep, weight loss, and difficulty in taking care of her daily activities and responsibilities.

Discussion: Catherine presented with a history of depression that occurred shortly after her mother died. She said she felt that her mother was "my whole life." Catherine started grieving the loss of her mother, and the grief carried on into a bout of clinical depression.

Treatment plan: Her treatment plan focused on helping her to become aware of and acknowledge her sadness and depression, then teaching her the skills to resolve her depression and feel better. This involved the following five steps of MRT:

Step 1. Understanding mood regulation and the MRT process: The first step was helping Catherine identify her feelings and mood state and then understand how her mood became dysregulated. The next step was to learn how the dysregulation led to depression and the accompanying physiological changes such as sleep disturbance, low energy level, and poor concentration. She started measuring her mood and charting it on a daily basis.

Step 2. Biological strategies: Catherine was started on the antidepressant Effexor, to which she responded very well as shown by improvement in her sleep pattern, energy level, and appetite. The antidepressant also helped to reduce her anxiety level and to improve her concentration and attention. Other biological interventions included education regarding her diet to ensure that she had three healthy and balanced meals each day. To motivate her, her husband started an exercise program with her where they went on one-hour walks every other day.

Step 3. Cognitive strategies: Through the re-thinking exercises, Catherine worked on developing skills to identify and correct her negative thoughts. She examined the basic assumptions behind these thoughts and identified the distortions in them. Her biggest distortion was that her mother had abandoned her and didn't care about her. She was able to challenge that negative thought and develop new corrective counterthoughts, which changed her outlook and mood. That also allowed her to get in touch with the underlying anger she had but was unable to express about her mother's departure. As the negative thoughts became apparent to her and she challenged and corrected them, her mood brightened and she felt how much control she had over her mood state via her thinking patterns.

Step 4. Social strategies: Interpersonal psychotherapy helped Catherine to deal with the loss of her mother by helping her to go through the grief process and talk about the loss, its effect on her, and how to let go of her mother. She joined a grief group and developed new supports that understood what she was experiencing and helped her grieve her loss. As she did that, Catherine was able to gradually end the grieving process and form new attachments with other people in her community. She also met an elderly lady in her neighborhood who lived alone and needed the attention and caring of a friend, and Catherine was there to help her and offer her caring friendship.

Step 5. Spiritual strategies: Spiritually Catherine got help from her pastor, who prayed with her and gave her comforting verses from the scriptures to read. He helped her to see the continuity of life and afterlife, which was part of her religious belief system. Praying and attending church proved most valuable in helping her to let go of her mother and deepen her faith while feeling that she was still connected with her mom spiritually.

Outcome: All of these changes helped to stabilize and regulate Catherine's mood. Gradually over the following months Catherine's depression lifted; she was feeling terrific and was able to resume her functioning at home, work, and socially at a level even better than that prior to her mother's death. After a period of ten months, she was able to discontinue the medication. She showed great growth and ability to learn and grow through this process.

Brian

Background: Brian was a 35-year-old computer engineer who remembered feeling depressed "all my life." His parents divorced when he was eight years old and he lived with his mother after that. He stated, "She was always busy and never there for me." He described feelings of "emptiness, loneliness, and depression" throughout his adolescence and adult life. He had difficulties in trusting people or forming relationships and had difficulties with his self-confidence and self-esteem. In his adult life, he started having weight problems. The only solace he got was from food, and he stated, "The only way I can deal with emotions is by bingeing." He lived alone and spent most of his weekends watching television or reading at home or at neighborhood libraries.

He went to therapy with several therapists and found that, even though he felt better temporarily at the outset of therapy, his depression later deepened as he started talking about his problems and loneliness. He had a sense of shame for feeling that way.

Physically, in addition to his increase in weight, Brian had difficulty sleeping, experienced nightmares, and woke up at 5 a.m. every day. He complained of a low energy level and poor motivation. At work he frequently made mistakes and had problems focusing his attention. He had periods of anxiety where he became overwhelmed in meetings and had to leave. The pervasive emotions he felt were loneliness and fear. He felt that he would be stuck in this depression for the rest of his life and nobody would be able to get him out of it because nobody understood what he was going through.

Discussion: Brian presented with a long history of a dysregulated mood, as noted by his depression. The depression affected his biological, social, and psychological functioning. A major part of his depression stemmed from developmental problems while growing up, the abandonment by his parents, and learned helplessness. He had an overriding sense of failure, low self-esteem, and poor self-confidence. This type of depression is called a dysthymic disorder (dysthymia). In addition, he had clinical depression (also called major depressive disorder) as exemplified by his symptoms, which exacerbated his long-standing dysthymia.

Treatment plan: The treatment was focused on helping Brian to identify the causes of his dysregulated mood so he could learn the skills necessary to attend to them. MRT strategies were used to teach Brian how to be attentive of his mood states and how to use each of the four strategies to regulate his mood and feel better.

Step 1. Understanding mood regulation and the MRT process: Brian was educated on the basics of mood regulation therapy and the relationship between mood regulation and mood dysregulation. He was taught how to be aware of his mood at all times and how to rate it, track it, and note any shifts in his mood. He learned the determinants of mood, which include the biological, cognitive, social, and spiritual dimensions, and was taught the strategies of how to use them and feel terrific.

Step 2. Biological strategies: Brian was introduced to a nutritionist who taught him how to make healthy diet selections, which included reducing the fat and carbohydrate content of his meals, watching his caloric intake, and eating three balanced meals a day. He initially had difficulty dealing with the diet, but once he became involved in regulating his food and saw results with his weight dropping, his motivation improved drastically and his self-esteem started improving. He was also started on an antidepressant, which helped to improve his sleep, energy level, and concentration.

Step 3. Cognitive strategies: The re-thinking process helped Brian identify his negative thoughts and learn how to challenge them and correct them appropriately. His basic negative assumption was that "I am a very boring and stupid person. No one would ever want to be my friend." He was able to work on challenging that distorted thought and develop several corrective thoughts like, "I am a good person, and I can contribute positively to a relationship in several areas." He was also taught how to refocus his attention when he felt very depressed or anxious, especially at times when he was hungry and felt like binge eating. He developed a list of people to call or activities to do that would shift his attention at such times, which proved most helpful in giving him control over his mood.

Step 4. Social strategies: Brian started attending group therapy and joined a group of men and woman dealing with relationship issues. The group members helped him learn new interpersonal skills, and he started to overcome his shyness through his active participation in group discussions. He learned new communication skills and practiced them in the group setting, and he was delighted by his ability to relate and communicate effectively with others. He found out that people liked him when they got to know him, which helped reduce his interpersonal vulnerabilities and false assumptions and improve his self-esteem.

Step 5. Spiritual strategies: Brian believed that his life was meaningless and that he had no purpose to be alive. He was encouraged to reconnect with his church and pastor. He found that his pastor and the church members were delighted to hear from him and invited him to social and religious functions. His pastor helped him discover and define his faith beliefs, and he joined a Bible study group. Over time he discovered that he could derive meaning in life through helping others who have been through depression like him. His mission was to help others get out of the deep throes of depression and darkness that he had known so well for most of his life. He started a self-help group for people who were depressed, which became very popular in less than a year. Brian had found a purpose in life, which in turn gave his life meaning, hope, and a great sense of joy.

Outcome: Once Brian started using the MRT strategies, his mood slowly but surely brightened, his depression lifted, and he eventually felt terrific. He developed good and close friendships within the first year and felt himself to be part of society. His self-esteem improved, as did his self-confidence, which helped him to start the self-help group. His mood has remained well regulated and stable since that time and he has not suffered another bout of depression.

Jacqueline
Background: Jacqueline was a 29-year-old woman who came for consultation because she was feeling depressed, down, and blue during the past two years. Her complaint was, "I'm feeling depressed but I have nothing to be depressed about."

She noted that she would wake up in the morning unable to face the day, feeling that she would rather pull the covers over her head than get out of bed.

She had been married within the last two years to a man who was most supportive. She had a good job working at a newspaper and had a lot of friends and a supportive family. Even though she convinced herself that there was nothing for her to be depressed about, she noticed that as time went on she was sinking lower and lower into an abyss. She was preoccupied with negative thoughts, and she felt hopeless and pessimistic about the future. She was irritable and would get into fights with her husband about small matters. At one point, after an argument with her husband, she took an overdose of sleeping pills and was taken to the emergency room for treatment.

Her mood continued to deteriorate, and she felt that her existence was meaningless. She started seeing a therapist, and her primary care doctor put her on an antidepressant medication. When she felt no improvement in three weeks, she stopped the therapy and medication. As her depression continued to worsen, her energy level became low, her concentration poor, and she felt that she was in a fog most of the day. She felt like she was a "slug" and could take a nap at any time. She had intermittent suicidal thoughts, where she thought that the only relief she could have was by dying, even though she did not have any active suicidal plan. She felt ashamed and guilty for feeling this way because she had a good husband, a supportive family, and a good job but was still feeling depressed. She felt that nobody could understand her pain and suffering and what she was going through.

Discussion: Jacqueline had a dysregulation in her mood that started gradually two years earlier and led to her clinical depression. The depression was characterized by changes in many areas in her life—for example, her physical symptoms (sleep pattern and energy level), difficulty with her cognitive processes (attention, concentration, and memory changes), socially in her relationships, and the loss of meaning in her life and her thoughts about wanting to die. Attempts at treatment by simply giving her medications or talking with her about her past issues did not seem to resolve any of her depression.

Treatment plan: Our treatment plan focused on regulating her mood rather than treating her symptoms by addressing the four strategies and axis of the MRT perspective.

Step 1. Understanding mood regulation and the MRT process: Jacqueline was educated on the process of MRT, how moods are normally regulated, how they get dysregulated, and how depression sets in. She was taught how to be aware of her moods, how to rate and chart them, and to be aware when her mood shifted downwards. She was taught how to identify the obvious reasons or stressors that destabilize mood. She was educated on the specific skills and strategies of mood regulation so she could correct her mood and feel better.

Step 2. Biological strategies: Jacqueline was started on an antidepressant, Wellbutrin, and later on a mood stabilizer, Neurontin, to help reduce her anxiety. The combination of the medications reduced her symptoms, which allowed her to work on the other aspects of mood regulation.

Step 3. Cognitive strategies: Jacqueline was taught how to identify her negative thoughts and to examine the underlying assumptions and distortions contributing to her mood dysregulation. Through the re-thinking process, she learned how to identify negative thoughts, challenge them, and correct them appropriately, which helped to give her control over regulating her emotions. She was also taught the skills of refocusing attention, which helped her to divert her attention in moments when she was anxious or feeling down. The sense of control that she developed with these skills made her feel in command of her feelings, and her depression started to lift.

Step 4. Social strategies: Jacqueline examined how the close relationships in her life affected her mood and, in return, how her negative mood was affecting these relationships. She clarified her expectations in her relationships with her husband and parents and learned communication skills that helped her to discuss her expectations with them. With that, she felt her husband and family were starting to understand her, and she felt their understanding, caring, and support. That helped her mood tremendously, as she was now able to talk to the key people in her life about her feelings and ask for their assistance when she felt down.

Step 5. Spiritual strategies: Through spiritual counseling Jacqueline was able to examine issues of faith, religion, and the meaning of her life. From that perspective she started looking at her purpose in life to try to define it. She joined a religious congregation, made connections spiritually, and found a lot of solace in discovering and deepening her faith. She found that she had a greater purpose in being able to help and serve others. In helping others she felt good and she felt that she was doing something purposeful. She joined a group that went to orphanages on weekends, and she later adopted one of the children from the orphanage. Her life had become meaningful; in giving, she was able to receive much more.

Outcome: Several months after Jacqueline started with the MRT plan, her mood turned around drastically and she was feeling terrific. She was able to use the strategies to regulate her mood on her own, and she became fully aware that, when her mood became depressed, she had a strategy to correct it and maintain the feeling-terrific state.

Margaret

Background: Margaret was a 38-year-old single woman who presented with a main complaint of "I'm feeling hopeless, and I have fantasies of driving my car over a cliff and ending it all." Margaret stated that she had been feeling depressed "all my life."

She grew up in a family that was very chaotic. Her father was an alcoholic who was unavailable and unable to support the family. Her mother had great difficulty raising Margaret and her two siblings. There was a lot of physical abuse in the family; when the father got drunk, he lost control and struck the children and mother viciously. Their life was very unstable due to evictions and constant relocations from one residence to another.

Margaret remembered feeling depressed since she was a child and described how she would stay awake at night, staring at the ceiling and wishing she would disappear and not be alive in the morning. Throughout her adolescence that depression continued, which led to difficulties in school. At age 18 she left home and started working in nurseries; she changed jobs eight times in ten years. She had great difficulty in relationships with friends and had difficulty keeping friends. Most of the time she felt that she was different from others and that nobody wanted to be her friend. Her self-esteem was very low; she felt that she was ugly. She felt that, no matter what she did, she was going to fail at it and that everybody could see what a loser she was. She had ongoing suicidal thoughts, even though she never actually hurt herself. Physically she complained of a low energy level, sleeping a lot, poor concentration, and low motivation.

Margaret had been in therapy for the last ten years, moving from one therapist to another and feeling that her therapists did not care for her and were not interested in helping or were unable to help her. She thought that nobody was able to feel the pain that she was feeling and that she was meant to stay miserable. Her mood was depressed most of the time. She saw her life through a dark lens, feeling hopeless and helpless most of the time. Even when she got a promotion at work, she could not accept the compliment and thought that people were trying to boost her morale and make her feel better. She had great difficulty in expressing her feelings and expressing her needs to others and felt very uncomfortable socializing with others.

Discussion: Margaret presented with a long-term depression that had colored all of her life, affecting her attitude, judgment, and decisions. She came from a disturbed family background, where she was deprived of the natural caring, nurturing, and affection a child should normally have. Her role models had major psychological and behavioral problems, with her father addicted to alcohol and her mother abused and emotionally unavailable. Margaret's mood was dysregulated, leading to the depression that affected her thinking, emotions, and behavior. Her depression was chronic, and even though she had attempted several talk therapies, she would only feel better afterwards for a brief period of time. Her primary depression type was a depressive personality and to a lesser extent she also had symptoms of a clinical depression, as well.

Treatment plan: The goal of treatment was to teach Margaret how to regulate her mood by learning about the multiple domains of MRT and the mood-regulating strategies. Her MRT plan was:

Step 1. Understanding mood regulation and the MRT process: Margaret was educated on the principles of mood regulation and dysregulation. She was educated on the normal stages of mood regulation and in this context she learned how her mood became dysregulated in childhood. She was educated on the types of depression that she had and the approaches to treatment through MRT strategies. She was introduced to the Daily Mood Scale, and she learned how to rate and monitor fluctuations in her mood.

Step 2. Biological strategies: Given the fact that Margaret had difficulties with her energy level, concentration, and sleep, she was started on the antidepressant Lexapro, which proved most helpful in improving her energy level, concentration, and mood. She was also started on an exercise program with a personal trainer in the gym for four days each week. She also joined a walking group that walked every weekend by the beach, where she met people and started socializing with them.

Step 3. Cognitive strategies: By developing re-thinking skills, Margaret learned how to identify her negative and distorted thoughts. She challenged her underlying assumptions that she was "no good" and that nobody wanted to deal with her. In challenging her thoughts and changing them, her feelings changed and she started feeling better. She was also taught how to utilize the technique of refocusing attention so that, when she was feeling down, she could change that mood state.

Step 4. Social strategies: Through interpersonal psychotherapy Margaret learned skills to help her relate to people, communicate with them, and clearly express her needs to others. She also learned how to be aware of her expectations from others in relationships and how to express these expectations. She joined a relationship therapy group, which helped her exercise and use these newly learned tools and get feedback from others in a safe setting. As her relationship skills improved, her self-confidence increased, and she started going on dates and making friends. The newfound friendships pulled her away from her isolation and loneliness, and she experienced the joy of having people in her life who cared about her.

Step 5. Spiritual strategies: Margaret started a spiritual counseling program with her pastor, who proved very understanding of her depression and predicaments. She joined a church group and started attending Bible study on a weekly basis, which gave her a sense of belonging and started her spiritual education process. In developing her faith she was able to look beyond her troubles and find meaning in her suffering and her newly found recovery. Discovering the spiritual dimension of her life gave her a lot of solace and comfort and became the leading force in her recovery and feeling terrific. Margaret became a very active member of her church and started a spiritual support group for anyone suffering or in pain, and she became an accomplished speaker and educator in the field.

Outcome: Within a few months after starting MRT, Margaret's mood brightened, and she felt joy in most of what she did. Margaret developed the ability to be aware of her mood at any time and to use mood regulation strategies whenever she felt that her mood was shifting downward. She developed mastery of all the mood-regulating strategies, and the growth she accomplished in her spiritual dimension opened a whole new life and opportunities for her. She was able to feel terrific and then give that gift to others. She discontinued the medication one year after she started it. She has not had a bout of depression since.

Mary

Background: Mary was a 40-year-old housewife who started feeling depressed six months before she came for consultation. She had gone through several losses in the prior three years and was feeling increasingly lonely and depressed the last six months. She had very few friends and supports in her life.

Mary had separated from her husband after a twenty-year marriage. He had left her for someone else. She was caring for her two young children on her own. She felt abandoned and overwhelmed, and stated, "I'm feeling very hopeless and helpless. I don't know how I can go on." She had to give up the house she had lived in for eighteen years and move to an apartment with her children. The move and the separation were followed by her having to get a new job and having to separate from the few friends she had at work.

Her life seemed to have changed in a sudden, drastic, and irreversible way. She felt alone, abandoned by her husband, away from her friends, and overwhelmed by her tasks as a single mother having to start over again on her own. She felt depressed and unhappy. She stated, "Most of my thoughts center on what a failure I am and how I can't do anything right. I must have screwed up this marriage." She dreaded facing each day and felt her existence was meaningless.

Physically Mary lost her appetite for food and lost fifteen pounds in three weeks. She was not sleeping well and woke up every morning before dawn, unable to go back to sleep. She felt irritable and easily annoyed with her children and screamed at them several times a day. She lost interest in her usual hobbies (gardening and reading). She felt isolated and stuck, cut off from the world around her. She felt that no one understood what she was going through and nobody empathized with her. The few friends and family members that she had stayed in contact with told her to "pull yourself up by the bootstraps and move on." That was the best advice they could give her; they had no other solutions or words of wisdom. Whenever she told them how she felt, they dismissed her feelings, which left her with a sense of being invalidated and unheard, which made her feel even worse. She regretted reaching out and asking for support. It seemed that nobody understood her predicament. Mary's mood continued to deteriorate until she had difficulty going to work. She went to see her general practitioner, who referred her for psychiatric consultation.

Discussion: Mary presented with a dysregulated mood state as evidenced by her clinical depression, reactive depression, and the marked changes in her mood state. Her mood dysregulation led to interruptions of normal function in several areas: biologically, as evidenced by the changes in her appetite, weight, sleep, and energy level; cognitively, with changes in her negative thinking pattern and in her emotions; and socially, as she became isolated and disconnected from people, she felt her life was meaningless and felt hopeless, helpless, abandoned, and angry. Mary became very isolated and depressed and was spiraling downward.

Treatment plan: The treatment plan focused on helping Mary to master the mood-regulating strategies to help her gain control over her mood and feel terrific.

Step 1. Understanding mood regulation and the MRT process: We concentrated on education so that Mary could understand the nature of her depression and the principles of mood regulation and dysregulation. She was taught how to rate and chart her moods and how to be aware of what influences them positively or negatively. The goal was to attain a stable mood state that she could regulate in order to feel terrific.

Step 2. Biological strategies: Mary was started on an antidepressant medication, Zoloft, to help her regulate her symptoms of clinical depression, primarily by improving her sleep cycle, energy level, appetite, and mood. She also started on an exercise program, walking two miles a day with a friend in the morning, which helped improve her energy level for the day.

Step 3. Cognitive strategies: Using the re-thinking process, Mary learned how to identify her negative distorted thoughts, which centered on "I am a failure. I am ugly. No one wants me." She learned how to examine the beliefs behind these thoughts, find the errors in them, and correct them. She found that through her distorted thinking she had blamed herself completely for the divorce and for being the cause of her husband leaving her. As she was able to correct her thoughts, she developed new thoughts, such as "Even though my marriage failed, I am not a failure." Her negative thinking slowly decreased as she learned how to change it, and her depression started lifting.

Step 4. Social strategies: Interpersonal psychotherapy helped Mary examine her role in the marriage, what went wrong, why it ended, and how to let go of the marriage, move on, and make other connections. It also helped her to learn new skills for building healthy friendships and making choices according to her needs and others' needs. She joined a divorce recovery group, which helped her heal her wounds faster and acquire new coping skills to deal with the divorce. Her network of friends and supports increased, and she no longer felt alone or isolated.

Step 5. Spiritual strategies: After her divorce, Mary felt disconnected from everything around her and felt she had no purpose in life. Through spiritual counseling, she developed her faith and found a new and comforting connection with her relationship with God. Prayer gave her a lot of solace and took all her loneliness away. She joined a local religious congregation, where she was accepted and adopted into that community. Within a short period of time she had a number of supportive people who were calling on her and inviting her to join them in their spiritual activities. That helped her tremendously in being able to feel like part of the community, and she shared with them the close ties of faith.

Outcome: Within a few months, Mary was able to have her mood well regulated and to feel terrific. Not only was she able to have such a great outcome, but she was remarried to a wonderful gentleman from her congregation within eighteen months from the start of treatment. She has not had a bout of depression since her treatment twelve years ago.

George

Background: George is a 56-year-old chief executive officer of a business company. He worked for the company for the last twenty-two years and moved up through the ranks to become the CEO. The company had been doing well in the past years, but after George took command, there was a rapid turnover in personnel and the company started losing a lot of its customer base. All the middle and senior managers recognized the problem; it was George. He was overwhelmed by the job and was making one mistake after another. He was unable to make decisions and he obsessed about every detail. He was unable to delegate many of his decisions and did not trust his senior officers. He felt anxious and irritable and moody most of the day, and people were scared to point out his shortcomings to him or ask him if he was having any difficulties or needed help.

His mood changed and he felt depressed. He had difficulty sleeping and was waking up in the middle of the night, feeling anxious and unable to go back to sleep easily. His energy level dropped, and his concentration was poor. He was preoccupied with negative thoughts and fears that he was going to run the company into the ground and that he could not do anything to stop it.

George was feeling very depressed and thought that nothing was going well in his life. He felt alone, with no supports, and very lonely. His primary focus was on turning the business around and being successful again, as he used to be. In evaluating his role at work, it became clear that George made all his business and managerial decisions based only on his subjective and often distorted perceptions of facts and reality and not on the objective reality of the work place. He reacted to what he perceived was happening and not to what was actually going on.

His subjective version of reality was colored by his fears ("Everybody wants my job, they are waiting for me to fail"); by his distortions ("Once you are at the top you can't trust anybody, I'm all alone, I have no friends anymore"); and by his insecurities ("I don't really think I can do this job; what if they find out I'm incompetent?"). This change in his behavior occurred six months after he took over the job of CEO. The company was going through a cyclically low time in sales. This happened every year during that season. However, George did not pay attention to the seasonal factor. He was focused on the fact that the company was not doing well and that the board of directors would expect of him, as a new leader, to show charisma and do something drastic. If he did nothing to turn the company around, then the board might think he was inept and unfit for the job. He obsessed for days on what to do, and when he felt time was running out, he panicked. Against the advice of his senior officers, he abruptly cancelled some product lines and fired two managers. He was responding only to his fears and distorted internal reality.

As his depression worsened, his thoughts became disconnected from reality and from the people around him. His judgment became poor. He was making irrational decisions, and he was not aware of what he was doing since he was out of touch with reality. He became isolated, suspicious, and paranoid in his thinking. He thought that people had bugged his office, home, and car, and wanted to poison him. He refused to talk on the phone because he thought it was tapped. Feeling desperate and trapped and with no way out, George tried to end his life by shooting himself in the abdomen. Fortunately he was saved by his neighbor.

Discussion: George presented with a dysregulated mood state, which is evidenced by the psychotic depression. This is a serious and life-threatening type of depression. His paranoid thinking and loss of touch with reality are characteristic of psychotic symptoms. George was depressed and ruminative, obsessing on his failures and negative thoughts. Untreated, his depression worsened till he hit bottom and attempted suicide.

George was having difficulty in regulating his mood for a long time before his suicide attempt, but he and others around him ignored it. The dysregulation in mood was evidenced by the negative changes of his mood, the physical symptoms of depression, and his negative thoughts and feelings. This dysregulation affected his functioning at work and outside of work, which led him to spiral downward.

Treatment plan: George's treatment plan focused on treating the psychotic symptoms, keeping him safe, and resolving his depression. He was hospitalized for seven days, where the treatment was started in a safe setting. After his psychotic symptoms cleared, the focus was in helping him regulate his mood and feel terrific. His treatment plan was comprised of the following steps:

Step 1. Understanding mood regulation and the MRT process: After the psychotic symptoms cleared (within five days), George was educated about depression, mood regulation, and dysregulation. He was taught how to identify and rate his mood and how to chart it to note any changes.

Step 2. Biological strategies: George was first started on the antipsychotic medication Zyprexa, which helped control his psychotic symptoms. He then was started on an antidepressant, Prozac, which helped lift his depression, treat the physical symptoms of depression, and control his obsessions. He became in touch with reality, and the paranoid and suspicious ideations stopped after the medications were started.

Step 3. Cognitive strategies: George's negative thinking was addressed with re-thinking skills and exercises, which helped him to identify his negative thoughts and challenge them in a corrective way. This helped him start facing his negative thoughts and distortions and to pay attention to facts. For instance, he was able to see that the shift in the company's performance for the last two months was due to a seasonal effect and not due to his leadership. His ability to recognize his negative thoughts and change them gave him a lot of control. As his mood improved, he started listening to people, became better able to gain their trust, and challenged his distorted thoughts as they occurred.

Step 4. Social strategies: George started learning interpersonal psychotherapy skills that helped him understand how he relates to others and how he gets into difficulties in relationships. The focus was on helping George to begin to understand how his relationship with people affects his mood directly, and how after every interaction he has with people, there may be a shift in his mood, positively or negatively. George worked on his communication skills, which helped him express his needs and thoughts to others without feeling threatened or vulnerable. This got him out of the isolation he was living in, and he started building a support system around him, slowly but surely.

Step 5. Spiritual strategies: George had very few supports and felt very detached and alone. He had many fears, which were related to his own sense of mortality. He was feeling all alone. Through spiritual counseling, George was able to start looking beyond himself and to a higher power. He found comfort in praying and reading a holy text and felt it gave him a lot of strength. It also gave his experience meaning, in that he saw his suffering a turning point in his life to help him find his faith and spirituality and live through them. George got very involved in his religious organization, where he became involved in many activities and later chaired many of their committees and functions.

Outcome: After a few months George's mood stabilized and he was feeling terrific. He was able to make major changes in his life. As soon as his mood improved and he had learned skills to deal with people and challenge negative thoughts, he made a remarkable turnaround. He returned to his job, explained to them what he had learned while he was in treatment, and was able to win the confidence of his team and felt connected with them.

George was able to overcome his depression, and he reached a point where he was feeling terrific. He learned how to maintain his mood in that feeling-terrific state. George found his experience with depression to be a life-changing event, having discovered many things about himself—most importantly, his spirituality. He has not had a bout of depression in fourteen years and writes and speaks extensively on his experiences with depression and the feeling-terrific state he has attained.

Samantha

Background: Samantha was a 38-year-old nurse who lived and worked in San Diego. She consulted for the treatment of her depression. When she first came in, she stated, "I am so miserable I can't think. I can't open my eyes in the morning and face another day."

Her depression started a year ago, soon after the youngest of her three children left home to go to college. At the time she attributed her feelings of depression to the separation from the youngest of her children, the last one to leave home, and to empty-nest syndrome. To counter that feeling of sadness, she tried to keep busy by taking golf lessons and art classes. As the months went by, however, her depression got worse. She noticed that she was losing interest in her usual pursuits and hobbies. She had difficulty falling asleep and staying asleep, and was irritable and short-tempered with her coworkers and especially with her husband. Life was not as enjoyable as it used to be.

Samantha had never experienced depressive feelings like this. She used to be an energetic person with a zest for life. She used to get involved in all her children's activities and was head of the PTA. She helped her children with their homework, their sports activities, and planned all the family vacations and trips. She took care of the pets at home, cared for the garden, and her home was always clean and spotless. In addition to this, she went to work as a nurse and was able to keep all those activities and duties well-coordinated.

Her primary role, though, was her role at home. She defined her primary purpose in life as keeping the family happy, and she did that very well. She felt that without her efforts everything at home would come to a stop; she felt that the family needed her. She noted that her main purpose in life was to be mother and wife.

After the children left home, Samantha no longer felt that her life was as purposeful. When she first came to consult, she stated, "I feel empty inside…I feel a big void…Everything I live for in life is purposeless…I need something to feel good about, something to give me meaning, I want to wake with a purpose every day…I need something that I can call mine. I want to fill this void inside."

Samantha noted that, no matter what she tried to do, she felt empty and detached. She did not enjoy seeing her old friends. Most of her thoughts were negative and she was starting to feel very hopeless and helpless. She was even having suicidal thoughts.

Discussion: Samantha was doing well until the youngest of her children went to college. Shortly after that she had a grief reaction marked by feelings of sadness and loss, which were natural to happen. Her sadness and grief, however, slowly progressed into a bout of clinical depression.

Her mood was dysregulated, and this dysregulation caused the depression that affected her biological, cognitive, social, and spiritual domains. Cognitively, she had negative thoughts. Socially, she felt isolated, detached, withdrawn, and unable to connect with people. Spiritually, she felt empty and unable to make connections with her congregation and her pastor, whom she used to be close to.

Treatment plan: The treatment goal focused on teaching her skills so she could regulate her mood and feel terrific. Samantha's treatment plan focused on the following points:

Step 1. Understanding mood regulation and the MRT process: Samantha learned about her grief reaction that had increased and become a clinical depression bout. She was taught the basics of how moods are regulated, what the underpinnings of mood are, how moods are affected and can affect her functioning biologically, cognitively, socially, and spiritually. She was given the Daily Mood Scale and was taught how to rate and monitor her mood on a daily basis.

Step 2. Biological strategies: Since Samantha had put on thirty pounds of weight during the time she was depressed, she was instructed on proper nutrition to help her deal with her weight, which was causing her to feel sluggish and slow. She started seeing a nutritionist and started an exercise and diet management program. Her increased weight had been affecting her self-esteem negatively; the negative feelings abated as she lost weight and stopped her carbohydrate binge eating. Her energy level improved, as did her sleep pattern. She was also started on an antidepressant, Celexa, to help her regulate her mood and help the physical symptoms of the clinical depression.

Step 3. Cognitive strategies: By developing re-thinking skills, Samantha was able to identify her negative distortions and assumptions that centered in the basic thought of "My role in life is over. No one needs me anymore." She examined and challenged those assumptions and found that they were not based on facts, as she had experiences and knowledge that could help many people. Her corrective thoughts were "Even though my role as mother is not needed as it used to be, there are many friends who want to be closer to me and need me. I can now go to school and get my graduate degree that I have been long waiting to do." The control over her negative thinking made her feel much better, as she recognized the power she had over changing her negative thoughts and feeling better.

Step 4. Social strategies: Since one of the biggest losses for Samantha was the feeling of void and emptiness after the children left, she was helped to find a new social role for herself as a person, working adult, and a woman. She reconciled the loss of her day-to-day parenting and homemaker role and started searching for a meaningful role in something that represented the other sides of herself. She also was able to develop close relationships with friends. She was also able to look at how meaning is derived through her work and through her role as a nurse. Samantha was able to deal with her feelings of grief with the loss of her children and the loss of her role and was able to forge a new role. She did this successfully, and as it helped her to be able to form a new definition of herself, her depression lifted and she started feeling much better.

Step 5. Spiritual strategies: Through spiritual counseling Samantha was able to derive meaning by strengthening her faith in God. She became active in her local church and found a lot of comfort and strength in prayer and reading the Bible. She volunteered at an orphanage that the church was helping and was able to contribute in her own way by helping others and caring for them. This was uplifting and contributed to great change in her mood and feeling terrific.

Outcome: Samantha went on to college, got her Ph.D., and became a very successful therapist. She wanted to teach others how to rise from their darkest moments and find within themselves purpose that was enriching and enduring. She learned how to feel terrific through who she is, how she feels, and how she regulated her mood, not simply through what she does. Samantha has not had an episode of depression in the last eleven years.

CHAPTER 9
Integration

This book has addressed three questions:
- What is depression or the depressions?
- Why do we get depressed?
- How do we beat depression and feel terrific?

The underpinnings of depression start with understanding the principles of mood regulation. Mood regulation is a neurobiologically mediated function that is influenced by biological, cognitive, social, and spiritual events in our life. For instance, inadequate parenting or traumatic experiences can be disruptive to the process of mood regulation and lead to anxiety and depression. Any disruption in the mood regulatory functions leads to abnormal or deficient emotional responses, such as a sad mood, withdrawal, and negative thinking as seen in depression.

The whole concept of mood regulation as we have described it is based on an imbalance within one or more of the four dimensions. These dimensions—biological, cognitive, social, and spiritual—form the foundation for the functioning of the person or self. These dimensions of the self are not independent of each other. What happens in one area affects the others directly or indirectly. Each dimension also has a range of function—from healthy to unhealthy. The influence and interactions of these dimensions are the processes that bring about mood stabilization and regulation through their direct and indirect effects on the mood-regulating network (Torres 2001). Feeling terrific is the state where all four processes are functioning in optimal fashion and within the healthy range, leading to a stable and well-regulated mood.

Even though each of the four interlocking dimensions must be understood individually, when treating depression there is no actual separation between working on all four of them; the depressed person works on them simultaneously and collectively. The lines of separation are theoretical; such a framework should occur only in our methods of explanation. In the real treatment setting, no such boundaries occur.

Depression is caused by dysregulation or disruption in the normal mood regulatory processes. Mood dysregulation can occur from an internal malfunction, as in a chemical imbalance, or in response to external stimuli—for example, hearing bad news—that results in depression.

The disruption caused by depression represents an opportunity to look within and make changes and feel terrific. By examining our depression, we come to understand the mind-body-spirit axis, as any one of those areas can be an entry port for intervention, change, and recovery. Making the appropriate interventions with the strategies outlined in this book leads to mood regulation and feeling terrific.

We emphasize in our work with people who are depressed that depression serves an information function, as a cue for action, notifying the individual of the need for change. Dr. Wong wrote, "It is through suffering that many have found enduring happiness and become fully alive. It is through weakness and losses that many have discovered their true identity and authenticity. Stars shine most brightly in the darkest night."

The important point is that depression is not a single entity but rather a broad spectrum of mood-dysregulated conditions, which is why we refer to them as "the depressions." Each condition differs from the other in severity more than in kind. The exception is the psychotic depressions, which are qualitatively different through the experience of psychotic symptoms. The common denominator to all the depressions is mood dysregulation, which is why mood regulation therapy (MRT) can be effective for all kinds of depressions. By focusing on the core and central deficits that occur in depression, effective management and treatment occur. The core deficit is a failure in mood regulation. This central and global deficit in mood regulation is the hallmark of depression and leads to characteristic changes seen in depression, such as changes in mood, thoughts, behavior, and other symptoms.

Once viewed from a mood regulation perspective, the depression isn't seen as caused distinctly by a "distorted thought," "relational deficit," "chemical imbalance," or "defense against repressed anger," but that all of these phenomena can be contributing in part or whole, or in conjunction with one another, to mood dysregulation.

Mood regulatory processes are varied and are always at work trying to keep the mood well regulated and balanced. When there is failure in maintaining regulation, depression sets in. Accordingly, mood dysregulation is the essential and dominant feature of depression that needs to be understood and focused on to recover and feel terrific.

Depression is rarely unilateral in its origin. A person gets depressed when multiple layers of the biological, cognitive, social, and spiritual dimensions start failing and the person can no longer compensate to regulate his or her mood. For instance, a negative distorted thought alone will not cause depression, but in combination with poor relationships, lack of support, loss of a relationship, and/or a biological hereditary tendency for depression, one may get depressed. It is the failure of the ability to regulate mood through all available primary and compensatory mechanisms or strategies that leads to depression.

Why is it that important? Because in the process of mood regulation therapy, we attempt to "build back" these layers while focusing on and monitoring not simply the symptoms of depression but how well the mood is regulated, and how to keep it regulated, and by monitoring the mood regulation by using the Daily Mood Scale.

Feeling terrific is an endpoint we seek in treatment with MRT by working with both the parts and the whole. This means that we move from the part or small picture of feeling depressed to the whole or the big picture of mood regulation and the four dimensions, and then we go to each of the specific parts to work on each dimension individually. This, in our experience, produces a lasting "feeling-terrific" mood state and not simply the reduction of symptoms of depression. Feeling terrific means that the person feels whole, with no residual symptoms or disabilities and a good ability to function socially and at work. It also entails acquiring a reserve of hardiness and resilience and developing a sense of coherence in one's life. In feeling terrific, you will appreciate all dimensions of yourself as you experience and grow in all four areas.

MRT offers interactive levels of therapeutic integration from the cell to the soul. MRT is not the summation of several therapies but an integration and harmonization of the modalities of therapies that have been specifically targeted for the treatment of depression and have been validated by research for their efficacy and success. Through mood regulation, the four approaches gain meaning in their connectedness as they influence and change mood from a dysregulated to a well-regulated state.

Mood regulation therapy is not a new technique for the treatment of depression; rather, it is a new perspective that encompasses proven theories and modalities for the understanding and treatment of depression. The importance of the mood regulation process has recently been recognized and considered by some researchers in the field to be "a fundamental mechanism of all psychiatric disorders" (Schore 2002). The strategies that are used in MRT have been validated by research for their efficacy. The MRT perspective focuses on these elements:

- Understanding depression as a disorder of mood regulation caused by dysregulation in the mood center. This necessitates the understanding of the physiology and neurobiology of mood regulation, circadian rhythms, and all influences on the mood-regulating center.

- The focus of treatment is not merely the reduction of symptoms but the restoration of mood to a well-regulated state.
- Knowing well the parameters of mood regulation, which are the biological, cognitive, social, and spiritual processes, and their effect on mood.
- Understanding the processes and their impact on the mood center leads to understanding the strategies, which increases the therapeutic modalities available to the clinician or therapist.
- MRT is outcome focused and no person is considered recovered until the endpoint of feeling terrific is attained and all dimensions are stable.
- MRT is quantitative in its approach to treatment and uses therapeutic measuring tools for all stages of depression and its treatment.
- MRT offers several therapeutic options and thus opens up more options to the person who may refuse, for instance, to take medications but may be willing to utilize other strategies or use other modalities.
- MRT broadens the therapeutic perspective and knowledge base to see depression from a wide angle. In that venue, MRT formulates depression as not being merely the result of "a bad thought" or a "sour relationship" but a multi-factorial end stage of several processes gone awry.
- MRT seeks to demonstrate that the understanding of the causes and treatment of depression is not about isolated domains of knowledge. Rather, it concerns conceptualization and problem solving that comes from understanding the linkages among the various disciplines.
- The MRT perspective links the body, brain, soul, and mind into an understandable and working format that is theoretically explainable and practically applicable in clinical practice. In our experience, it is very effective and leads to excellent results as evidenced by the recovery rates in persons we have treated over the last twenty-five years.

We have tried to show in this book that there are two sides to depression. One is the dark, negative side marked by anguish, despair, confusion, hopelessness, and physical, emotional, and spiritual pain. The other side is a bright positive side with joy, contentment, coherence, and hope. MRT is a path that takes you to the bright side, where you may find your full potential and happiness. Every dark shadow has its brighter side. Depression seen in that context may be seen as an opportunity to change, break free, and feel terrific. Feeling terrific may be the best mood state that you've ever experienced. We want you to experience it, embrace it, and know that you have the ability to maintain it for as long as you wish.

APPENDIX

On the following pages are extra copies of the Depression Questionnaire, Daily Mood Graph, Daily Mood Strategies Inventory, and Daily Mood Strategies Profile. These are provided for the convenience of the reader who may be using these tools over an extended period of time.

		NOT AT ALL	MINIMALLY	MILDLY	MODERATELY	SEVERELY	EXTREMELY SO
1.	I feel sad, blue, down, or depressed.	0	1	2	3	4	5
2.	I believe I am a failure.	0	1	2	3	4	5
3.	I feel hopeless about the future.	0	1	2	3	4	5
4.	I do not enjoy the things I used to enjoy.	0	1	2	3	4	5
5.	I feel guilty.	0	1	2	3	4	5
6.	I feel dissatisfied.	0	1	2	3	4	5
7.	I have lost interest in people and in my surroundings.	0	1	2	3	4	5
8.	I have trouble with my sleep.	0	1	2	3	4	5
9.	My energy level has decreased.	0	1	2	3	4	5
10.	I am hard on myself.	0	1	2	3	4	5
11.	I break into tears easily.	0	1	2	3	4	5
12.	My interest in sex has decreased.	0	1	2	3	4	5
13.	I have difficulty concentrating.	0	1	2	3	4	5
14.	I have difficulty making decisions.	0	1	2	3	4	5
15.	I am more irritable than usual.	0	1	2	3	4	5
16.	I have difficulty getting started on a task.	0	1	2	3	4	5
17.	I feel physically tired.	0	1	2	3	4	5
18.	I have experienced an increase or decrease in my appetite.	0	1	2	3	4	5
19.	I have trouble with my memory.	0	1	2	3	4	5
20.	I am worried about my health.	0	1	2	3	4	5

Add the numbers you have circled for each of the 20 questions.

TOTAL: _____

FIGURE 25. THE DEPRESSION QUESTIONNAIRE

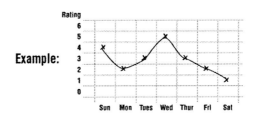

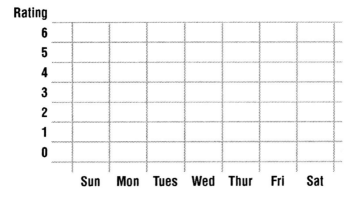

FIGURE 26. DAILY MOOD GRAPH

In front of each mood regulation strategy below, write the letter that indicates the frequency with which you use it when you are depressed. **I** - *Infrequently;* **S** - *Sometimes;* **F** - *Frequently*

A. Biological
___ Rest, take a nap, close your eyes, sleep
___ Take a bath or shower, Jacuzzi, splash water on your face
___ Eat something
___ Exercise/participate in sports activities
___ Have sex
___ Smoke cigarettes/drink coffee
___ Drink alcohol
___ Take drugs or medication

B. Cognitive
___ Evaluate the situation
___ Try to put feelings into perspective
___ Control your thoughts (calm yourself or try to not think about it)
___ Reframe the way you view the situation
___ Tend to chores (housework, homework, gardening, etc.)
___ Engage in hobby
___ Engage in stress management activities (organizing, planning)
___ Read or write

C. Social
___ Be with family
___ Talk it out with someone
___ Spend time with friends
___ Play with a pet
___ Go to a support group
___ Engage in activity with friend (go for a walk)
___ Go to a public place (coffee shop, mall)
___ Chat on the Internet

FIGURE 27-1. MOOD REGULATION STRATEGIES INVENTORY (CONTINUED ON NEXT PAGE)

D. Spiritual
___ Pray
___ Meditate
___ Talk to spiritual advisor
___ Read spiritual literature (Bible, Koran, Torah, Kabbalah)
___ Engage in a spiritual/religious activity
___ Rituals (fasting, chanting, etc.)
___ Go to church, mosque, or temple services
___ Listen to inspirational speakers/tapes

Write the total number of strategies that you marked in each group in the blanks below.

A. Biological _____   **C. Social** _____
B. Cognitive _____   **D. Spiritual** _____

FIGURE 27-2. MOOD REGULATION STRATEGIES INVENTORY (CONTINUED FROM PREVIOUS PAGE)

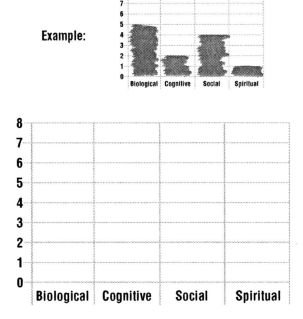

FIGURE 28. MOOD REGULATION STRATEGIES PROFILE

REFERENCES CITED

Angst, J. and K. Merikangas. 1997. The depressive spectrum: Diagnostic classification and course. *Journal of Affective Disorders* 45:31-40.

Artal, M. and C. Sherman. 1998. Exercise against depression. *The Physician and Sportsmedicine* 26(10):55-60.

Aspinwall, L.G. 1998. Rethinking the role of positive affect in self regulation. *Motivation and Emotion* 22:1-32.

Barrett, K.C. and M.E. Lamb. 1983. Socioemotional development. In *Handbook of Child Psychology*. Volume 2. Edited by M. Haith and J.J. Campos. New York: Wiley Publishing.

Beck, Aaron T. and R.R. Greenberg. 1974. *Coping with Depression (A Booklet)*. New York: Institute for Rational Living.

Beck, Aaron T., John Rush, Brian Shaw, and Gary Emery. 1979. *Cognitive Therapy of Depression*. New York: Guilford Press.

Borg, J., A. Bengt, H. Soderstrom and L. Farde. 2003. The serotonin system and spiritual experiences. *The American Journal of Psychiatry* 160:1965-1969.

Bouchard, T.J. Jr. and M. McGue. 2003. Genetic and environmental influences on human psychological differences. *Journal of Neurobiology* 54(1):4-45.

Bouchard, T.J. Jr., M. McGue, D. Lykken, and A. Tellegren. 1999. Intrinsic and extrinsic religiousness: Genetic and environmental influences and personality correlates. *Twin Research* 2(2):88-98.

Bouchard, T.J. Jr., D.T. Lykken, M. McGue, and N.L. Segal. 1990. Sources of human psychological differences: The Minnesota study of twins reared apart. *Science* 250:223-228.

Bower, Gordon H. 1994. Monograph based on a speech delivered at the Capitol Hill Science Seminar sponsored by the Federation of Behavioral, Psychological, and Cognitive Sciences.

Bowlby, John. 1969. *Attachment and Loss, Volume 1: Attachment*. United States: Basic Books.

———. 1980. *Attachment and Loss, Volume 3: Loss*. United States: Basic Books.

———. 1998. *Secure Base*. United States: Basic Books.

Bradburn, N.M. 1977. The measurement of psychological well-being. In *Health Goals and Health Indicators*. Edited by J. Elinson et al. Washington, D.C.: Westview Press.

Brown, C.W., T.O. Harris and J.R. Copeland. 1977. Depression and loss. *British Journal of Psychiatry* 130:1-18.

Burns, D.D. 1981. *Feeling Good.* New York: Signet N.A.L. Penguin, Inc.

Byrne, A. and D.G. Byrne. 1993. The effect of exercise on depression, anxiety, and other mood states: A review. *Journal of Psychosomatic Research* 37(6):565-574.

Cahill, L. and B. Prins. 1994. B-Adrenergic activation and memory for emotional events. *Nature* 371:702-704.

Cannon, Walter B. 1932. *The Wisdom of the Body.* New York: W.W. Norton and Co.

Carr, D.B., B.A. Bullen, G.S. Skrinar, M.A. Arnold, M. Rosenblatt, I.Z. Beitins, J.B. Martin, and J.W. McArthur. 1981. Physical conditioning facilitates the exercise-induced secretion of beta-endorphin and beta-lipotropin in women. *New England Journal of Medicine* 305(10):560-563.

Carter, T.M. 1998. The effects of spiritual practices on recovery from substance abuse. *Journal of Psychiatric and Mental Health Nursing* 5:409-413.

Chaouloff, F. 1997. Effects of acute physical exercise on central serotonergic systems. *Medicine and Science in Sports and Exercise* 29(1):58-62.

Ciarrochi, J.V., J.P. Forgas, and J.D. Mayer. 2001. *Emotional Intelligence in Everyday Life.* Philadelphia: Psychology Press.

Cicchetti, D. and D. Tucker. 1994. Development and self-regulatory structures of the mind. *Development and Psychopathology* 6:533-549.

Clore, G.C. 1994. Why emotions are felt. In *The Nature of Emotion*. Edited by P. Ekman and R.J. Davidson. Oxford: Oxford University Press.

Clore, Gerald L. and Karen Gasper. 2000. Feeling is believing: Some affective influences on beliefs. In *Emotions and Beliefs: How Feelings Influence Thoughts*. Cambridge: Cambridge University Press.

Close, R. 2000. Logotherapy and adult major depression: Psychological dimensions in diagnosing the disorder. *Journal of Religious Gerontology* 11(3/4):119-140.

Cohen, Ronald. 1997. Neuropsychiatric aspects of disorders of attention. In *Neuropsychiatry*. Third Edition. Washington, D.C.: APA Press.

Corsini, Raymond J. et al. 1984. *Current Psychotherapies.* Third Edition. Itasca, Ill.: F.E. Peacock Publishers.

Costello, C.G. 1973. Depression: Loss of reinforcers or loss of reinforcer effectiveness. *Behavioral Therapy* 3:240-247.

Creech, F. Reid. 1985. About Depression. An unpublished article written by Dr. Creech and shared with the author. San Diego, Calif.

Damasio, A. 1994. *Descartes' Error.* New York: G.P. Putnam's Sons.

———. 1999. *The Feeling of What Happens.* New York: Harcourt.

Damluji, Namir F. and Donna Genett, Ph.D. 1988. *The Depression Treatment Workbook.* La Mesa, California: Alvarado Parkway Institute.

Davidson, R.J. 1984. Affect, cognition, and hemispheric specialization. In *Emotions, Cognition, and Behavior.* Edited by C.E. Izard, J. Kagan, and R.B. Zajonic. Cambridge: Cambridge University Press.

Depue, R.A. and P.F. Collins. 1999. Neurobiology of the structure of personality: Dopamine, facilitation of incentive motivation, and extraversion. *Behavioral and Brain Sciences* 22:491-569.

Derryberry, D. and M.A. Reed. 1994. Temperament and attention: Orienting toward and away from positive and negative signals. *Journal of Personality and Social Psychology* 66:1128-1139.

Descartes, R. 1967. Treatise on the passions of the soul. In *The Philosophical Works Of Descartes.* Translated by E.S. Haldane and G.R.T. Ross. Cambridge: Cambridge University Press.

Domar, Alice D. and Henry Dreher. 1999. *Self-Nurture: Learning to Care for Yourself as Effectively as You Care for Everyone Else.* New York: Viking Press.

Dunn, A.L. and R.K. Dishman. 1991. Exercise and the neurobiology of depression. *Exercise and Sport Sciences Reviews* 19:41-98.

Ekman, P. 1994. Moods, emotion, and traits. In *The Nature of Emotion.* Edited by P. Ekman and R.J. Davidson. New York: Oxford University Press.

Elmer, Eddy. 2003. *Transcending the Black Dog: Living with Depression.* Retrieved February 12, 2005, from the author's website. www.eddyelmer.com/articles/dogmean.htm

Erber, Ralph. 1996. *Striving and Feeling.* Edited by Leonard Martin and Abraham Tesser. Mahwah, N.J.: Lawrence Erlbaum Associates.

Fabry, J. 1994. *The Pursuit of Meaning.* Abilene, Texas: Institute of Logotherapy Press.

Flach, Frederic F. 1974. *The Secret Strength of Depression.* Philadelphia: J.B. Lippincott Co.

Forgas, J.P. 1992. Affect in social judgment and decisions: A multiprocess model. *Advances in Experimental Psychology* 25:227-275.

Forgas, J.P. 2000. *Feeling and Thinking.* Cambridge: Cambridge University Press.

Frankl, Viktor E. 1984. *Man's Search for Meaning.* New York: Touchstone Books.

Frijda, N.H. 1986. *The Emotions.* Cambridge: Cambridge University Press.

Gibran, K. 1926. From *Sand and Foam.* Retrieved February 13, 2005, from the 4umi website http://4umi.com/gibran/sand_and_foam/6.htm.

Gold, M. 1987. *The Good News About Depression*. New York: Villard Books.

Goodwin, F.R. 1977. Diagnosis of affective disorders. In *Psychopharmacology in the Practice of Medicine*. Edited by Murray Jarvik. New York: Appleton-Century-Crofts.

Goodwin, F.R. and K.R. Jamison. 1990. Manic depressive illness. In *The Manic Depressive Spectrum*. New York: Oxford University Press.

Gray, J. and T. Braver. 2002. Integration of emotion and cognition in the lateral prefrontal cortex. *Proceedings of the National Academy of Sciences of the United States of America* 99(6):4115-4120.

Gross, J. 1989. Emotional expression in cancer onset and progression. *Social Science and Medicine* 28:1239-1248.

Gross, J.J. and R.F. Munoz. 1995. Emotion regulation and mental health. *Clinical Psychology-Science and Practice* 2:151-164.

Gross, J.J. and R.W. Levenson. 1997. Hiding Feeling: The acute effects of inhibiting positive and negative emotions. *Journal of Abnormal Psychology* 106:95-103.

Gross, J.J. 1998. The emerging field of emotion regulation: An integrative review. *Review of General Psychology* 2:271-299.

———. 1999. Emotional regulation: Past, present and future. *Cognition and Emotion* 13(5):551-573.

Hamer, Dean. 2004. *The God Gene: How Faith Is Hardwired Into Our Genes*. United States: Doubleday.

Harlow, H.F. and M.K. Harlow. 1971. From thought to therapy: Lessons from a primate laboratory. *American Scientist* 59:538-549.

Hassed, Craig S. 2000. Depression: Dispirited or spiritually deprived? *Medical Journal of Australia* 173:545-547.

Hatch, R.L., D.S. Naberhaus, L.K. Helmich, and M.A. Burg. 1998. Spiritual Involvement and Beliefs Scale: Development and testing of a new instrument. *Journal of Family Practice* 46:476-486.

Heun, R., A. Papassotiropoulos, and U. Ptok. 2000. Subthreshold depressive and anxiety disorders in the elderly. *European Psychiatry* 15(3):173-182.

Huddleston, J. 1993. Perspectives, purposes, and brotherhood: A spiritual framework for a global society. In *Transition to a Global Society* by S. Bushrui, I. Ayman, and E. Laszlo. Oxford, England: Oneworld Publications Ltd.

Hury, J. and P.E. Bebington. 1987. Psychiatric symptoms and social disablement as determinants of illness behavior. *Australian New Zealand Journal of Psychiatry* 21:68-74.

Idler, E. 1987. Religious involvement and the health of the elderly: Some hypotheses and initial tests. *Social Forces* 66:226-238.

Iles, George. Retrieved February 12, 2005, from the Quote Garden website, www.quotegarden.com/hope.html.

James, William. 1890. *The Principles of Psychology.* New York: Henry Holt and Co.

James, William. 1922. *The Varieties of Religious Experience.* London: Longmans, Green and Co.

Jarrett, David B. 1989. Chronobiology. In *Comprehensive Textbook of Psychiatry.* Fifth edition. Edited by Harold Kaplan and Benjamin Sadock. Baltimore: William & Wilkins.

Juchli, L. 1991. The spiritual dimension of depression. *Schweizerische Rundschau fur Medizin Praxis (Revue Suisse de Medecine Praxis)* 80(38):980-983.

Judd, L.L., M.P. Paulus, K.B. Wells, and M.K. Rapaport. 1996. Socioeconomic burden of subsyndromal depressive symptoms and major depression in a sample of the general population. *American Journal of Psychiatry* 153(11):1411-1417.

Julkunen, J., R. Salonen, G.A. Kaplan, M.A. Chesney, and J.T. Salonen. 1994. Hostility and the progression of carotid atherosclerosis. *Psychosomatic Medicine* 56:519-525.

Jung, C.G. 1968. *Psychology and Alchemy: Collected Works of C.G. Jung, Vol. 12.* Princeton: Princeton University Press.

Kagan, J. 1994. On the nature of emotion. In *The Development Of Emotion Regulation: Biological And Behavioral Considerations.* Chicago: The University of Chicago Press.

Kaufman, I.C. 1967. The reaction to separation in infant monkeys: Anaclitic depression and conservation withdrawal. *Psychosomatic Medicine* 29:648-675.

Kendler, Kenneth S. 1998. Boundaries of depression: An evaluation of DSM-IV criteria. *American Journal of Psychiatry* 155:172-177.

Khavari, K. 1999. *Spiritual Intelligence.* White Mountain Publications: New Liskeard, Ontario.

King, Martin L. *Strength to Love.* 1981. Minneapolis: Augsburg Fortress Publishers.

Klein, M. 1948. A contribution to the psychogenesis of manic-depressive states. In *Contributions to Psycho-Analysis, 1921-1945.* London: Hogarth Press.

Klerman, G.L. 1983. The significance of DSM-III in American psychiatry, in *International Perspectives on DSM-III.* Edited by R.L. Spitzer, J.B. Williams, and A.E. Skodol. Washington D.C.: American Psychiatric Press, Inc.

Klerman, G.L., M.M. Weissman, B. J. Rounsaville, and E.S. Chevron. 1984. *Interpersonal Psychotherapy of Depression.* New York: Basic Books, Inc.

Kline, Nathan S. 1974. *From Sad to Glad.* New York: Ballantine Books.

Koenig, H.G. 1997. *Is Religion Good for Your Health: The Effects of Religion on Physical and Mental Health.* Binghampton: Hayworth Press.

————. 2001. Religion and medicine II: Religion, mental health, and related behaviors. *The International Journal of Psychiatry in Medicine* 31(1):97-109.

Koenig, H.G., D.K. Weinger, B.L. Peterson, K.G. Meador, and F.J. Keefe. 1997. Religious coping in the nursing home: A biopsychosocial model. *International Journal of Psychiatry in Medicine* 27(4):365-376.

Kokkonen, M. and L. Pulkkinen. 1996. Emotion and its regulation. *Psykologia* 31:404-411.

————. 2001. Examination of paths between personality, current mood, its evaluation and emotion regulation. *European Journal of Personality* 15:83-104.

Kraeplin, E. 1921. In *Manic Depressive Insanity and Paranoia.* Edited by G.M. Robertson. Edinborough: E & S Livingstone.

Kubler-Ross, E. 1999. *The Tunnel and the Light.* New York: Marlowe and Company.

Laird, J.D. 1989. Mood affects memory because feelings are cognitions. *Journal of Social Behavior and Personality* 4:33-38.

Lam, D., N. Smith, S. Checkley, F. Rijsdijk, and P. Sham. 2003. Effect of neuroticism, response style and information processing on depression severity in a clinically depressed sample. *Psychological Medicine* 33(3):469-479.

Lavretsky, H. and A. Kumar. 2002. Clinically significant non-major depression: Old concepts, new insights. *American Journal Geriatric Psychiatry* 10(3):239-255.

Lawler, K.A. and J.W. Younger. 2002. Theobiology: An analysis of spirituality, cardiovascular responses, stress, mood, and physical health. *Journal of Religion and Health* 41(4):347-362.

LeDoux, Joseph. 1998. *The Emotional Brain: The Mysterious Underpinnings of Emotional Life.* London: Weidenfeld and Nicholson.

Lechin, F., B. van der Dijs, B. Orozco, M.E. Lechin, S. Baez, A.E. Lechin, I. Rada, E. Acosta, L. Arocha, and V. Jimenez. 1995. Plasma neurotransmitters, blood pressure, and heart rate during supine-resting orthostasis, and moderate exercise conditions in major depressed patients. *Biological Psychiatry* 38:166-173.

Leuba, James H. 1896. Studies in the psychology of religious phenomena. *American Journal of Psychology* 7:345-347.

Levin, J. 1994. Religion and health: Is there an association, is it valid, and is it causal? *Social Science and Medicine* 38:1475-1482.

Lewis, A.J. 1938. States of depression: Their clinical and aetiological differentiation. *British Medical Journal* 2:875-878.

Lipsey, John R. *How to Evaluate Your Psychiatrist or Other Therapist If You Have (Or Possibly Have) a Depressive Disorder.* Retrieved February 12, 2005, from the Depression and Related Affective Disorders Association (DRADA) website, www.drada.org/ReferenceShelf/lipsey.html.

Lloyd-Jones, D.M. 1965. *Spiritual Depression: Its Causes and Its Cure.* Grand Rapids, Mich.: Eerdmans Printing.

Lobstein, D.D., C.L. Rasmussen, G.E. Dunphy, and M.J. Dunphy. 1989. Beta-endorphin and components of depression as powerful discriminators between joggers and sedentary and middle-aged men. *Journal of Psychosomatic Research* 33(3):293-305.

Mandell, A.J. 1980. Toward a psychobiology of transcendence: God in the brain. In *The Psychobiology of Consciousness.* Edited by J.M. Davidson and R.J. Davidson. New York: Plenum.

Marks, Tracy. 1972. *The Meaning of Life According to Seven Philosophers, Psychologists and Theologians.* Retrieved October 12, 2004, from the author's website, www.geocities.com/~webwinds/frankl/meaning.htm.

Martinez-Pons, M. 1997. The relation of emotional intelligence with selected areas of personal functioning. *Imagination, Cognition and Personality* 17:3-13.

Maultsby, Maxie C. Jr. 2005. The ABCs of where emotional feelings come from. Drawing provided by author.

Mawdudi, Abul A'la. 1997. *Towards Understanding Islam.* Translated by Khurshid Ahmad. Lahore: Idara Tarjumanul-Quran.

Mayberg, H.S. 1997. Limbic-cortical dysregulation: A proposed model of depression. *Journal of Neuropsychiatry and Clinical Neuroscience* 9(3):471-481.

———. 2002. Modulating limbic-cortical circuits in depression: Targets of antidepressant treatments. *Seminars in Clinical Neuropsychiatry* 7(4):255-268.

Mayer, J.D. and A.A. Stevens. 1994. An emerging understanding of the reflective (meta-) experience of mood. *Journal of Research in Personality* 28:351-373.

McCullough, M.E. and D.B. Larson. 1999. Religion and depression, a review of the literature. *Twin Research* 2(2):126 136.

McHugh, P.R. and P.R. Slavney. 1986. *The Perspectives of Psychiatry.* Baltimore: The Johns Hopkins University Press.

McLean, P.D. and A.R. Hakstian. 1979. Clinical depression: Comparative efficacy of outpatient treatments. *Journal of Consulting and Clinical Psychology* 47:818 83.

Meehl, P.E. 1975. Hedonic capacity: Some conjectures. *Bulletin of the Menninger Clinic* 39:295-307.

Mennin, Douglas S., Richard G. Heimberg, Cynthia L. Turk, and David M. Fresco. 2002. Applying an emotion regulation framework to integrative approaches to generalized anxiety disorder. *Clinical Psychology: Science and Practice* 9:85-90.

Miller, P. and J.G. Ingham. 1976. Friends, confidants, and symptoms. *Social Psychiatry* 11:51-58.

Miller, Michael C. 2003. Stop Pretending Nothing's Wrong. *Newsweek*. 16 June. 141(24):71.

Mitchell, Ross. 1981. *Depression*. Great Britain: Penguin Books, Ltd.

Mueller, P.S., D.J. Plevak, and T.A. Rummans. 2001. Religious involvement, spirituality, and medicine: Implications for clinical practice. *Mayo Clinic Proceedings* 76:1225-1235.

Nathanson, D.L. 1996. *Knowing Feeling: Affect, Script, and Psychotherapy*. New York: W.W. Norton and Co.

———. 1988. Affect, affective resonance, and a new theory for hypnosis. *Psychopathology* 21:126-137.

Newberg, A.B. and J. Iversen. 2003. The neural basis of the complex mental task of meditation. *Medical Hypotheses* 61(2):282-291.

Newberg, A. and E. D'Aquili. 2001. *Why God Won't Go Away*. United States: Ballantine Books.

Newberg, A., M. Pourdehnad, A. Alavi, and E. D'Aquili. 2003. Cerebral blood flow during meditative prayer: Preliminary findings and methodological issues. *Perception Motivation Skills* 97(2):625-630.

Nix, G., C. Watson, T. Pyszczynski, and J. Greenberg. 1995. Reducing depressive affect through external focus of attention. *Journal of Social and Clinical Psychology* 14(1):36-52.

Nygard, Mark. 1996. The Muslim concept of surrender to God. *International Journal of Frontier Missions* 13(3):125-130.

Oatley, K. and P.N. Johnson-Laird. 1987. Towards a cognitive theory of emotions. *Cognition and Emotion* 1:29-50.

Paquette, V., J. Levesque, B. Mensour, J.M. Leroux, G. Beaudoin, P. Borgouin, and M. Beauregard. 2003. Change the mind and you change the brain: Effects of cognitive-behavioral therapy on the neural correlates of spider phobia. *Neuroimage* 18(2):401-409.

Paykel, E.S. and M.M. Weissman. 1978. Social maladjustment in the severity of depression. *Comprehensive Psychiatry* 19:121-128.

Payne, J., A. Bergin, A.K. Bielema, and P. Jenkins. 1991. A review of religion and mental health: Prevention and the enhancement of psychosocial functioning. *Prevention in Human Services* 9:11-40.

Persinger, Michael A. 1983. Religious and mystical experiences as artifacts of temporal lobe function: A general hypothesis. *Perceptual and Motor Skills* 57(3/2):1255-1262.

————. 2001. The neuropsychiatry of paranormal experiences. *Journal of Neuropsychiatry and Clinical Neurosciences* 13:515-524.

Phillips, Mary. 2003a. Neurobiology of emotion perception I: The neural basis of normal emotion perception. *Biological Psychiatry* 54:504-514.

————. 2003b. Understanding the neurobiology of emotion perception: Implications for psychiatry. *British Journal of Psychiatry* 182:190-192.

Posner, Michael I. and S.E. Petersen. 1990. The attention system of the human brain. *Annual Review of Neuroscience* 13:25-42.

Powell, J. 1989. *Happiness Is an Inside Job.* Valencia, Calif.: Tabor Publishing.

Rahwan, J. 2000. *The Transmission to God: The Limbic System, The Soul, and Spirituality.* San Jose: University Press.

Reps, Paul and Nyogen Senzaki. 1994. *Zen Flesh, Zen Bones.* Boston: Shambhala.

Rippere, V. 1976. Antidepressive behaviour: A preliminary report. *Behaviour Research and Therapy* 14(4):289-299.

————. 1980. More historical dimensions of common sense knowledge: Spiritual consolation for the depressed. *Behaviour Research and Therapy* 18:549-563.

Rowe, Dorothy. 1992. *Wanting Everything.* London: Fontana.

Salovey, P., J.D. Mayer, S. Goldman, C. Turvey, and T. Palfai. 1995. Emotional attention, clarity, and repair. In *Emotion, Disclosure, and Health.* Edited by J. Pennebaker. Washington, D.C.: American Psychological Association.

Saver, J.L. and J. Rabin. 1997. The neural substrates of religious experience. *Journal of Neuropsychiatry and Clinical Neuroscience* 9(3):498-510.

Schore, A. 2001. The effects of a secure attachment relationship on right brain development, affect regulation, and infant mental health. *Infant Mental Health Journal* 22:7-66.

————. 2002. Dysregulation of the right brain: A fundamental mechanism of traumatic attachment and the psychopathogenesis of post-traumatic stress disorder. *Australian and New Zealand Journal of Psychiatry* 36(1):9-30.

Schutte, N., J.M. Malouff, M. Simunek, J. McKenley, and S. Hollander. 2002. Characteristic emotional intelligence and emotional well-being. *Cognition and Emotion* 16(6):769-785.

Seidl, L.G. 1993. The value of spiritual health. *Health Progress* 74(7):48-50.

Seligman, Martin E.P. 1992. *Helplessness: On Depression, Development, and Death.* New York: W.H. Freeman.

Shelley, Percy Bysshe. 1909. *The Cenci.* New York: P.F. Collier and Son.

Solomon, Andrew. 2001. *The Noon Day Demon: An Atlas of Depression.* New York: Scribner.

Solomon, Robert C. 2000. The philosophy of emotions. In *The Handbook of Emotions.* Edited by M. Lewis and J.M. Haviland-Jones. New York: Guilford Press.

Stahl, Samuel M. *The Legacy of Abraham Joshua Heschel.* Sermon given March 6, 1998. Retrieved October 14, 2004, from the Temple Beth-El website, www.beth-elsa.org/be_s0306.htm.

Stewart-Brown, S. 2000. Parenting, well-being, health, and disease. In *Promoting Children's Emotional Well-Being: Messages From Research.* Edited by A. Buchanan and B.L. Hudson. Oxford: Oxford University Press.

Strauman, T. 1999. Is depression a dysfunction in self regulating the brain-behavior system for approach? *Behavioral and Brain Sciences* 22:3.

Sullivan, Harry S. 1953. *The Interpersonal Theory of Psychiatry.* Edited by Helen Swick Perry and Mary Ladd Gawel. New York: W.W. Norton and Co.

The Open University in association with the Health Education Council and the Scottish Health Education Unit. 1980. *The Good Health Guide.* Pan Books: London.

Tiebout, Harry. 1953. Surrender versus compliance in therapy. *Quarterly Journal of Studies on Alcohol* 14:58.

Tkachuk, G.A. and G.L. Martin. 1999. Exercise therapy for patients with psychiatric disorders: Research and clinical implications. *Professional Psychology: Research and Practice* 30(3):275-282.

Torres, Michael. 2001. *The Effects of Stress on the Body, Mind, and Spirit.* Retrieved October 16, 2004, from the author's website, www.imhm.com/aboutthepresident.htm.

U.S. Department of Health and Human Services. 1993. *Depression is a Treatable Illness.* AHCPR Publications Clearinghouse: Silver Springs, Md.

U.S. Surgeon General. 1996. *Surgeon General's Report on Physical Activity and Health Report.*

Vedantam, Shankar. 2004. *Antidepressant Use by U.S. Adults Soars.* Washington Post. 3 December.

Walden, T.A. 1991. Infant social referencing. In *The Development of Emotional Regulation and Dysregulation.* Edited by J. Garber and K.A. Dodge. Cambridge: Cambridge University Press.

Weissman, M.M. and S.V. Kasl. 1976. Help seeking in depressed outpatients following maintenance therapy. *British Journal of Psychiatry* 129:252-262.

Wender, Paul H. and Donald F. Klein. 1981. *Mind, Mood, and Medicine.* New York: Farrar, Straus and Giroux.

Weyerer, S. and B. Kupfer. 1994. Physical exercise and psychological health. *Sports Medicine* 17:108-116.

Wittgenstein, Ludwig. 1958. *Philosophical Investigations.* Second Edition. Translated by G.E.M. Anscomb. New York: Macmillan.

Wong, Paul T. 1999. Towards an integrative model of meaning-centered counseling and therapy (MCCT). *The International Forum for Logotherapy* 22(1):47-55.

———. 2000. Meaning-centered counseling workshop. Workshop presented July 2000 at the International Conference on Personal Meaning, Richmond, British Columbia.

———. 2001. *Logotherapy.* Retrieved February 2004 from the International Network on Personal Meaning website, www.meaning.ca/articles/logotherapy.html.

———. 2003a. *The Transcendental Life: An Impossible Dream?* Retrieved July 2003 from the International Network on Personal Meaning website: www.meaning.ca/articles/presidents_column/transcendental_life_july03.htm.

———. 2003b. *Finding Happiness Through Suffering.* Retrieved August 2003 from the International Network on Personal Meaning website: www.meaning.ca/articles/presidents_column/happiness_aug03.htm.

World Health Organization. 2001. *The World Health Report 2001 Mental Health: New Understanding, New Hope.* Geneva: World Health Organization.

World Health Organization. 2003. *Investing in mental health.* Department of Mental Health and Substance Dependence. Geneva: World Health Organization.

INDEX

FOR MORE INFORMATION

To learn more about MRT, you may wish to attend one of our workshops. Information regarding the workshops can be found at our website: http://www.moodregulationinstitute.com.

The authors would also like to recommend their workbook, *Mood Regulation Therapy: The Depression Workbook,* which has specific exercises and practical information on MRT strategies. The workbook is available through The Mood Regulation Therapy Institute.

The Mood Regulation Therapy Institute was established to provide information, education, and consultation services. Our mission is to contribute to our field through research and training, and to support individuals, families, and communities through personal and spiritual growth with Mood Regulation Therapy strategies.

For more information about Mood Regulation Therapy, upcoming workshops, consulting services, training for clinicians, or to order workbooks, please visit our website at http://www.moodregulationinstitute.com or e-mail MRTInstitute@aol.com.

To contact Dr. Damluji directly, you can e-mail him at MoodDoc@msn.com.

978-0-595-35508-2
0-595-35508-0

Printed in the United States
34795LVS00004B/109-330

9 780595 355082